The Progressive Conservative Party of Canada has been in opposition in Ottawa for forty-seven out of the past fifty-eight years, having lost twelve out of the last eighteen federal elections. In *The Tory Syndrome* George Perlin argues that Conservative electoral weakness can be ascribed at least in part to persistent internal conflict which has focused on or involved the party's leaders. Perlin explores the causes for the party's instability in a case study of events from the cabinet revolt against John Diefenbaker in 1963 to Robert Stanfield's resignation following the 1974 election. His analysis is based on research that included interviews with most of the people who held key roles in the party during this period and surveys of delegates who attended party conventions in 1967, 1971, and 1976. It is set in the context of a review of the history of earlier conflicts and their relationship to the Conservative decline from dominant to minority party in federal politics.

Perlin analyses the effects both of long-term cleavages in the values and social composition of the party and of attitudes and dispositions that are part of its internal political culture. In his conclusion he draws attention to the influence on conflict of attitudes and dispositions that have developed as a result of the party's habituation to the role of the opposition. He says these have helped create a mutually re-enforcing cycle of conflict and defeat that is independent of the original causes for the party's decline. Perlin believes the Progressive Conservative party will continue to win office from time to time because it is the only party strong enough to challenge Liberal hegemony in federal politics. But he argues that the party will require exceptionally adroit leadership and some considerable luck if it is to use such opportunities to break free of this cycle and achieve a more competitive position.

George Perlin is a political scientist who teaches at Queen's University. He has written about Canadian parties, voting behaviour, regionalism, and provincial politics.

The Tory Syndrome

LEADERSHIP POLITICS IN THE PROGRESSIVE CONSERVATIVE PARTY

George C. Perlin

McGill-Queen's University Press
MONTREAL

ISBN 0-7735-0350-1 (cloth)
ISBN 0-7735-0352-8 (paper)
Legal deposit 1st quarter 1980
Bibliothèque Nationale du Québec

Printed in Canada by John Deyell Co.

This book has been published with the help of a grant from the Social Science Federation of Canada, using funds provided by the Social Sciences and Humanities Research Council of Canada.

CONTENTS

TABLES

ACKNOWLEDGEMENTS

This book is based on a number of separate pieces of research. Some of the work on the 1967 convention was undertaken as part of a joint project in which I was invited to participate by Professor Hugh Thorburn. Funding for that project was provided by the Canada Council and by the Donner Foundation. Some of the funding for the 1976 survey was provided by the Canadian Broadcasting Corporation in preparation for its coverage of the convention. Support for other parts of the research was provided in the form of research assistance and computer grants by Queen's University.

Among the many people who have worked on this project I especially want to thank the students in my political parties seminar who conducted interviews at the 1976 convention, the friends who assisted me with interviews with members of Parliament in 1973 and 1974, and Peter Snow, who worked on the analysis of data from these two parts of the research.

Anyone familiar with the scholarship of John Meisel will recognize his influence on the interests and concerns of this book. Professor Meisel has been one of the few truly original students of Canadian politics, contributing as much by his insights as a teacher and critic as by the substantial body of his own published work. He, Ed Black, Jock Gunn, Jack Grove, and Hugh Thorburn have also given me the deeply valued support of their friendship and encouragement at times when it was most needed. These colleagues, Bill Irvine, and Peter Leslie have all read and made useful comments on portions of the manuscript.

My most notable debt is to Patti Peppin. In dedicating this book to her I have tried to express my gratitude both for the constancy of her support and for the unique contribution she made to the substance of the research in designing and carrying out the analysis of the 1967 delegate survey.

Several people have worked on the typescript for the book: Sheilagh Dunn, Jayne Hinchey, Gail Hogarth, Fanny Calucag, Dawn Snow, and Ann Young. While thanking them all, I particularly want to mention Mrs. Hinchey who was generous with her time in every emergency. I also wish to express my appreciation to Rene Hogarth, administrative officer of the Department of Political Studies at Queen's University, who has been responsible for the administration of various parts of the research.

As editor, Joan Harcourt has provided not just her technical skill, but also her morale-sustaining enthusiasm. In the final production of the manuscript I gratefully acknowledge both her contribution and that of Eleanor Gunn who prepared the index.

Finally, I owe a special debt to the many members of the Progressive Conservative party who co-operated in my research. In submitting to interviews and complying with requests to complete questionnaires, they have been notably generous with their time and patience. Whatever their opinions of my conclusions, I hope they will appreciate that the book is written not with the intention of criticizing their party, but with the intention of contributing to an understanding of its problems.

1

Introduction: Some Theoretical Considerations

Since the death of its first leader, Sir John A. Macdonald, in 1891, the Progressive Conservative party has been subject to recurring crises of internal conflict focused on its leadership. Nearly all of Macdonald's successors have had to deal with open and often continuous challenges to their authority. Most have resigned under the pressure of manifest or incipient rebellion.

The need for internal unity is a concern to all political parties for at least two reasons:

First, no party can achieve optimum organizational effectiveness when its members are engaged in internal conflict because internal conflict saps their energies and diverts them from the performance of their organizational tasks. As John Diefenbaker succinctly put it from the leader's perspective: "No leader can lead when he has to turn to see who is trying to trip him from behind."[1]

Second, the appearance of disunity is symbolically harmful to a party, raising doubt about its competence to govern. A party which is unable to manage its own affairs is unlikely to be convincing in its claim to manage public affairs. This problem will be the more acute if the party leader is at the centre of controversy. It will be difficult for any leader to win public confidence if members of his own party openly criticize him or appear to reject his leadership.

Leadership politics in the Conservative party has never been more acrimonious or divisive than during the two decades from 1956 to 1976.

This period began with a cabinet revolt against John Diefenbaker who, in 1957, had led the party to victory for the first time in twenty-two years. Diefenbaker survived in the leadership but his government was defeated in Parliament and in the ensuing general election was forced from office. For the next three years there were repeated challenges to Diefenbaker's authority which he vigorously resisted. But in November 1966 the party's annual meeting voted to call a leadership convention. At the convention, held in September 1967, Robert Stanfield was chosen as Diefenbaker's successor. From its very outset Stanfield's tenure was beset by conflict which he struggled unsuccessfully to contain. His failure to unite the party contributed to three successive electoral defeats which ultimately forced him to resign. Stanfield's farewell address to the party was a blunt warning to its members of the dangers in continued disunity. Commenting from his own experience, he observed that it seemed "Some Tories would rather fight than win."[2]

This book is concerned with the instability of the Conservative party's leadership. It seeks to identify the causes of this problem with a view to assessing the chances that it may be overcome. The analysis focuses on events in the Diefenbaker-Stanfield period.

THE THEORETICAL CONTEXT

The analytical perspective of this book is derived from the growing body of literature that seeks to apply concepts from psychology to the study of the behaviour of political elites.[3] The central concept in the analysis is that of motivation. Motives are dispositions (attitudes and feelings) that stimulate people to act in particular ways. They consist both of general dispositions that influence a person in everything he does and of specific dispositions that are related only to particular roles. A person's motives are formed through his experiences in interacting with other people. They are acquired through the processes of socialization to which he is exposed and through his activities in the roles which he occupies in society.

The motives that concern us here are those that govern support relationships between a party leader and members of his party. We are interested in the motives that may induce a party member to prefer the leadership of one person rather than another; to accept as leader a person who was not his first choice; to refuse to comply in the leadership of a particular person; or to reject a leader he had once supported. For the purpose of explaining these support relationships we can classify the motives of party activists as belonging to one of three main types which I shall call affective motives, policy motives, and patronage motives.[4]

The word affective belongs to the realm of liking and disliking. It refers to an emotional dimension of social interaction which inheres in the interaction itself. *Affective motives* are positive and negative emotional dispositions toward others—either individuals or groups. Such dispositions may have a bearing on leadership politics in a variety of ways. Support may be based on emotional attachments created through the intrinsic appeal of a personality, on bonds of friendship, or on feelings of affinity for people with some shared social characteristic. Conversely, opposition may be based on dislike of a person because of attributes of his personality, negative feelings toward some group with which he is associated, or prejudice against him because of some social characteristic he possesses.

The strongest bonds of political support are those built on emotional attachments. These attachments can transcend all objective evaluations for, as the old aphorism puts it, love is blind. Such attachments are likely to endure beyond all others. If a leader who has support of this kind is challenged, intense conflict almost certainly will ensue.

But the most intractable conflicts will be those in which participants act from negative affective dispositions. This point may be illustrated by considering the role of affective motives in conflicts over the choice of a leader. In such conflicts, even when a party member acts from positive feelings, it may be difficult to get him to accept a leader other than his first preference. This is because his gratification is inherent in the relationship itself.[5] His motive lies in his feeling of attachment to that particular person. But a person acting from this kind of disposition, although disappointed if his own candidate is unsuccessful, may be willing to transfer his support or he may simply be indifferent to a leader other than his first preference. In contrast, a person who is motivated by his dislike of another person or group will reject any accommodation with that person or group. If that person or group wins control of the leadership, he is likely to try to renew the conflict at the first opportunity. In this regard it should be noted that the process of conflict itself—whatever the original motives of participants—tends to produce negative feelings towards rivals.[6] This tendency may inhibit the settlement of any conflict, even when there appear to be alternative outcomes which would satisfy the original purposes of the participants. It is also likely to have a residual effect—influencing the behaviour of participants after the settlement of the immediate issue around which the conflict revolved.

Policy motives are motives with objectives related to actions of government that have generalized effects. Usually we think of them as expressing attitudes toward issues of public policy. But in leadership politics we may also think of them as expressing judgements about a person's general fitness for leadership—that is, about his ability to give competent direction to public affairs. What distinguishes this kind of response to a personality from the kind assigned to the category of affective motives is that it is evaluative rather than emotional and that it relates to the effectiveness of the process of government. However, this is a special case. Normally, when we think of policy motives we are concerned about the substance of policy, about choices between alternative courses of government action. And it is in this sense—unless I otherwise indicate—that I shall refer to policy motives. Our interest will be in the effect of differences in opinion about issues on the choice of and support for a leader.

When there is conflict over the leadership based on disagreements about policy, the possibility of reaching accommodation will depend on the nature of the issues that are (or are perceived to be) involved. Almost any issue may rouse strong feeling among some people because there is bound to be a group with a special interest in it, but there are some disagreements about policy which are in a general sense less amenable to compromise than others. One important variable in this regard will be the extent to which the participants believe the issues raise questions of basic principle. A person who perceives policy disagreements in terms of basic principles is likely to feel more intensely about his position and to be less willing to make any compromise.[7] Another variable is the extent to which policy disagreements are based on social cleavages that generate affective dispositions. The cleavages that have this property are those that involve ascribed group characteristics directly related to an individual's sense of personal identity. In the broad sense, this would embrace any characteristic distinguishing a person as belonging to some culturally-defined group. The most common examples are characteristics of ethnic or racial identity. Issue conflicts that rouse feelings along cleavages of this kind will invariably be difficult to resolve.

Patronage motives are motives that involve wholly individual gratifications associated with the possession of power. They include the power motive (the desire to exercise dominance over others); status motives (aspirations for social prestige or for the esteem of others); the achievement motive (the desire to possess power because it is a measure or means of achievement); and material motives (the desire for personal financial rewards). The objectives of motives in this category may be to occupy positions of power, to receive some benefit (either a material reward or a status-enhancing honorific reward) within the prerogative of power-holders; or to associate with or be seen to be associated with those who hold positions of power.

Normally the conflicts that will be most easily resolved are those in which participants act from patronage motives. The person who is patronage-motivated will view the relationships he forms in instrumental and dispassionate terms, being willing to leave existing relationships and to enter new ones with relative ease in return for some share of power or its benefits. Even in situations in which his specific aspirations are unfulfilled, he will want to avoid total exclusion from the circle of power.

Thus, he is likely to be flexible in his view of alternative benefits. Moreover, he has the most to lose from violating party discipline. The career costs of challenging a party leader are potentially high. It is not just the risk of failure that must be weighed. There is the danger of incurring the disapproval of other party members if one's actions appear to do the party harm. But compliance based on the support of the patronage-motivated is inherently unstable because it is contingent upon the party's winning office. Without office there are obviously serious constraints on the leader's ability to satisfy aspirations for patronage. At the same time, any politician who is patronage-motivated is likely to have a strong drive for success as an end in and of itself. The test of leadership in the eyes of this person is whether it brings victory, and the support he has accorded a leader can be withdrawn as readily as it has been given. Thus, the compliance of a party member who is ambitious for the rewards of office is unlikely to endure for long if the leader does not bring the party electoral success.

This discussion suggests three propositions that may assist us in analysing conflict in party leadership politics:

1. The more party members act on the basis of affective motives, the more intense will be their conflicts and the more difficult it will be to get them to reach accommodation. The most intractable conflicts will be those which involve negative affective motives.

2. Conflicts based on disagreements about policy will be difficult to resolve when the participants believe the issues involved raise questions of principle or when the issues involved touch on ascriptive social cleavages related to feelings of personal identity.

3. The party members most favourably disposed to accommodation will be those who are motivated by ambition for patronage rewards. But support accorded a leader on the basis of patronage motives is inherently unstable, being contingent on the leader's ability to bring the party electoral success.

These propositions provide a starting point for our analysis of Conservative leadership politics.

In building from these propositions I should emphasize that the distinctions I have made are analytical distinctions. In reality, the motives that activate people in their party roles are likely to be more complex than the distinctions imply. We would expect all politicians to be motivated to some extent by personal ambition, to have sets of attitudes that establish boundaries to what they will accept as public policy, and to respond emotionally to the people with whom they associate. However, we may equally expect variations in the primacy of particular motives in each person's orientation to party activity. Different motives will have different weights in the behaviour of different people. Thus, there are some people whose primary motivation will be ambition for the rewards of office. They will be relatively single-minded in the pursuit of this ambition and they will therefore be likely to adopt an instrumental and calculating approach to questions of policy and to be more controlled in their emotional responses to their associates. Similarly, there are some people whose primary motivation for political activity is a preoccupation with particular issues or a general orientation that "finds politics intrinsically interesting because it expresses a conception of the public interest."[8] These people may be expected to respond to conflicts mainly on the basis of their policy concerns. Finally, recent research has shown that there are some people who are active in parties primarily because of the emotional gratifications that they find in their associations with other people.[9] The basic orientation that these people bring to their roles is likely to predispose them to respond to the politics of the party on the basis of affective motives. Again, this is not to say that the weighting in a person's motivation is immutably fixed. Motives are, after all, dispositions shaped by experience. A person who enters party activity primarily for one kind of motive may through his experiences in the party begin to give primacy to another kind of motive. (I have already suggested how this may occur in discussing the effect of the process of conflict in producing affective dispositions.) But my basic assumption is that there will be some constancy in the weighting of each person's motives that will reflect the totality of his experiences outside the party and within it.

The fact that motives are shaped by experience is of considerable importance for our analysis. To explain the instability of the Conservative leadership, we must not only identify the motives that give rise to instability but also the factors which account for these motives. I have said that a person's motives in his party role will reflect both the experiences he has had outside the party and the experiences he has had within it. Thus, to explain leadership conflict in the party, we must consider two kinds of factors. First, there are characteristics of the party that attract people with particular dispositions to active membership; second, there are characteristics of the party which influence the dispositions of members once they have joined it. The first set of characteristics may be described as those that relate to the party's role in the party system. These will include the nature of its ideology, the kinds of social groups to which it directs its appeal, and its competitive position. The second set of characteristics may be described as those that relate to its internal culture. These will include its internal social composition (that is, the characteristics of its active members as distinct from those of the people to whom it appeals), its institutional structure, norms governing the role of the leader, and the effects of its historical experience.

In applying this approach we will be concerned with the behaviour of two groups in the party: the party elite (that is, those people who occupy designated leading positions in the formal structures of the party or in ad hoc organizations formed for such purposes as the conduct of a candidate's leadership campaign) and the active party membership. For the purpose of analysing the behaviour of the party elite, I have relied primarily on extended personal interviews. Not everyone who had a role in the events that concern us has been interviewed, but the sample is a large one.[10] The interviews include most of the people who had leading roles in the conflict over Diefenbaker's leadership, most of the candidates and representatives of the organizations of all of the candidates in the 1967 leadership convention,[11] most of the leading members of the extra-parliamentary party during Robert Stanfield's tenure, and 80 percent of the Conservative caucus elected in 1972. Data for the analysis of the behaviour of the party's active membership are derived from surveys of delegates at the 1967 leadership convention, the 1971 annual meeting of the National Association, and the 1976 leadership convention. The first two surveys were conducted by mail after the conventions while the third was conducted in face-to-face interviews during the convention.

SOME PROBLEMS OF ANALYSIS AND INTERPRETATION

There are some general problems of analysis and interpretation which derive from the nature of the approach that has been adopted here.

First, people often may not explain their motives in terms which fit the categories of the typology. The typology is an analytical construct and, while in the abstract the categories may be relatively distinct, in application it may not always be easy or possible to make all responses and explanations fit neatly into them.

Second, motivation is often not easy to articulate and indeed may not even be consciously understood.

Third, there are approved and disapproved ways of perceiving motives and this may colour responses. For example, one might expect a person to have some disposition to explain his or her motivation in terms of other-serving rather than self-serving ends. A special difficulty arises in this regard because there is a tendency to explain all conflict at the public level in terms of policy ends. The articulation of policy differences has an instrumental as well as an expressive function; politicians seek and use policies as a means of mobilizing support. Thus, while conflict may be articulated in terms of policy differences, these differences may not reflect what is really at issue.

I have tried to deal with problems of this kind as they arise. The effectiveness of the controls I have used in particular cases is a matter of judgement. Each piece of the analysis may be tested in its own context. But it should also be seen in the larger context of the study as a whole.

Ultimately, the cogency of the explanations which are developed rests on how well the separate pieces of analysis can be seen to constitute a coherent whole.

Comment is also required on the nature of the evidence and the form of its presentation.

To build the highest level of confidence into evidence from the interviews, three tests have been applied:

1. Is what the respondent said internally consistent?
2. Is what the respondent said consistent with what he did?
3. Can what the respondent said be corroborated by evidence from other interviews or published sources?

In the case of evidence relating to a person other than the respondent I have followed the rule of looking for corroboration from three or more independent sources.

The evidence from the interviews, which is the principal source for the chapters on elite-level politics, is presented in summary form in a narrative-analytical style that has been adopted to make the presentation more interesting for the reader. Direct quotations from the interviews are used in the text to illustrate general points. In a few cases, the source of a particular quotation cannot be identified because confidentiality was requested.

The delegate surveys provide data of a quite different kind which require careful interpretation. Insofar as it was possible to make tests for representativeness, there does not appear to be any significant bias in any of the samples.[12] It is difficult in any survey to make subjective evaluations of the accuracy of individual responses, impossible in surveys conducted by mail. The limited number of questions which can be asked in surveys of this kind and the broad range of concerns which the surveys sought to embrace made it impossible to include control questions for every topic. Another problem is created by the fact that the 1967 questionnaire was not designed exclusively for the purpose of pursuing the questions raised here. For all of these reasons there is obvious need for caution in drawing conclusions from the survey data. Quantitative analysis, therefore, has been conducted at a relatively simple level and the most conservative statistical tests have been used.

The book is divided into three main sections. The first section—chapters 2 and 3—establishes the context for the analysis of the conflicts of the Diefenbaker-Stanfield period. Chapter 2 describes the role of the leader within the party, while chapter 3 reviews the history of conflict in the party. The second section—chapters 4, 5, and 6—discusses elite-level politics during the period from the cabinet revolt against John Diefenbaker in 1962 to Robert Stanfield's announcement of his intention to resign in 1974. Chapter 4 deals with the conflicts over Diefenbaker's leadership, chapter 5 with the events which led to Stanfield's election as leader, and chapter 6 with the conflicts that occurred during Stanfield's tenure. The third section—chapters 7, 8, and 9—discusses mass-level politics in the party as represented in the behaviour of convention delegates. Chapters 7 and 8 analyse the behaviour of delegates at the 1967 convention, while chapter 9 uses data from the survey of delegates to the 1976 convention to discuss the extent to which observations about the nature of cleavage in elite-level politics during the Stanfield period apply to the party as a whole.

At the end of these three sections there is one further chapter which suggests a general explanation for the instability of the party's leadership and discusses the implication of this explanation for the party's future.

Part I

2

The Leader's Role in the Party

In one of the first textbooks on Canadian politics Hugh McD. Clokie wrote: "The dominant position of the party leader in Canadian politics has often been commented on by foreign observers. It is far greater than in Britain where the adherence to party principles or programme competes with loyalty to the leader as a bond of partnership. It is also far greater than in the United States where party candidates are nominated locally without any obligation to support the national leader of the party. In Canada more than anywhere else it is possible to define a party as being a body of supporters following a given leader."[1]

Clokie's view of the pre-eminence of Canadian party leaders is widely shared. Competition between the Liberal and Conservative parties is most often described in both scholarly and popular literature in terms of the activities and attitudes of their leaders. It is fairly common to identify the differences between the parties as an expression of differences in their leaders' personalities.[2]

Party campaign strategists clearly agree that the personality of the leader has an important effect in federal politics. They all direct their research at the study of the impact of the personal attributes of leaders and devise their campaign plans in response to their analyses of strengths and weaknesses in the personal images of the rival leaders.[3]

Studies of voting behaviour have not dealt extensively with the effect of leader images on popular perceptions of the parties, but there is enough evidence to indicate that it is significant. For example, in a national survey in 1968, John Meisel found that when voters were asked what party aspect was most important in their voting choice, the largest number (42 percent) said it was the party leader.[4]

Several factors have contributed to the pre-eminent role of the leader in the Liberal and Conservative parties.

One, as Clokie pointed out, is that there have not been significant long-term differences in the policies of the two parties. Both parties are committed to the principles of capitalist economics and liberal-democratic politics.[5] When in office both have built incrementally on the social and economic policies laid down before their election. Both have been prepared to resort to public ownership and both have contributed to the development of the welfare state.[6] In the absence of fundamental disagreements about policy the one means the parties have of forming distinctive appeals for public support is to emphasize the personal attractiveness, political style, and competence of their leaders.

A second factor is the regionally plural character of Canadian society. Regionalism—based both on affective attachments to regional cultures and on differences in regional economic interests—has impeded the development of a strong sense of national identity in the Canadian political culture.[7] Parties which seek national support must create a conception of national interest transcending and reconciling regional outlooks. Some group or person in each party must be able to stand above sectional interests and give expression to the party's conception of the national interest. This responsibility has fallen on the leader. At the same time, the leader has a symbolic role within his party, providing, through loyalty to his office, a common focus for the diverse regional groups which the party includes among its active membership.

A third factor is the central role of the prime minister in the Canadian system of parliamentary government. The office of prime minister has always been endowed with an impressive array of powers. History has so re-enforced and extended these powers that some students have described the position as presidential—without the checks and balances which hedge presidential power in the United States.[8]

More recently, another factor enhancing the role of party leaders has been the use of radio and television for political communication. Before the development of these media, leaders could communicate with the electorate only through a chain of regional and local intermediaries. Now they are able to appeal directly to voters.

In the Conservative party there are two additional reasons for the leader's pre-eminence.

First, there is good reason to believe that the political ideas of Canadian Conservatives have been influenced by British toryism, which puts considerable emphasis on the value of strong leadership.[9] Their connection to the British tradition is frequently cited by Canadian party members as a characteristic which makes them different from American conservatives.[10]

Second, there is the way in which the party came into existence. The Conservatives were forged from an unstable alliance of legislators into a united national party through the drive of one man, Sir John A. Macdonald. Macdonald's ideas, Macdonald's leadership skills, and Macdonald's personality provide the one constant through the first three decades of the party's history.[11] In this period Conservatives led or formed the government for twenty-five out of twenty-nine years. Thus, in party lore, a myth of heroic leadership has developed around Macdonald. His career is commemorated as the expression of the highest standard of achievement.

Macdonald also left his mark on the leadership in a much more concrete way. The precedents of his actions shaped the leader's role during its formative stage. With enormous personal prestige and the patronage of office with which to command support, he built the leadership into a position of transcendent authority in the structure of the party.

THE LEADER'S AUTHORITY

The leader's authority has its most important manifestation in his exclusive right to declare party policy. This right is clearly expressed in party statements about the participation in policy-making of the National Association—the institution through which the extra-parliamentary membership is represented in the conduct of party affairs. The constitution of the National Association affords it a role in policy-making, but this role has been carefully limited, both by the wording of the constitution and by the declarations of successive leaders. The constitution says only that the association shall convene meetings to *discuss* policy. It gives no official status to any resolutions or declarations which may result from such discussions. While it is the normal practice to conclude policy meetings by voting on a series of resolutions, leaders or their spokesmen have repeatedly stated that these resolutions have no official status. For example, the party newspaper *Communique* reported in 1972 that delegates to the December 1971 annual meeting "were invited to vote on some 350 resolutions *that will act as a guide to the leader* in the exposition of where the Progressive Conservative Party stands on what"[12] (emphasis added).

In practice, this does not mean that the leader acts alone or arbitrarily in making policy. The principles which govern the process are derived from the parliamentary system in which the party operates. The legislative function rests with the parliamentary party, or caucus; the executive function rests with the leader and a group of associates whom he chooses. When the party is in office the leader is of course legally bound to share his executive responsibility with a cabinet, but when the party is in opposition no such obligation exists. Leaders in opposition since the turn of the century have established caucus committees to deal with policy in specific areas and the chairmen of these committees have been designated as the principal opposition spokesmen in the House. But the committee chairmen are not officially described as shadow ministers and no Conservative leader has ever established a shadow cabinet. The committee chairmen do not meet as a body to discuss policy and there is no collective commitment to a particular committee chairman's stance. The committee chairmen work independently of one another and are required to report not to an executive committee of the parliamentary party but to the leader.

The policy-making role of the caucus as a whole has depended on whether the party has been in government or in opposition. When the party has been in government, caucus has had little more than the right to be informed about legislation proposed by cabinet before it is submitted to the House. But when the party has been in opposition, caucus has had a larger role because it is the only forum for the collective discussion of policy. However, even in this situation there is no requirement that committee chairmen submit their proposals to caucus before they can become policy and, while caucus may question the chairmen, their accountability is clearly to the leader.

The leader's authority in policy-making is enhanced by two aspects of caucus procedure.

First, regular meetings of caucus are held for only one half day each week and special meetings are convened infrequently. Therefore, caucus has almost no opportunity to engage in systematic and thorough discussion of most areas of policy.

Second, no votes are taken in caucus. The leader is left to determine the sense of discussion and to act upon it as he sees fit. And it is the leader who gives instructions to the party whips. Accordingly, it is left to him to decide whether the position to be taken on a particular issue will be treated as requiring the sanction of party discipline.

In summary, the leader is viewed as the authoritative voice of the party in Parliament. He is recognized to have the continuing and untrammelled right to make overriding pronouncements on behalf of the caucus or to designate who may make such pronouncements. Thus, as one official put it in an interview, party policy consists only of those statements which have been made by the leader or by a person speaking with the leader's approval.[13] The Conservative party has no official policy except that which the leader decides.

A second manifestation of the leader's authority is the unlimited scope of his prerogative of appointment. As prime minister, of course, he would select all of his colleagues in the ministry. As leader of the opposition, he appoints the policy committee chairmen and their deputies, the party house leader, the whips, and the chairman of caucus. Formally, these appointments are made by caucus on the recommendation of the leader. In fact, the leader's recommendations are submitted as a single list to caucus, when he deems fit, and are never discussed or voted on.

The significance of the leader's authority in this respect may be illustrated by a comparison with the British Conservative party. Within the British party's parliamentary structure, there is an independent committee of backbenchers, called the 1922 committee. The 1922 committee elects its own chairman and acts without direction or interference from the leader.[14] The only position in the Canadian party comparable to the chairmanship of the 1922 committee is the chairmanship of caucus. As I have just noted, however, this position is filled by the appointment of the leader and not by the election of caucus. In effect, this means that there is no recognized independent body within the Progressive Conservative caucus that can challenge the leader.

The leader's authority to make appointments in the extra-parliamentary party is also subject to few formal restrictions. The party's national director, its principal administrative officer, is formally appointed by the steering committee of the National Association, but only on the recommendation of the leader. Other appointments are made directly by the leader or subject to the leader's approval.

While some of these appointive positions are defined in the constitution, their number and powers are not restricted. Thus, the leader has the right to create any ad hoc committee he wishes and to delegate extensive authority of these committees, authority which may supersede that of the National Association and its elected officers. The best illustration is provided by the organization of the party in election campaigns. The leader creates the organization for the conduct of the campaign, defines the positions within it, and makes appointments to these positions—all without any requirement of consultation with any other officer or group within the party.

A third manifestation of the leader's authority is his control over the allocation of party resources. The budget for national headquarters is prepared and administered by the national director who is appointed, as we have observed, by the leader and is accountable only to the leader. Thus, the leader enjoys an absolute right to approve the budget for the continuing activities of the party organization. Until the adoption of the Election Expenses Act in 1974, his control over the allocation of national campaign funds was equally unrestricted. His appointees in the campaign committee were accountable only to him for their disbursement of funds. The implementation of the Election Expenses Act has limited the leader's authority by compelling the party to establish a legal entity subject to external scrutiny to account for the collection and disbursement of party funds. However, within this requirement of public law, the leader's control over national party finance remains unimpaired.

The one area in which the primacy of the leader's authority has appeared to be qualified is that of nomination. The choice of candidates for Parliament has always been a carefully guarded prerogative of party members at the local level. This prerogative antedates the formation of the party, arising from the democratic spirit which led to the establishment of representative government in Canada. Thus, as formal organization developed in the Conservative party, the right of nomination was recognized to lie with constituency (or, as they are also called, riding) associations. The only suggestion of an implicit national party right to intervene in this process is a provision of the constitution of the National Association requiring that constituency associations adopt a constitution which establishes "definite rules and regulations for the conduct of a nomination meeting" and that copies of this constitution be available to the members and filed with national headquarters.[15] There is no central list from which the constituencies get the names of approved candidates, as is the case in the British Conservative party, and there is no requirement for national party approval of the nominees of the constituency associations once they have been chosen.

However, while it has been tested in only one case, the leader does appear to have the right to reject a candidate. The case in point was Robert Stanfield's refusal to accept the candidate nominated by the constituency association for Moncton, New Brunswick, in 1974. Although there was considerable local protest and there was no evidence that party rules had been violated, the Moncton association followed Stanfield's instruction to nominate another candidate.[16] The fact that it did comply with the leader's order would appear to establish that even in this area the leader's word is ultimately the final law of the party.

Of course, no matter what the extent of his authority, every party leader is bound by constraints which arise from his need to maintain the support of the party. The exercise of the rights of leadership is possible only with the consent of those who are led. To explain what this implies for the politics of the Conservative leadership it will be necessary to describe the structure of the party.

ORGANIZATION AT THE PROVINCIAL LEVEL

The development of Conservative organization outside Parliament has closely followed the development of the Canadian federal system. Associated with the establishment of strong independent-minded provincial governments was the development of strong independent-minded provincial parties. As a result, parallel federal and provincial structures have grown up at the local level and the national party has had to organize itself on the federal principle.

In all of the provinces there is a provincial women's association, and a provincial youth association. Provincial constituency organization is maintained in every province except Quebec, and Quebec is the only province in which the party does not have a provincial leader and does not run candidates in provincial elections. In Quebec, the party has maintained a connection with provincial politics through an informal association with the Union Nationale which absorbed most of the members of the provincial Conservative party that disappeared in the mid-1930s. The extent of this association is reflected in data from the survey of 1967 convention delegates. Seventy-four percent of the delegates from Quebec said they were supporters of the Union Nationale and 54 percent said they worked for the Union Nationale in provincial elections.

The strength of provincial organization varies considerably. The critical factor is the competitive position of the provincial party. Provincial organization is strongest where the party holds office, but a tendency toward single-party dominance in provincial politics suggests the need for caution in generalizing about the situation of parties in opposition. For example, while Conservatives formed the official opposition in Alberta and Newfoundland during the 1960s, they had few resources because they faced very powerful and entrenched governing parties. Provincial organization in these two provinces was a good deal weaker than in New Brunswick and Prince Edward Island where the party, although in opposition, had recently formed the government and retained a solid electoral base. In the period of this study, the strongest provincial party was that of Ontario which has held office continuously since 1943. Apart from Quebec where, as I have already mentioned, there is no provincial party, provincial party organization was weakest during this period in British Columbia and Saskatchewan. In British Columbia, most of the party's support was absorbed by the provincial Social Credit party in 1952, while in Saskatchewan, until very recently the party has never been effective in provincial politics.

Regardless of the strength of provincial parties, the locus of power in party organization is at the provincial level. One reason is simply that the lines of communication are shorter from the provincial level to party organization in the constituencies. It is much more efficient in a country as large as Canada to mobilize support by organizing in a decentralized structure. As a result, whatever central direction and support may be required for constituency campaigns comes from provincial campaign committees. Since it is these committees that control the supply of services and money to the constituencies, they are in the best position to exercise external influence in the conduct of constituency affairs.

A second and equally important reason for the decentralized structure of power in party organization is the force of regionalism in the Canadian political culture. As I have already pointed out, this is not just a function of competing regional claims for the allocation of national resources. It also reflects the widespread tendency for Canadians to identify with and express themselves through regionally defined cultural communities. This dimension of regionalism has been manifest in, among other things, strong attachments to provincial political institutions. In fact, in most of the provinces there is evidence that a majority of the population feel closer to the provincial government than to the federal government.[17] It should not be surprising, therefore, that most party activists seem to view their role in the federal party from a provincial perspective.

CONSTITUENCY ORGANIZATION

The basic unit of mass participation in the party is the constituency association. The conditions of membership in constituency associations are minimal. The constitution of the National Association requires only that the constituency associations "admit all bona fide Progressive Conservative supporters to their membership."[18] The associations can prescribe their own conditions, but by custom in most constituencies the only requirement is the purchase of a party card at a nominal fee.

Constituency associations have several important functions. They nominate the party's federal candidates; they are the main agencies for the recruitment of party workers; they have a symbolic role as the representative of the party in the constituencies; and they are expected to provide resources for the conduct of the party's constituency campaigns.

Despite its importance to the party, constituency organization has never been strong. There are very few constituencies in which the active continuing membership exceeds the dozen or so persons who comprise the executives of the local association and affiliated bodies. In many constituencies the associations consist of little more than local cliques. Most constituency associations rarely hold more than one meeting of the general membership each year and then meet only to elect a new executive as required by the constitution of the National Association. In many constituency associations even this minimum requirement is not met.

It is difficult to get any accurate count of the number of constituencies which do have active federal associations.[19] In the report on party organization which led to the reforms of 1943, it was claimed that 204 of the then 243 ridings had inadequate organization.[20] Some party officials estimate that in spite of repeated efforts to overcome this problem, even during the tenure of the Diefenbaker government, as many as one-quarter of the constituencies did not have active associations.

One measure of the continuing weakness of the constituency associations is provided by data from the 1976 convention survey. Delegates from the constituencies were asked how many members had attended the meetings at which they were chosen to be delegates. Since the choice of convention delegates is one of the most important functions of the constituency associations one would expect them to be well attended. But, only 11 percent of the delegates said they were chosen by meetings attended by 200 or more people, while 69 percent said they were chosen by meetings attended by less than 100 people.

The quality of local organization varies considerably from province to province. It has been weakest in Quebec where the party has been able to maintain a local presence only by creating regional structures embracing clusters of constituencies. Most of the constituency associations outside the pockets of anglophone population in Quebec are paper organizations. In other provinces, the number of constituencies with active associations changes with the circumstances of the time. For example, after the defeat of the Diefenbaker government in 1963, particularly as the party became involved in the conflict over Diefenbaker's leadership, constituency associations were weakened by a decline in the enrolment of new members and the withdrawal into inactive roles of substantial numbers of their existing members.

All Canadian parties have had difficulty in establishing active local organization. One reason is the wide dispersal of the population in constituencies outside the main urban centres. The problems of communications in these constituencies have made it very difficult to assemble any kind of functioning constituency-wide organization. A second reason is that parties do not contest municipal elections in Canada. As a result, there is no local focus for party activity.

For the Conservative party there have been special problems created by its electoral weakness. In this respect, the party appears to have been handicapped in the development of local organization in three ways.

First, because it has had so little electoral success, the party has had considerable difficulty in raising funds for inter-election activity. It has always had a struggle just to maintain a minimum budget for national headquarters. As a result, there has been little sustained support for constituency organization. The constituency associations have had to rely on voluntary local labour to develop programs which could attract and maintain membership.

Second, the Conservative party has had little patronage to offer as an incentive for participation.[21] Even the symbolic rewards are very few in the constituency association of a party with such a long history of electoral defeat.

Third, electoral failure is probably also a deterrent to persons who might seek an active role in the party to pursue policy objectives, since the Conservative party is committed to the same basic principles that guide the Liberal party. The person who hopes to influence public policy through partisan activity and operates within the framework of these principles is unlikely to choose the party which has the poorer chance of achieving office.

The membership base of the party has been broadest where a provincial Conservative party has held office or had a good chance to win office. But the presence of a strong provincial party does not necessarily produce strong federal constituency organization. The problem is that there is little congruence between federal and provincial constituency boundaries which has meant that it has been necessary to maintain separate federal and provincial constituency organization. This imposes conflicting demands on local activists.

The complexity of this problem varies with the number of provincial constituencies encompassed by a federal constituency. There is a closer fit between federal and provincial associations in Ontario because the ratio of provincial to federal constituencies there is about four-to-three. In the other provinces with competitive provincial parties—Newfoundland, Prince Edward Island, New Brunswick, Nova Scotia, Manitoba, Saskatchewan, and Alberta—the ratio of provincial to federal constituencies varies from about three-to-one to five-to-one. In these provinces, as a result, a federal constituency association will include part or all of several provincial associations.

There have been different patterns of accommodation to this problem. Independent federal organization is maintained in some cases through the activity of an independently elected federal executive which has little or no overlapping membership with provincial executives. But data from the survey of delegates to the party's 1971 annual meeting suggest that in about three-quarters of the federal constituencies most executive members also hold positions on provincial constituency executives. Given that the main focus of interest for most Conservatives appears to be the provincial party, this suggests that many federal constituency associations may be little more than dependencies of provincial associations.

THE NATIONAL ASSOCIATION

For the first half century of Confederation there was no association of the members of the extra-parliamentary party and there was no provision for their participation in the direction of national party affairs.

In 1924 a national association was established to represent the rank and file but it did not develop a strong base. Despite its weakness, it had symbolic significance because its formation constituted a step toward recognition of the right of the extra-parliamentary membership to share in the decisions of the party. This right was finally recognized in 1943 with the formation of the Dominion Progressive Conservative Association. The constitution of the Dominion Association—which later changed its name to National Association—became the basic constitutional document of the party.

Provincial parties occupy a particularly important role in the National Association. Provincial party leaders, provincial association presidents, provincial women's association presidents, provincial youth organization presidents, and Progressive Conservative supporters in provincial legislatures all have ex officio delegate status at general meetings of the association. In addition, each provincial delegation elects a national vice-president and two directors with ex officio delegate status and each provincial association has the right to appoint delegates-at-large in proportion to the number of federal constituencies in the province. Other voting members in the association are representatives of the constituency associations, representatives of the university and other Progressive Conservative clubs, national officers of the association, members of the association standing committees, members of the Senate and Commons, candidates in federal districts which the party does not hold, privy councillors, the leader, former national leaders, and former national presidents of the association, officers of the national women's association and national youth federation, and representatives of the Yukon and Northwest Territories.

Normally the association meets biennially. Its constitution therefore has delegated its continuing authority to a variety of executive institutions. These are the national executive, a body of some 150 members which is required by the constitution to meet once a year; an executive committee that has varied from twenty to twenty-five members, which is required to meet semi-annually; and a steering committee of eleven members which meets at the call of the association president. Until 1969 there was no constitutionally designated body smaller than the executive committee, although it had been the practice from time to time for consultations to take place among the executive officers of the association. Provincial leaders, officers of provincial associations, women's associations, and youth organizations, and provincially elected vice-presidents and directors of the national association constitute close to half the membership of the national executive. The ten vice-presidents of the provinces are also members of the executive committee. With some minor changes, other members of the executive committee have been the president, secretary, treasurer, three national vice-presidents, leader, national director, and three representatives of the caucus. The steering committee—which consists of the national officers, the leader, the national director, the president of the national women's association, and the president and vice-president of the national youth federation—is the only executive body which does not include specifically designated representatives from the provincial parties.

While the association is presumed to be controlled by the party's mass membership, until 1969 the apportionment provisions of the constitution were such that ex officio delegates and delegates-at-large made up a majority of those entitled to vote at association meetings. For example, in the constitution of 1964, each constiutency association was entitled to elect only two delegates for a total from the constituencies of 528, while the number of ex officio delegates and delegates-at-large was approximately 830. In 1969, constituency representation was increased to five per association, for a total of 1320, while the number of ex officio delegates and delegates-at-large remained about the same.

But, despite this change in the constitution, association meetings continue to be dominated by ex officio delegates because few constituency associations send all of the delegates to which they are entitled. One reason is the weakness of constituency organization, particularly in Quebec. Another is the prohibitive cost of attending. Not many constituency associations are in a position to help defray the costs of attendance and these costs are sufficiently large to deter many delegates from attending at their own expense. These two factors have always been an obstacle in the way of achieving full participation from the constituencies.

Even when there is full or substantial participation from the constituencies, data from the surveys conducted for this study show that meetings and conventions of the association are by no means popular assemblies of Conservatives. First, the surveys show the delegates are almost entirely middle-class and predominantly upper-middle class, while voters who identify themselves as Conservatives constitute a broad cross-section of status groups.[22] Second, most of the delegates from the constituencies are people who hold executive positions in the local constituency associations.

THE SELECTION AND ACCOUNTABILITY OF THE LEADER

As we have already seen, the functions of the National Association have been substantially limited by the prerogatives of the leader. But the association has been conceded one vitally important function that gives it a central role in the politics of the party. It is the association which is authorized to call and manage party leadership conventions.

Before 1927 every Conservative leader, with one exception, was chosen while the party was in office. As a result, the ultimate decision was taken by the governor general acting on the advice of members of the cabinet or the retiring prime minister. On the one occasion that a change took place while the party was in opposition, the choice was made by a meeting of the caucus. However, in 1927, following the precedent established by the Liberal party in 1919, the Conservatives chose their leader in a national convention. A convention was again used when the party next changed its leader in 1938. However, in 1941, Arthur Meighen had the leadership conferred on him by a meeting, ostensibly representing the extra-parliamentary party, whose claim to be a legitimate assembly of the party was seriously in doubt. It was not until the following year, when Meighen resigned, that the national convention was finally established as the permanent procedure for leadership selection. The constitution of the National Association in 1943 gave formal legitimacy to this procedure. In addition it gave the National Association the right to decide when a convention should be called.

The institutionalization of the extra-parliamentary party's right to choose the leader raised the question of the leader's accountability. So long as the choice lay within the parliamentary party—either the cabinet or the whole caucus—there could be little doubt that the leader's accountability was there. But with the decision to delegate this decision to a convention and the granting to the association of the right to decide when a convention should be called, the line of accountability was no longer clear.

Because he occupies a distinctive role in Parliament, with rights and duties established both by custom and by the written law, the leader still retains a line of accountability to the caucus. Although this line of accountability is not mentioned in the written constitution of the party, it is hardly likely to be challenged, since a leader of the party who is not accepted as leader by the caucus cannot secure recognition in Parliament. It is, after all, through the parliamentary party that the ultimate purpose of the party—the achievement of office—is realized. The leader, therefore, has the problem of trying to maintain the support of two bodies—the caucus and the association.

This is a problem of considerable importance in conflicts over the party leadership. Until 1969, its effect was aggravated by a lack of clarity in the rules governing the selection and tenure of leaders. The party constitution did not stipulate under what conditions or by what procedures a leadership convention could be called. Nor did it specify any limit to the leader's tenure or provide for any effective form of leadership review. The only test of confidence in the leader was a voice vote taken as a matter of custom at the end of each general meeting of the association. As we shall see, the leader's dual line of accountability and the absence of effective procedures for leadership review helped to intensify and extend the conflict over John Diefenbaker's leadership.

In 1969 the party adopted a formal procedure requiring a review of the leader's mandate at each annual meeting of the association. In the form in which it was adopted it was both ambiguous and a source of contention. As a result, it was amended in 1974. The constitution now requires that at each annual meeting there shall be a secret ballot putting the question "'do you wish to have a leadership convention?' In the event that more than fifty per cent of the votes cast indicate desire for a leadership convention, the Executive Committee shall call a leadership convention at the earliest date."[23]

This device, however, dealt with only one aspect of the problem. The fact remains that the leader is accountable to both the caucus and the association—a situation which is inherently unstable. The problems created for party leaders by this dual line of accountability are seriously aggravated by three factors.

First, the extra-parliamentary party and the caucus are almost always likely to represent different sets of social interests. This is because the institutions of the extra-parliamentary party have been deliberately designed to ensure representation for all parts of the country, regardless of the distribution of the party's electoral support. Therefore, social groups excluded from representation in the caucus by cleavages in the party's voting support are likely to be represented in the extra-parliamentary party.

Second, members of the caucus and the extra-parliamentary party are likely to have different institutional perspectives on national affairs. The caucus is a national institution functioning in a milieu whch emphasizes national interests and a "centralist" outlook on the country's problems. In contrast, the extra-parliamentary party is composed of people whose outlook is formed primarily through roles in provincial institutions or under the influence of provincial elites. They are therefore likely to view national affairs in terms of provincial interests and from a "provincialist" perspective.

Third, the leader is likely to be much more effective in mobilizing patronage-motivated support in the caucus. His prerogative of appointment means that his favour is essential for career advancement in the parliamentary party. In addition, he controls other resources which can be vitally important to the ambitious member of Parliament, including the right to determine who will have prominent seats in the House, who will speak for the party in major debates, and who will get preferred assignments in House committees. Even when the party is in office, he has relatively few benefits of comparable value to confer on members of the extra-parliamentary party. And when the party is in opposition, he has virtually nothing of significance to offer them except the promise of reward if office is attained.

CONCLUSION

The institutional context of Conservative politics embodies constraints that have an important effect on the nature of conflict over the party leadership. These may be summarized in two main points.

1. The Progressive Conservative party is a leader-centred party. This is true in two senses. First, in his person the leader gives symbolic expression to the party in the country. Second, the role of the leader is endowed with transcendent authority in the structure of the party.

2. Leadership politics in the Conservative party takes place in two quite different arenas; the leader must have the support of both the caucus and the extra-parliamentary party. The complexity of the problems that this creates is increased by the fact that the two bodies tend to represent different sets of social interests, that the extra-parliamentary party is dominated by provincial elites and people with a "provincialist" outlook, and that the leader has less effective patronage resources for dealing with the extra-parliamentary party.

The importance of these and other points discussed in this chapter will be developed more fully later.

3

The History of Conflict in the Party

The history of the Conservative party has been profoundly influenced by conflict over its leadership, as this chapter will demonstrate. The chapter is not intended to be an analysis of the episodes it describes. It is, rather, a summary based on secondary sources which lays out the main features of the role of conflict in party history. Some episodes are more fully described than others because they have been more extensively treated in the secondary literature. An overview of the general points to be drawn from the party's past experience with conflict will be provided at the end of the chapter.

When Sir John A. Macdonald died in 1891, the Conservative party had held federal office in Canada—with one brief interruption from 1873 to 1878—ever since Confederation. But the party's electoral base had begun to erode and its internal unity had begun to weaken.[1] The party's strength under Macdonald's leadership had been its ability to win support across the historically divisive cleavages between Catholics and Protestants, the French and the English, Ontario and Quebec. The constitution of 1867 had helped make this possible by giving jurisdiction to the provinces in areas which seemed most likely to raise linguistic and religious controversy but, despite Macdonald's efforts, federal politics could not be insulated from issues of racial and sectarian concern. The emergence of conflict along these old cleavages struck directly at the foundation of the party's success under Macdonald's leadership.

Ironically, it was Macdonald's policy of western development—a policy which was central to his plan for achieving national unity and, thus, for preserving the strength of his party—that precipitated the strains in racial and sectarian relations. With the opening of the West to immigration, conflicts occurred over the rights of the French-speaking and Roman Catholic *Métis* population already settled there. As early as 1869 there had been an armed rising by the *Métis*. The rising was suppressed and its leader Louis Riel escaped to the United States, but not before the *Métis* provisional government had executed Thomas Scott, a Protestant prisoner captured early in the fighting. Sixteen years later, Riel returned to Canada to lead a new revolt. This time he was captured, tried for treason, and sentenced to hang. There was widespread opposition to Riel's sentence in Quebec and Macdonald was urged by leaders of French-Canadian opinion to commute the sentence. In Ontario Riel's involvement in the execution of Scott was used to stir the English Protestant population against commutation. After some delay Macdonald decided against intervention and, in the fall of 1885, Riel was hanged.

Macdonald might have followed a different course had there been a strong French-Canadian leader among his colleagues. But there was none. The Quebec wing of the party was badly split—by factional conflicts over the control of patronage, by regional competition between Quebec and Montreal, and by the doctrinal cleavage between moderate and ultramontane Roman Catholics. There was no one who had both the stature and the support to be able to speak authoritatively on behalf of French-Canadian opinion.[2]

Riel's hanging evoked an emotional response in Quebec. Prominent Conservatives joined in the nationalist reaction from which there emerged a *Parti National*, launched and led by the provincial Liberal leader, Honoré Mercier. In the provincial election of 1886, Mercier cut deeply into Conservative support. Subsequently, with the assistance of Conservative nationalists he overturned the Conservative majority in the legislature and formed a government.

In the federal election which followed, early in 1887, the Conservative share of Quebec's sixty-five seats was reduced from fifty-one to thirty-three. While the party retained a one-seat majority in Quebec, the fact remained that its hold on French Canada had been badly shaken. The effect was to aggravate the divisions within the Quebec wing and to weaken even further the French-Canadian voice in the Conservative caucus.

This was all the more serious because, once ignited, the flames of religious and racial conflict could not be contained.[3] Another contentious issue was provided by the decision of the Mercier government to pay compensation for lands seized from the Jesuit order after its disbandment in the eighteenth century. The Jesuit Estates Act had the support of Protestant members of the Quebec legislature and dealt with a matter which was purely of provincial concern, but it incensed Protestant extremists in Ontario who demanded that it be struck down by the federal government—using the federal power to disallow provincial legislation. In 1888 a Conservative member of Parliament introduced a disallowance motion. This motion was easily defeated but the debate it provoked gave additional stimulus to extremist opinion. One result was the formation by Ontario Protestants of an Equal Rights Association, the purpose of which was to curb the influence of French Canadians and their religion outside Quebec.

D'Alton McCarthy, a prominent Conservative member of Parliament, put himself at the head of the Equal Rights Association and carried its message into western Canada. Soon after his visit, the Territorial Assembly of the Northwest Territories adopted a resolution asking Ottawa for repeal of the section of the Northwest Territories Act which recognized French as an official language. In January 1890, McCarthy brought the resolution into Parliament. The resolution raised a difficult issue because it concerned not just the question of the status of French, but also the question of the right of the assembly to regulate territorial affairs. At one stage in the debate there was a vote in which French- and English-speaking members coalesced across party lines in opposition to one another, but ultimately a compromise acceptable to moderate opinion was devised and adopted.

McCarthy's activities in Manitoba helped precipitate a problem which was less easy to solve. In 1890 the Manitoba legislature adopted a Public Schools Act which denied government support to denominational schools and thereby attacked the right to a separate education which the French-Catholic minority in Manitoba believed had been guaranteed in the Manitoba Act—the act by which Manitoba had been established as a province. Now it was the Catholic community (English as well as French) which demanded that the federal government intervene. One course was disallowance; another was to invoke a provision of the Manitoba Act which permitted the federal government to adopt remedial legislation. Macdonald avoided an immediate response by persuading Manitoba Catholics that before the federal government took any steps to intervene it would be better to test the constitutionality of the Public Schools Act in the courts. This manoeuvre averted a decision which would have forced the Conservative party to choose between offending either Catholics or Protestants.

Macdonald managed to keep the election campaign of 1891 off the sensitive ground of the Public Schools Act. Two factors helped him. One was the diversion provided by the Liberal commitment to unrestricted free trade with the United States, a proposal that roused fears in both Quebec and Ontario about Canada's absorption by the United States. The other was the continued support he received from the hierarchy of the Roman Catholic church in Quebec. Despite a net loss of ten seats, the Conservative party won the election. Twelve weeks later Macdonald died.

The party was ill prepared for the problem of choosing a new leader.

The Quebec wing was in complete disarray. In the election the support of the church had helped stave off a substantial defeat, but there were further losses and, for the first time since 1874, victory in Quebec had gone to the Liberal party. Moreover, the divisions among Quebec Conservatives had been driven more deeply and were more widely exposed. Before the election, Israel Tarte, a prominent party organizer, had made charges of corruption against the senior Quebec minister, Sir Hector Louis Langevin. Tarte may have been trying to help Langevin's principal rival for control of the Quebec party, Joseph Chapleau.[4] In any event, his actions did nothing to improve the relationship between Langevin and Chapleau and he himself moved to the fringe of the Conservative party from which he was to defect altogether in 1893. The Quebec wing now had neither enough members in the caucus nor a cabinet representative with sufficient support from his own province and sufficient respect from his English-speaking colleagues to give French Canada an effective voice in the decisions of the national party.

The balance of power in the selection of Macdonald's successor therefore lay with English-speaking Protestants. Most of them were moderates but they were sensitive to the effect on their constituents of the intemperate and intolerant rhetoric of Protestant extremists.

Since the party was in office, the formal designation of the new leader lay with the governor general who took advice from members of the cabinet. For reasons which are not clear, Sir Charles Tupper, who was the most prominent of Macdonald's surviving colleagues, was not wanted by the cabinet. Sir John Thompson, the minister of justice, evidently had considerable support, but Thompson was a Catholic convert from Methodism and, therefore, believed that the climate of sectarian hostility made his candidacy unacceptable. As a result, the succession fell to Sir John Abbott, a member of the Senate, who observed that he had been chosen because he was 'not particularly obnoxious to anybody."[5]

The lack of enthusiasm for Abbott's appointment was quickly reflected in criticism of his leadership.[6] He apparently had neither the desire nor the physical ability to give direction. As a result, the real power soon passed to Thompson who had been chosen to lead the party in the Commons. In December 1892, because of continued ill health Abbott resigned and advised the governor general to appoint Thompson in his place. Thompson, believing that there had been some moderation in the intensity of religious feeling against his succession, agreed to accept.[7] He demonstrated his own willingness to find an accommodation within the party by appointing to the cabinet one of the eight Conservatives who had voted for disallowance of the Jesuit Estates Act in 1888.

In 1894 the strength of this alliance was faced with a fundamental test, because the federal government was finally forced to deal with the Manitoba public schools issue. In separate decisions the Privy Council had ruled that while the act was within the legislative competence of Manitoba, the federal government had the authority to provide redress to the minority by enacting remedial legislation. Thompson moved slowly, seeking to avoid the accusation of bias toward his fellow Catholics. Then, quite unexpectedly, while he was on a visit to London, Thompson died.

Complicating the selection of a leader this time was the fact that the country had a new governor general, Lord Aberdeen, who was ill disposed toward Tupper. The prejudice of Lord Aberdeen, along with the hostility of the "knot of jealous and feuding individuals in the Cabinet, who in pursuit of their own ambitions disregarded the undoubted wishes of the rank and file"[8] ensured that Tupper was once again rejected. The leadership passed instead to Senator Mackenzie Bowell who, whatever his other qualifications, had the distinction of having been a former grand master of the Orange Order. Bowell's selection was a disaster for the party, as Macdonald's former secretary, Sir Joseph Pope, observed: "Then followed days which I never recall without a blush, days of weakened, incompetent administration by a cabinet presided over by a man whose sudden and unlooked-for elevation had visibly turned his head, a ministry without unity or cohesion of any kind, a prey to internal dissensions until they became a spectacle to the world, to angels, and to men."[9]

For a year Bowell procrastinated over the Manitoba schools issue. A majority of the cabinet was committed to remedial action, but the prime minister continued to delay. His indecision, together with the restiveness of those who had opposed and were reluctant to accept his leadership, produced a situation of virtually permanent crisis in the cabinet.

On March 19, 1895, the governor-in-council ordered the Manitoba government to restore support for the separate schools. It had been understood among the ministers that this order would be followed by an election in which the government would seek a mandate to proceed, but on March 21, Bowell informed the cabinet that he planned another session of Parliament. Sir Charles Hibbert Tupper, the minister of justice and son of Bowell's rival for the succession, immediately proposed to resign. After a week of negotiations he was persuaded to remain.

In July, Manitoba told the federal government of its refusal to comply in the March order. Bowell now proposed to defer the introduction of a remedial bill until January 1896, in order to try to find a compromise with Manitoba. In the face of this further delay the three French-Canadian ministers submitted their resignations. Once again there were negotiations to try to restore party unity. Two of the rebellious ministers finally agreed to withdraw their resignations, but the third, A. R. Angers, said he could no longer accept Bowell's assurances and insisted on leaving the cabinet. Equally damaging for the party in Quebec was a subsequent vote of non-confidence in the House of Commons in which six Quebec Conservatives voted with the opposition.

Bowell's desperate efforts to avoid the final step are not difficult to understand because he was under increasing pressure from both flanks. For example, during the July cabinet crisis, forty Ontario members of the caucus signed a petition urging him not to introduce remedial legislation. But the majority in the cabinet believed further delay could achieve nothing except to re-enforce the growing public impression of a weak, divided, and indecisive government.

The dissidents found confirmation of their suspicions of Bowell's incompetence and a rationale for action against him in his failure to secure a replacement from French Canada for Angers. Using this as a pretext, at the opening of Parliament in January 1896, seven ministers announced to the House of Commons that they could no longer serve under Bowell's leadership. Their action was part of a plan developed in December to force Bowell out and install the elder Tupper in his place.[10]

Over the next ten days Bowell struggled to retain the leadership, bolstered by Tupper's enemies in the party and by the governor general who twice refused to accept his resignation. A compromise was finally struck by which Bowell was permitted to save face while the rebels were afforded ultimate satisfaction. Bowell continued as prime minister with the understanding that he would be replaced by Tupper at the end of the session; Tupper entered the cabinet and assumed the leadership of the party in the Commons; six of the seven ministers who had resigned were reappointed; a French-Canadian replacement was found for Angers; and in February the remedial bill was introduced.

The government's action on the remedial bill came too late. By a narrow majority the bill was passed through second reading, but the opposition was able to hold up its progress at the committee stage until the impending expiry of the term of Parliament forced its withdrawal. As a result, the party entered the 1896 election with the matter still unsettled.

Quebec was the chief battleground for the 1896 election. The Conservatives retained the support of the Roman Catholic hierarchy because the Liberals had helped block the remedial bill in Parliament and probably because church leaders continued to mistrust "radical" Liberal ideas.[11] However, French Canadians had reason to be suspicious of the Conservative commitment. For one thing, there had been the government's long delays in dealing with the Manitoba problem. In addition, the campaign revealed contradictions between the Conservative party's official policy and that adopted by many of its candidates. In Ontario, even though the most militant Protestants were now outside the party,[12] fully half of the Conservative candidates said they were opposed to any further effort to pass remedial legislation. More than once in Ontario, Tupper was forced to couch his statements in guarded language as he found himself speaking in support of a candidate who had renounced the official policy. He was, therefore, exposed to the charge of having one policy for Quebec and another for the rest of the country.

The Liberal party's position may have been equally suspect,[13] but the

Liberals had two advantages. First, they had not had the responsibility of office and therefore escaped blame for the provocations against French Canadians which had been such an important feature of political life over the preceding decade. Second, their leader, Sir Wilfrid Laurier, was a French Canadian.

Tupper had tried hard to find a Quebec leader who could rival Laurier's appeal among French Canadians, but the one man whose popularity was thought to be sufficient to the task, Joseph Chapleau, could not be induced to join the cabinet. There was an irony in the Conservative party's efforts to persuade Chapleau to assume the Quebec leadership because only five years before when he had wanted the position the party had spurned him.[14] With Chapleau unwilling, the shattered Quebec wing was ineffectual against Laurier.

The outcome of the election in Quebec was decisive in the national result. The Conservatives won only sixteen seats while the Liberals won forty-nine. This substantial Liberal victory in Quebec provided Laurier with the majority he needed to defeat the government.[15]

Historians agree on the importance of the internal conflicts within the Conservative party in bringing the government down.[16] To some extent, the instability in the leadership was a matter of historical accident. Abbott's illness and Thompson's premature death are both illustrations of the intervention of chance. Yet there was more to the extended crisis of leadership than mere bad luck. The parameters of leadership choice were defined by sectarian and linguistic conflict. In addition, relationships among the principals were coloured by their personal ambitions or their desire to frustrate the ambitions of others.[17]

The rivalries, jealousies, and shifting personal loyalties within the Quebec wing of the party had an independent impact on the national crisis. These forces were at work long before the hanging of Riel and the re-emergence of inter-communal conflict in national politics. The Quebec wing had been engaged in its own succession conflict ever since the death in 1873 of Macdonald's ally in the formation of the party, Sir George-Etienne Cartier. Cartier exercised what amounted to baronial control over the party in Quebec. Thus, the succession there was a considerable prize. In the struggle to achieve it, the Quebec wing was so weakened that French-Canadian Conservatives ceased to have an effective voice in the national party at the time when it most needed a strong counterweight to English Protestant opinion.

The 1896 election marked the end of the period of Conservative ascendency in federal politics. It was to be fifteen years before Canada had another Conservative government and the party was never again to achieve the extended success it had enjoyed under Macdonald's leadership.

In 1900 Sir Charles Tupper resigned the Conservative leadership and was succeeded by Robert Borden, the first leader who had not been a minister under Macdonald. Borden's accession symbolized change, but it could not mean a complete break with the past and this created problems for the new leader. For one thing, he had to contend with the opinions of those who contrasted his own style and performance with the style and performance of the selectively remembered days of power. In addition, there were tensions between new members and the generation with ties to the Macdonald period over the extent to which the party should reformulate its policy of national development to meet new conditions. Finally, there were the continuing instability in the Quebec wing of the party and the persistence of sectarian and religious cleavage in national politics.

Internal conflict continued to impair the effectiveness of the Quebec Conservative party. Borden tried to impose order from outside by designating Frederick Monk as Quebec leader, but Monk's efforts were frustrated by rivals, and Borden himself in the face of their complaints began to deal bilaterally with each of the various factions and cliques. As a result, he so undercut Monk's authority that Monk felt compelled to resign.[18] No new Quebec leader was appointed in his place.

To add to the party's difficulties in Quebec, there was another open split along religious and racial lines in 1905 when English-Protestant members of the caucus took the position that the two new provinces of Alberta and Saskatchewan—which were being created out of the Northwest Territories—should have complete self-determination in education policy. In so doing, they explicitly denied claims by French-Catholic members that minority education should have the same protection in the two new provinces that it had been given in the Manitoba Act. Borden tried to minimize the effects of this disagreement by declaring the issue a matter of conscience not subject to party discipline in the House but when it came to a vote, he took his own stand with the majority. He thereby publicly identified himself with the anti-French, anti-Catholic elements of the party and weakened both his personal prestige and the image of the party among French Canadians.

The breach between French- and English-speaking Conservatives was further widened in 1910 by a conflict over Canada's role in imperial naval defence. At the heart of this issue was the tension between the French Canadians distaste for involvement in European affairs and the English Canadians emotional attachment to the British connection. In 1909 Parliament had debated, and both the government and the opposition had supported, a resolution providing for the establishment of a Canadian navy. During the debate, the British government had announced that the imperial preponderance of naval power was threatened by Germany's dreadnought construction program. The British announcement provoked demands from English-speaking Canada—demands taken up by several prominent Conservatives—that Canada make an immediate and direct contribution to the imperial navy. These demands were anathema to a large number of French Canadians who were already afraid that the proposed Canadian navy might become a device for entangling the country in unwanted overseas commitments.

The Laurier government introduced a bill to establish the Canadian navy in January 1910. It proposed that in an emergency the navy could be placed under imperial command by order-in-council—subject to subsequent approval by Parliament. French-speaking Conservatives insisted that nothing short of a referendum on the issues raised by the bill would be sufficient to meet Quebec concerns; English-speaking Conservatives opposed a referendum and urged the government to go further and make an immediate contribution to the imperial navy. Borden tried to reconcile the two views, but his francophone colleagues would not accept any compromise that called for an immediate contribution. Ultimately, both sections of the party opposed the government's legislation but the French-speaking members did so through a separate amendment which ran counter to the general policy declared by Borden.

In the aftermath of the parliamentary debate, the francophone members opened a general attack on Borden's leadership. This precipitated a revolt by a group of anglophone members with grievances of their own.

> Once the dam had been breached, a great flood of discontent in the parliamentary party broke loose. Many parliamentarians deeply resented the way Borden had treated his colleagues over the years. He had been distant, moody, imperious, sometimes almost scornful of their worth. He had seldom consulted with them. If a caucus was stormy he might go away and not call another for the remainder of the session. From the beginning of his leadership he had made policy by memoranda with outsiders; businessmen, journalists, provincial potentates, men who understood little and cared less about the demands, the whims, and the welfare of the parliamentary party. And now all the long smouldering unrest came out in a great disorganized rush of revolt. The Quebeckers had wounded the leader. The malcontents moved in for the kill.[19]

On April 5, 1910, Borden offered to resign. One week later the caucus met to consider his resignation and after some debate voted by a substantial majority to reject it. This was not the end of the affair. Early in 1911 Laurier announced that the government had agreed to terms for general free trade with the United States. As a result, a number of prominent Liberals—whose business interests were well-served by the tariff—negotiated an agreement with Borden to support the Conservative party. The rebels in the Conservative caucus seized on this agreement to renew their attacks on Borden, denouncing any suggestion of cooperation with Liberals. Once again a strong display of support for the leader by other members of the caucus forced them to withdraw.

Borden had less success in dealing with the French-speaking Conservatives. In an attempt at conciliation, in 1911 he conceded that before any direct naval contributions were made to Britain there should be an appeal to Parliament and if that failed there should be an appeal to the country. He also pledged to seek a role for Canada in the formulation of imperial foreign policy. These concessions were not sufficient to reunify the party but they helped preserve an arms-length association. In the general election which followed, the French-speaking Conservatives formed an alliance with other Quebec nationalists and constituted themselves an independent Conservative party, finding common cause with the rest of the party in their determination to defeat Laurier.

In the 1911 election the Conservative party was returned to power. The reciprocity issue had split the Liberal party and given the Conservatives an opportunity to appeal to the strong sentiment of anti-Americanism in Ontario and other parts of English-speaking Canada. In Ontario alone the Conservatives piled up a majority of sixty seats. The Liberals again won Quebec although the nationalist alliance with the Conservatives cut Laurier's majority there from forty-three to eleven. The Conservative party, therefore, had an opportunity to try to rebuild its base in French Canada.

To this end, Borden included in his cabinet Frederick Monk, the leader of the Conservative nationalists from Quebec, and three other French Canadians. Within a few months, however, the increasing threat of war in Europe led to a renewal of the conflict over naval policy. When the rest of the cabinet agreed to ask Parliament for an emergency contribution to the British navy, Monk, who wanted the question put to a plebiscite, resigned.

Borden's rapprochement with the French-speaking Conservatives was dealt a further blow by a new controversy over minority education rights. In 1912 the Conservative government of Ontario issued an order which effectively put an end to French-language instruction in Ontario schools.[20] Franco-Ontarian protests of this order led to the closing of schools under the administration of the separate schools authority in the city of Ottawa. To get the schools open, the legislature enacted a law which would permit the minister of education to place them under the administration of a special commission responsible to his department.

The federal cabinet was immediately pressed by the francophone and Catholic communities to disallow this piece of provincial legislation. Shortly after, the Liberal government in Manitoba secured legislative approval for a bill which abolished bilingual schools in that province. The agitation roused by this additional assault on French language rights prompted the three French-speaking members of the cabinet to ask Borden to have the whole question of the status of French outside Quebec referred to the Judicial Committee of the Privy Council. On the ground that this would be an unacceptable interference in provincial autonomy, Borden refused. The cabinet also subsequently rejected the petition to disallow the Ontario act.

For the time being, although the three French-Canadian ministers had come to the brink of resignation,[21] the unity of the government was preserved. However, the cabinet's decisions had created new stress in the relationship between French- and English-speaking Conservatives and added to the sense of grievance throughout the francophone community just at the time when the country was beginning to debate the deeply divisive issue of conscription.

Underlying the conflict over conscription were the differing views of national identity which had been at the centre of the naval controversy. Canadians of English descent had strong ties to Britain and the Empire and were therefore emotionally committed to the war. French Canadians, in contrast, had no close ties either to Britain or to continental Europe. Their approach to European politics was pragmatic, not emotional. While they had agreed that Canada should support the allies, they did not have the English Canadians passionate sense of dedication to the allied cause. As a result, when the heavy drain on military manpower created pressure for the introduction of conscription, there was widespread opposition in Quebec. The French-Canadian view was heard in the Conservative cabinet and caucus but there is little evidence that it received much sympathy. In any event, in 1917 the government introduced a conscription bill.

Both government and opposition split over the bill. One of the French-speaking ministers resigned and most French-speaking members of the Conservative caucus voted with Quebec Liberals against the bill. A large number of English-speaking Liberals supported conscription and subsequently agreed to join a coalition government under Borden's leadership. In the fall of 1917, the newly constituted Union government went to the country and won a substantial majority. Unionists swept the English-speaking provinces, taking 150 out of 170 seats. But for the Conservative party it was a truly pyrrhic victory. Out of the sixty-five seats in Quebec, the Unionists won only three—all in predominantly English-speaking districts. For the first time since Confederation, not one French Canadian was elected as a Conservative—regular or independent.

Borden continued as prime minister until 1920 when he was succeeded by Arthur Meighen, the minister of the interior. Meighen's appointment was not universally popular with his colleagues. His forensic skills had earned him wide support on the Conservative back-benches, but most members of the cabinet were opposed to him. In fact, Borden had recommended him to the governor general only after Sir Thomas White, the minister of finance, had refused to accept. Meighen's biographer, Roger Graham, ascribes the opposition to him to a belief that he would be unacceptable to French Canadians, to resentment at his rapid rise to power (until 1917 he had been the most junior member of the cabinet), and to a concern that he was temperamentally unsuited to be leader.[22] This last objection evidently was the most important. Meighen's style was intellectual, dispassionate, and blunt. "[B]y the very power of his mind, the perfection of his speech, the manifest sincerity of his beliefs"[23] he had demonstrated a singular capacity to inspire support. But he was reserved, aloof, and deficient "in the small, personal arts of politics."[24] He had already made enemies and he would continue to do so—both outside the party and within it.

One of the first problems Meighen had to face was the condition of the party in Quebec. He believed that if the party could find a prominent French Canadian to assume the leadership in Quebec it might be able to restore itself there. But he was at some disadvantage in attempting the search for such a figure. For one thing, he was closely identified with conscription, having been the sponsor of the conscription bill in the House. In addition, his own views were not sufficiently open to make the kind of commitments necessary if French Canadians were to be convinced that the party had become more sensitive to their concerns.[25] It may well be argued that no leader, however accommodating on specific issues, could have overcome the hostility of French Canadians towards the Conservative party at that time. In any event, Meighen's efforts to find a French Canadian of stature to lead the Quebec wing of the party were to no avail. The remnant of the Conservative party in Quebec was disorganized, fractious, and clique-ridden.

Although the situation in Quebec was serious, it was just one of Meighen's problems. Another was the conflict between the interests of the party's supporters in agricultural sections of the country—particularly in Manitoba, Saskatchewan, and Alberta—and the interests of its supporters in the urban commercial and manufacturing areas of central Canada. The post-war economic decline had created hardship for farmers, aggravating their complaints against the federal policies which seemed to contribute to their exploitation by central Canadian business. Agrarian discontent grew into a movement for economic and political reform which rapidly spread through the prairie provinces and rural sections of Ontario. One of the main objectives of this movement was the elimination of the protective tariff, long the centrepiece of Conservative doctrine and the policy on which the party had built the hard core of its support in the manufacturing communities of central Canada. In 1919 when the government refused to reduce the tariff, T. A. Crerar, a Liberal member of the Unionist cabinet, and nine other Liberal-Unionist members of

Parliament withdrew from the coalition. In the following year Crerar assumed the leadership of a new Progressive party which quickly cut into Unionist support in the prairies and rural Ontario.

A third problem for Meighen was the dissatisfaction of several prominent Conservative businessmen with the government's railway policy. Free enterprise principles and powerful special interests had both been offended by the nationalization in 1918 of the Grand Trunk and Pacific Northern railways. As it happened, Meighen had also been the author of this policy and in defending it he had earned the personal as well as the political animus of those who opposed it. These men—who controlled important resources of money and prestige—remained cool toward Meighen and ambivalent toward the party under his leadership.[26]

The new leader had a fourth problem in the opposition among Conservatives to the continuation of the alliance with Unionist Liberals. The decision to continue the alliance had been taken before Meighen assumed the leadership, but he had supported it and continued to do so because he believed it might help the party retain some of the Liberal votes it had won in 1917. Underlying the objections of opponents of the decision there appear to have been two kinds of motives. First, it required them to share, and therefore reduced, their opportunities for patronage. Second, it compelled them to work with people toward whom through years of often bitter rivalry they had developed strong feelings of personal antipathy. Many old Conservatives refused to cooperate in the alliance. While some simply would not work with Unionist Liberals, others publicly attacked Meighen and took steps to disrupt the alliance.[27]

All of these factors—the condition of the party in Quebec, the alienation of the party's agrarian support, the hostility toward Meighen of some Conservative businessmen, and the conflicts within the party organization—contributed to a crushing defeat for the Meighen government in 1921. The Liberals won every seat in Quebec and made gains in Ontario, the maritime provinces, and British Columbia. Progressive candidates won all but three seats in the prairie provinces and most of the seats in agricultural sections of Ontario. Altogether, the Liberals won 116 seats, the Progressives 65, and the Conservatives 50. As a result, a new Liberal administration took office under the leadership of William Lyon Mackenzie King.

Despite the fact they had won fewer seats than the Progressives, the Conservatives remained secure in their position as the only alternative governing party. The Progressives were interested more in achieving their program of reforms than in competing for office and when Parliament met allowed the Conservatives to assume the role of official opposition.[28]

Meighen's hold on the leadership of the Conservative party was less certain. His opponents in the party used the election defeat to justify their efforts to force him to resign. A caucus, in March 1922, temporarily stalled these efforts by unanimously refusing to accept his resignation. However, there was little abatement in the attacks on him from outside the caucus.

One source of these attacks was Robert Rogers, a minister under Borden whose exclusion from the cabinet when the Union government was formed had made him a bitter foe of the Unionist alliance. Rogers may have felt he had some reason to blame Meighen for the loss of his cabinet seat since Meighen had replaced him as the minister representing Manitoba. In any event, he had been a rival and a public and private critic of Meighen for many years.[29] In 1922 Rogers began a campaign for a leadership convention which he continued until the end of 1923, when he apparently became convinced that his efforts were futile.

The Conservative proprietors of the leading English-language newspapers of Montreal—the *Star* and the *Gazette*—were more persistent. Their main purpose was to find a leader who would be more amenable to the Montreal view of railway policy, that is, a policy which served the interests of the Canadian Pacific Railway. Lord Atholstan, the publisher of the *Star*, pursued Meighen with a particular vigour and virulence. The two men had formed a mutual dislike which came to dominate their relationship. Both in his role as a prominent figure in Conservative organization and through the *Star*, Atholstan was an unrelenting critic whose attacks continued to the end of Meighen's leadership.[30]

But internal conflict was not just a problem for the Conservative party. The Progressives, upon whose support the King government relied to sustain it in office, were divided on important issues of policy and strategy. These divisions were such that by 1922 the Progressive movement had begun to break apart. At the same time disagreements within the Liberal party and the need to attract Progressive support led King to follow a cautious policy which left his government with few solid achievements on which to base an appeal for re-election.[31]

To take full advantage of this opportunity, Meighen needed to rebuild the Conservative party. The main problem continued to be in Quebec. To deal with it, he invited E. L. Patenaude, the French-Canadian minister who had resigned from Borden's cabinet over conscription, to assume the leadership of the Quebec wing. Patenaude had turned Meighen down in 1921; now he found the national leader more accommodating to his views on French-English relations[32] and agreed to accept. There were still two difficulties. First, Patenaude had so delayed his decision that he did not have sufficient time to establish effective organization and, second, even though he insisted on complete autonomy for the Quebec party and the complete separation of the Quebec campaign from the national campaign he could not escape the taint of association with Meighen.

In the 1925 election, outside Quebec the Conservatives won 112 seats while within Quebec they won only four. The Liberal hold on French

Canada had given Mackenzie King enough seats to enable him, with continued Progressive support, to preserve his government.

Meighen was briefly restored to office in 1926 after the King government, while facing defeat in the House, was denied a dissolution by the governor general, and resigned. When Meighen was unable to secure the support of the Progressives he was granted the dissolution King had been refused. King made this a central issue in the campaign, arguing that the governor general had exceeded his authority in denying the Liberal request for a dissolution and then giving one to the Conservatives. Whatever its constitutional merits, King's argument had a nationalist appeal which probably had some general effect and certainly buttressed his party's position in Quebec. Once again the Conservatives were held to four seats in Quebec. Elsewhere peculiar local circumstances, the continued decline of the Progressives, and the effects of tax cuts enacted by the King government before its resignation, all helped contribute to Liberal gains.[33] As a result, the second Meighen administration was defeated.

Immediately following the 1926 election Meighen resigned from the leadership. The Conservative caucus appointed Hugh Guthrie to serve as interim leader until a leadership convention could be arranged.

When the convention met in October 1927, there were five candidates for the succession: Guthrie, R. B. Bennett, C. H. Cahan, R. J. Manion, Robert Rogers, and Sir Henry Drayton. Bennett, who had been a minister both in 1921 and in 1926 but was not closely identified with Meighen, was elected on the second ballot. The campaign for the leadership was notably free of contention. In fact, Meighen, in his one official appearance before the convention, generated more controversy than any of the candidates. In his address Meighen defended a speech from November 1925, in which he had declared that before the government undertook to send Canadian troops to fight in any future European war, it should test public opinion in a general election. This declaration had upset many English-speaking Conservatives and Meighen's defence of it provoked a heated response from Howard Ferguson, the premier of Ontario. Ferguson, who apparently feared that Meighen might try to use the issue to seek re-election, accused the former leader of enunciating a policy which could only contribute to national disunity.[34] The leadership candidates remained aloof from this debate and there is no evidence that it had any bearing on the outcome of the convention. It was a reminder, however, of the continuing vulnerability of the party on any issue which evoked the cleavage between the French and English communities.

In 1930 Bennett led the Conservatives back to office. Although the party had a net gain of twenty-six seats in the English-speaking provinces, the decisive factor in the election was its success in Quebec, where it won twenty-five seats. In surveying the explanations offered for this improvement, Murray Beck argues that an environment was created conducive to an appeal on economic issues. One factor which helped create this environment was the retirement of Meighen, whose image had been fixed in French Canada as the author of conscription. A second was a more sympathetic attitude toward the Conservatives in the hierarchy of the Roman Catholic church. A third was King's shift toward imperial preference and the resultant Conservative assertion of a "Canada first" trade policy.[35] As it was, the deep-rooted nature of anti-Conservative feeling among French Canadians ensured that the Liberals retained a sixteen-seat majority in Quebec, but the twenty additional seats the Conservatives picked up were enough to give them a national majority.

Bennett's success was brief. Just five years later the Conservatives suffered a defeat even worse than that of 1921. An important contributing factor was the conflict which developed in the relationship between the prime minister and H. H. Stevens, the minister of trade and commerce. Early in 1934 Stevens made a speech, blaming large retail firms for holding down prices paid to manufacturers and, therefore, for contributing to the exploitation of manufacturing workers. There was an immediate reaction from the big retailers which led to an angry meeting between Bennett and Stevens. Bennett accused Stevens of going "further in formulating policy without reference to the head of the government or his colleagues than a minister should go under sound constitutional practices"[36] and implied that Stevens should resign.[37] On the following day Stevens submitted a letter of resignation. However, the prime minister had not desired this result and arranged a second meeting. At this meeting, Bennett agreed to a proposal by Stevens for an inquiry into price spreads which would examine the questions raised by the speech. To conduct this inquiry a select committee of the Commons was established with Stevens as its chairman.

Stevens used the committee's hearings to secure evidence sustaining his charges. The general thrust of the case he developed was that farmers, workers, and the proprietors of small business were the collective victims of increasing corporate concentration. By June, when the committee's life was about to end, it was apparent that Stevens had struck a popular chord. Thus the cabinet agreed to appoint him chairman of a royal commission to continue the inquiry. A few weeks later the Toronto *Star* published a summary of a speech Stevens had made to a private meeting of Conservative members of Parliament.[38] There were two problems with the speech. First, it laid out the policy implications of the case Stevens was developing which suggested that as chairman of the royal commission he had prejudged the questions he had been asked to investigate. And, second, it contained charges, for which there was no substantiation, that there had been improprieties in a share transaction involving the principal shareholder of the Robert Simpson Company, one of the firms which had appeared before the inquiry.

The Liberal press and Simpson's demanded some response from the prime minister. There was too much political risk to interfere with the inquiry or remove Stevens who had earned a wide popular following, but Bennett wanted Stevens to apologize to the Simpson Company. This proposal was made to Stevens at a cabinet meeting which discussed the matter in October. Stevens agreed to consider the proposal and the meeting was adjourned until the following day. Stevens did not attend; instead he sent a letter of resignation to the prime minister. His decision was prompted by an account of the previous day's meeting which had been leaked to the press by another member of the cabinet:

> . . . to my annoyance I found that there appeared in the press a fairly complete résumé of what had happened in council, in regard to which a very solemn oath had been taken. The gist of this publication was that I had been asked to make amends, and to whom? To Mr. C. L. Burton of the Robert Simpson Company . . . who had complained to the Prime Minister regarding the utterances in the [speech]. . . . And the newspaper account of the meeting of the cabinet was to the effect that if I did not make these amends I would be asked to resign. Sir, I would not take that position for anybody, and I resigned and refused to go back to cabinet under those conditions. I resigned for that purpose and for that reason, that the secret and private discussions of cabinet had been spread upon the pages of the press. Had I gone back and had an amicable arrangement been made between my colleagues and myself it would have been on record that I had gone back because I had been publicly spanked in the press, and I had no intention of placing myself in that humiliating position.[39]

This time Bennett accepted the resignation because, he later explained, "what else could we do when he had resigned twice in the same year."[40]

One popular interpretation held that the resignation was a repudiation of Stevens' views on policy by a reactionary prime minister. There are three reasons to reject this interpretation. First, Bennett had long since demonstrated his willingness to give the government a more active role in the economy.[41] Second, he had already indicated sympathy for Stevens' ideas by agreeing to initiate the price spreads inquiry. And, third, just two months after Stevens resigned, Bennett announced a comprehensive program of social and economic reform modelled on the American New Deal. Some other members of the cabinet did disagree with Stevens about policy. A key figure was C. H. Cahan, the secretary of state, who had been a persistent critic of the price spreads inquiry. Cahan led the attack on Stevens in the discussion in cabinet and was believed to have been responsible for the leak to the press.[42] In the final analysis, however, it was the relationship between Stevens and the prime minister which counted and in this relationship a personal animus developed which was to be the decisive influence in their responses to the situation.

Both Stevens and Bennett were proud men, but it was Bennett's unpredictable temperament, insensitivity, and unbending nature[43] which led to the final break.[44] The resignation provoked an acrimonious exchange of correspondence, all of which was published. Soon further strain was added by rumours that Stevens planned either to attempt a coup against Bennett's leadership or to form a new party. This was a serious problem because Stevens remained a popular figure both in the party and in the country. Despite the obvious dangers if these rumours were true, despite pleas from other leading members of the party, and despite indications that Stevens would be receptive, Bennett refused to seek a reconciliation. In fact, he finally took a completely different course and instructed the party to exclude Stevens from the caucus.

In July 1935, just three months before the general election required by the expiry of Parliament's term, Stevens announced the formation of the Reconstruction party. Many local Conservative workers defected to the new party which nominated candidates in 171 ridings. Party organization had already been weakened through inattention[45] and provincial defeats. Not one Conservative provincial government remained in office in 1935. In Quebec the provincial party had completely disappeared, having merged with nationalist Liberals to form a new party, the Union Nationale.

The Depression, of course, was the central issue in the election. King had no alternative to Bennett's New Deal, but Bennett's reforms had come too late to have any effect and his credibility as a reformer was challenged by the defection of Stevens. Bennett's record and program were also attacked by two new radical parties, the Cooperative Commonwealth Federation (CCF) on the left and Social Credit on the right. Both of the older parties were threatened by the national preoccupation with economic problems. Established party loyalties had been formed when the country was mainly concerned with issues that related to sectarian and linguistic cleavages. Since the 1935 campaign was free of debate about issues of this kind there was no stimulus to re-enforce traditional party ties. The Conservative party was more seriously affected because it was the governing party and therefore was the immediate focus for frustrations generated by the Depression.

The magnitude of the government's defeat was unprecedented. It won only one seat in the maritimes, five seats in Quebec, and three in the prairies. In Ontario, where in the fourteen previous elections the Conservatives had never done worse than a tie, they elected only twenty-five out of eighty-two members. Altogether, the Conservatives won only forty seats while the Liberals won 173, Social Credit seventeen, the CCF seven, and the Reconstruction party one.

Although they won relatively few seats, the three new parties had an important effect on the outcome of the election by taking votes from Conservative candidates. Their significance is indicated by the fact that compared to 1930, the Conservative share of the popular vote dropped 19 percent while the Liberal share increased only 5 percent. The Reconstruction party with 9 percent of the popular vote had a particularly damaging effect on the Conservatives. One analysis concludes that there were sixty-two constituencies in which the combined Conservative and Reconstruction vote was larger than that of the winning Liberal candidate.[46]

Despite its important role in the election, the Reconstruction party quickly disappeared. This is hardly surprising since, as an organization, it was nothing more than a faction of dissenting Conservatives. In contrast, both the CCF and Social Credit were committed to sets of ideas which challenged the prevailing value consensus in Canadian politics. Their modest electoral success was sufficient to give them a platform from which to spread their ideas and set down a more enduring base. As a result, the Conservatives and Liberals were forced to compete on narrowed ground. Moreover, while Social Credit seemed likely to have little appeal outside the agricultural communities of the West, the CCF posed a threat in the industrialized sections of central Canada where the two established parties were most securely entrenched. There was the possibility, therefore, of an ideological polarization between the CCF and the established parties in which one of the established parties would be destroyed.

The Conservative party was so badly shaken by its defeat that it seemed unable to respond to this danger. Organization, which had been neglected before 1935, was now virtually ignored, while policy was allowed to drift. Although Bennett was reluctant to retire, he made no effort to deal with these problems. This situation continued until March 1938, when, in the face of growing dissatisfaction with his leadership, Bennett resigned. Fairly quickly it became apparent that the candidate most likely to win the convention called to choose his successor was R. J. Manion who had been minister of railways and canals in Bennett's government. The main source of Manion's strength was his appeal in Quebec. In this respect he had three assets. He was a Roman Catholic; he had married a French Canadian; and he had maintained a conciliatory view on issues related to French-Canadian concerns. Manion had a solid bloc of support among French-Canadian delegates and he was able to present himself to other delegates as a man who could help the party win Quebec. But precisely because he had French-Canadian support he was viewed with mistrust by some members of the anglophone wing of the party.

There was opposition to his candidacy as well from elements of the business community, in particular, E. W. Beatty, the president of the Canadian Pacific Railway. As minister of railways, Manion had resisted Beatty's efforts to get the government to rescue the CPR from its Depression difficulties by merging it with the publicly owned Canadian National Railway. Manion remained adamant in his stand on this issue and appeared "almost openly hostile" toward all big business.[47]

In addition, Manion had to contend with the personal enmity of Bennett. The two men had quarrelled on the floor of the House of Commons in 1935 when Bennett reprimanded Manion for his intervention in a debate on the estimates of another minister[48] and in 1936 Manion had published an autobiography in which he criticized Bennett for his arrogant and intemperate dealings with members of his cabinet.[49] As a result, the relationship had become so strained that Bennett and Manion were no longer on speaking terms.[50]

The problem for Manion's opponents was to find a suitable alternative. There was an element of desperation in their search. Beatty was even prepared to consider Stevens who had decided to return to the Conservative party.[51] Bennett wanted Arthur Meighen to run and, when Meighen could not be persuaded, Bennett began to think of running himself. In fact, an eleventh-hour Bennett candidacy was averted only by Meighen's warning that it might be unsuccessful and would certainly cause a serious rift in the party.[52] The anti-Manion groups finally converged in support of Murdoch MacPherson, a former attorney general of Saskatchewan who had had no previous federal experience.

Although he did not become a candidate, just as in 1927, Meighen was at the centre of controversy at the convention, and once again it was because of a speech on defence policy. The difference was that this time, by asserting the identity of Canadian and imperial defence, he upset the French-Canadian delegates. "The Quebec delegation was thrown into a state of open rebellion . . . and threatened to quit the Conservative party if asked to endorse his British Empire defence plea."[53] Supporters of Manion believed the speech was aimed at splitting the convention—to Manion's disadvantage.[54] Whatever the truth of this accusation, MacPherson tied his candidacy to Meighen's position. It was to no avail; Manion was elected on the second ballot.

Manion's strategy for restoring the party consisted of two parts. The first was to develop a reformist social program in order to appeal to voters who might be attracted to the CCF. He had some difficulty in establishing the sincerity of the party's commitment in this respect because Meighen, who had been leader of the party in the Senate since

1932, made public statements which appeared to contradict the official policy. Meighen's independence had the additional effect of undermining the leader's authority in the party.[55]

The second part of Manion's strategy depended on exploiting his potential appeal in Quebec. By the end of 1938 he had laid the groundwork for an alliance with Maurice Duplessis, the Union Nationale premier of Quebec, and in 1939 Duplessis formally promised Manion the full support of his provincial organization in the next federal election. However, with the increasing likelihood of war, it became more difficult to maintain the Quebec strategy. In March, anticipating a similar declaration by Mackenzie King, Manion announced that, in the event of war, a Conservative government would support Britain but it would not adopt conscription. This policy did not sit very well with anglophile extremists, although it provoked no overt resistance in English Canada. At the same time it permitted Manion to take the initiative for his party in French Canada. As a result, by mid-summer 1939 there seemed good prospect for Conservative gains in Quebec.

The outbreak of war destroyed this prospect. In October 1939 Duplessis called a provincial election, making the war the central issue. His pretext was that King would use the war to intrude upon the jurisdiction of the Quebec government. Faced with this challenge, the federal Liberals committed themselves in full force to the provincial campaign and helped the provincial Liberal party defeat Duplessis. For the Conservative party there were three consequences. First, without provincial office, the Union Nationale could do little to give effective organizational assistance in a federal campaign. Second, the election had created a new division between French- and English-speaking Conservatives in Quebec. Third, although the Conservatives had reaffirmed their opposition to conscription, the election had given the Liberals an opportunity to establish themselves as the party most likely to protect French-Canadian interests during the war.

The collapse of Manion's Quebec strategy deprived him of badly needed credibility. Public and private sniping at his leadership had persisted since the day he assumed it. From the autumn of 1939 he was pressed with suggestions to bring Meighen and Bennett back into the caucus. Manion believed that at least some of these were thinly veiled schemes to have him replaced by one of the former leaders.[56] In fact, there were public suggestions that he should step aside for Bennett as late as January 1940, when King caught the Conservatives with a surprise election. The attacks on his leadership were manifestly damaging to Manion's public image, undermining the effectiveness of his efforts to give direction to the party and disrupting party organization.

Two other factors had contributed to the weakening of party organization. One was the reluctance of Conservative businessmen to make financial contributions to the party while it was under Manion's leadership and the other was Manion's decision to follow a "national government" policy and run the Conservatives in 1940 as the National Government party. Since Manion's selection as leader, the shortage of funds had prevented effective efforts to overcome Bennett's neglect of party organization. In the 1940 campaign the level of contributions was so curtailed that the party was unable to meet its campaign requirements.[57] The National Government decision had an adverse effect on party morale at the constituency level, particularly when efforts were made to open nominations to candidates from other parties. More than that, it failed as an electoral tactic because both King and J. S. Woodsworth, the leader of the CCF, said they would not serve in any government under Manion's leadership.

The 1940 election was even more disastrous for the Conservative party than the election of 1935. While the Conservatives were again limited to forty seats, the Liberals increased their strength to 184. Among the Conservatives who were defeated was Manion.

Six weeks after the election, in May 1940, the Conservative caucus accepted Manion's resignation from the leadership and appointed R. B. Hanson, who had already been chosen to lead the party in Parliament, as interim leader.

The war and the condition of the party delayed action on the selection of a permanent leader for more than a year. In November 1941 a special conference of members of the parliamentary party and representatives of provincial and constituency associations met to plan a leadership convention. One group at the conference wanted to appoint Meighen to the leadership without a convention. The difficulty was that not all of the participants wanted Meighen and there were some who believed that the conference had no authority to do anything but call a convention. After considerable debate these objections were overcome and it was resolved to draft Meighen.

His selection was a victory for the conscription wing of the party. He had long been convinced of the necessity of conscription and in the summer of 1941 had begun a series of speeches advocating its adoption. Even before the conference met there was a warning of the likely consequences in Quebec if Meighen's position became party policy. "Alarmed by the rising tide of conscriptionist sentiment . . ."[58] in the party, J. S. Roy, the only French-Canadian Conservative member of Parliament, resigned from the caucus.

Meighen's second term as leader lasted barely a year. In February 1942, he was defeated in a by-election called in the Toronto constituency of York South in an attempt to open a seat for him in the Commons. There had been no Liberal candidate, but Meighen's vigorous criticism of King's war policy had provoked Liberal support for his only opponent, a CCF candidate.[59] In addition, he had underestimated the appeal of the CCF campaign among working class voters.[60] With Meighen's defeat, the party was faced with divided leadership—Hanson in the House and Meighen outside. Differences soon developed between Meighen and Hanson over the extent to which the party should carry its criticism of the government's conduct of the war. Since no other member of the caucus was prepared to assume the leadership in the House, it was apparent by the end of July that an impasse had been reached.

At about the same time a group of Conservatives, organized by a Toronto trust company executive, J. M. Macdonnell, announced plans for a conference of members of the extra-parliamentary party to discuss policy reforms that would help the party meet the increasing threat from the CCF. The conference, which met in Port Hope, Ontario, in September, formulated proposals for a full-employment policy, a broadly based social security system, recognition of trade union rights in collective bargaining, and a freer trade policy.

While Meighen had little enthusiasm for these proposals, he saw in them an opportunity to launch the party in a new direction.[61] Even before his own return to the leadership a year earlier he had tried to persuade John Bracken, the premier of Manitoba, to accept the position. The fact that Bracken was a Progressive with no previous connection to the Conservative party was one of the qualities which made him attractive. Meighen believed his identification with the reform tradition of Progressivism could help broaden the party's popular appeal, particularly in Manitoba, Saskatchewan, and Alberta, where the Conservatives had had little success since 1921. The Port Hope proposals constituted a platform which could make the Conservative party acceptable to Bracken. Thus, just two weeks after the conclusion of the conference, Meighen called a leadership convention and began a campaign to get Bracken chosen as his successor.

Meighen had hoped to prevent serious competition for Bracken but there were four other candidates: Murdoch MacPherson, John Diefenbaker, Howard Green, and H. H. Stevens. This was an obstacle which evidently gave Bracken pause. Another was his desire to secure assurances, which Meighen could not give, that the party would officially adopt the Port Hope proposals and that it would change its name to *Progressive* Conservative.

There was no basic disagreement at the convention about public policy; in its resolutions the convention embraced the Port Hope proposals with little apparent dissent. The main focus for controversy was provided by Bracken's candidacy. One reason was resentment at his sponsorship. Some critics argued that he was being imposed on the party by an "old guard" or party establishment, based in Toronto and Montreal and closely linked with powerful financial interests. This argument evoked cleavages between elites and non-elites in the party, between central Canada and the hinterland provinces, and between big interests and "ordinary Canadians." A second reason for opposition to Bracken was the fact he was an outsider.[62] Bracken's demands that the party make itself over before he would become a candidate only served to emphasize this point. The hostility of delegates was directed in particular at his proposal to change the party's name. Twice before the leadership vote, efforts to put a motion to effect this change were frustrated by the heated response the motion aroused.

In the voting, Bracken was more successful. On the first ballot he had the support of 46 percent of the delegates and on the second he was elected. Following his election, party unity was symbolically restored when, on the motion of one of the most outspoken opponents of his candidacy, the delegates adopted the new party name.

Bracken did not fulfil the expectations for his candidacy—for three reasons.

First, he refused to look for a seat in the House. While this freed him to work on party organization and to carry the party message across the country, it kept him away from the centre of public debate and created the problems of dual leadership. As a result, he lost his best opportunity to establish his personal qualities as a leader and made it more difficult for the party to project a united image.

Second, the Liberal government developed its own response to the CCF, introducing a program of reforms which included a national income supplement in the form of family allowances, a guarantee of price supports for agricultural products, and a commitment to a full-employment policy. The Conservative party was thus deprived of control of the centre ground between the Liberal party and the CCF. Bracken's efforts to preserve the party's position in this area were further weakened when the Conservative premier of Ontario and a Conservative member of Parliament both publicly criticized family allowances.

Third, in 1944 the party was trapped in debate over a manpower crisis in the European war. At first the issue was more damaging to the government which, with great reluctance, was forced to adopt conscription. But the Conservatives, by following a course of vigorous and unqualified advocacy of conscription, suffered the greater long-term harm. By the time a general election was called in June 1945, the war in Europe had ended and conscription no longer had the same compelling appeal among the English-speaking population. In Quebec, on the other hand, the posture adopted by the Conservatives had had the effect of reviving all the negative images associated with the party's conscription policy in the First World War.[63]

In the 1945 election the Conservatives made gains in only one province, Ontario, where they won forty-eight out of eighty-two seats. In

Quebec they were able to find candidates for only twenty-nine out of the sixty-five ridings and elected only two. In the three prairie provinces, where Bracken had been expected to have a large personal following, the CCF won twenty-three seats, the Liberals fourteen, Social Credit thirteen, and the Conservatives five. Although its majority was reduced, the King government was re-elected with 125 out of the total of 245 seats.

The Conservative defeat was a serious blow to Bracken's leadership. His own election to the House probably forestalled any immediate effort to remove him, but his support quickly disappeared. The desire to remove him became so strong that it was reported that a fund was being established to provide him with a guaranteed income if he would retire. In the summer of 1948, having learned that he could no longer be sure of the confidence of the caucus, Bracken resigned.[64]

Bracken's fall has been ascribed to his failure to project the kind of image needed to help the party win.[65] In part, he suffered by comparison with George Drew, the premier of Ontario. Drew had formed a majority government in 1943 following an election in which the CCF won the second largest number of seats. In 1945, running a "Red scare campaign," he had led the party to a substantial victory and in 1948—although he lost his own seat—his government was comfortably re-elected. Thus not only had Drew brought the Conservatives their first success since 1930, he had demonstrated his ability to deal with the threat of the CCF.

There were three candidates for the leadership at the convention which met in the early autumn of 1948: Drew, John Diefenbaker, and Donald Fleming. Only Diefenbaker seriously challenged Drew. He ran a populist campaign as a candidate who represented the party rank and file and who could appeal to the average Canadian. By inference, Drew was portrayed as a candidate backed by the party establishment and the "big interests" of Toronto and Montreal. The issue of party democracy figured prominently in Diefenbaker's campaign. Some of his supporters claimed that delegate-at-large appointments were being rigged for Drew, a charge which Diefenbaker believed[66] and did nothing to suppress, although he formally dissociated himself from it in a comment to journalists.[67]

On questions of government policy the candidates were at least publicly agreed. Both adopted the same themes in their speeches to the convention, emphasizing national unity and the need to protect the autonomy of provincial governments from the expansion of federal power. Although he had once criticized family allowances, Drew now advocated their extension. Noting the adoption of a proposal to this effect in the convention's policy resolutions, the Toronto *Globe and Mail* observed its significance "in view of past opposition to family allowances from some sections of the party."[68]

Drew won the leadership on the first ballot with two-thirds of the votes cast. While there was the usual demonstration of support for the new leader from both defeated candidates, the convention left some deep wounds, particularly in the relationship between Diefenbaker and people in the party establishment who had backed Drew. The depth of personal feeling in this rift is suggested by an incident Diefenbaker reports in his memoirs: "On the night of Drew's victory, I went up to his suite in the Chateau Laurier. They were celebrating. I was an intruder. I went to congratulate him. I walked into that gathering and it was as if an animal not customarily admitted to homes had suddenly entered the place."[69]

One of the virtues asserted for Drew's candidacy was that he would help the party win seats in Quebec. This claim was based on his connection with Maurice Duplessis, whose Union Nationale had been returned to office in 1944. Drew and Duplessis had found common cause in opposing the incursions of the federal government on provincial jurisdiction and Duplessis was now expected to give Drew the organizational help he needed to establish a strong Conservative presence in Quebec. However, no matter how well disposed he was toward Drew, Duplessis could not risk an open commitment—for two reasons. First, the Liberal party had chosen a new French-Canadian leader, Louis St. Laurent, who was immensely popular in his native province. Second, Drew was a staunch anglophile[70] whose record included widely publicized and provocative criticisms of French Canadians.

In the 1949 election, St. Laurent's strength and Drew's weaknesses were fully exploited in the Liberal campaign in Quebec. As a result, the Conservative party once again failed to make any significant gains there. Elsewhere the party fared just as badly. In fact in Ontario, where Drew received little help from his provincial successor, Leslie Frost, it lost most of the seats it had gained in 1945. The St. Laurent government was re-elected with 193 seats, 152 more than the Conservative party.

Despite this defeat, Drew was accorded a unanimous vote of confidence by the national executive when it met in the autumn of 1949 and for the next four years he continued to enjoy at least the outward support of his party. Even after the St. Laurent government won another large majority in 1953 there was still no challenge to Drew's leadership. But behind the facade of unity there was a growing restiveness in the party. Drew had created problems for himself in the caucus by confining positions of influence to a small inner circle, identified with the group to which some other members of the party referred as the old guard.[71] Outside the caucus, his leadership was beset by public and private disagreements with provincial leaders[72] and by complaints from some constituency associations that he had become an electoral liability.[73] The mounting pressures from within the party, together with the demands imposed by a particularly difficult period in the House,[74] subjected Drew to increasing stress with the result that in August 1956, he collapsed from emotional and physical exhaustion. Although Drew wanted to continue in leadership, members of his own inner circle felt compelled to persuade him to resign.[75]

John Diefenbaker was widely perceived to be the candidate with the best chance of succeeding Drew. He had been a leading figure in the federal party since 1940, was recognized as one of its most able parliamentarians, and had acquired a national reputation for his advocacy of civil rights and progressive social legislation. Even some members of the party establishment from which he had long felt excluded supported his candidacy. There were others, however, who viewed the prospect of his leadership with such dismay that they tried to launch a stop-Diefenbaker campaign. They did not think either of the other two candidates, Donald Fleming and Davie Fulton, who were also members of Parliament, had sufficient national following or reputation to be able to compete effectively with Diefenbaker. They, therefore, tried to find a candidate of national stature and appeal from outside the caucus.[76] When these efforts failed most of them reluctantly gave their support to Fleming.

Although Diefenbaker had no difficulty in winning the leadership, his election was not accomplished without controversy. The problem arose when he decided not to invite a French Canadian to propose or second his nomination. The dominant clique in the Quebec wing of the party was anti-Diefenbaker and he felt there was little to be gained by a symbolic gesture designed to win Quebec votes. Some of his advisers warned him that the omission of a French Canadian might be seen to be a deliberate insult to Quebec because it appeared to defy tradition.[77] But he would not be dissuaded. The news of his decision provoked the reaction of which he had been warned. Léon Balcer, the nominal leader of the Quebec delegation, who was also president of the National Association, abandoned his position of formal neutrality to work against Diefenbaker. It was to no avail; Diefenbaker was elected on the first ballot with a substantial majority. When the new leader rose to make his acceptance speech a majority of the French-Canadian delegates refused to applaud and several demonstrated their disapproval of his election by leaving the convention hall.

Despite the obvious effect of this episode on his image among French Canadians, Diefenbaker's performance at the convention had earned him the support of a powerful ally in Quebec—Premier Duplessis. On the morning following the convention Duplessis telephoned Pierre Sévigny, one of the few delegates from Quebec who had worked for Diefenbaker, to tell him of his support:

> John Diefenbaker, [Duplessis] claimed, had made two outstanding speeches which indicated both a faith in Canada and a correct appreciation of the necessary and desired relationship between the central and provincial governments. This man was sincere and a winner, he

> said. He almost ordered me to stand with the Prince Albert politician in the forthcoming campaign. The Quebec Conservative wing, he claimed, would cool down and rally within the next few weeks. They had nowhere to go but with us, and he would make sure of the fact.[78]

Duplessis's commitment was applied discreetly, selectively, and covertly. In the general election of 1957, Union Nationale organizers were directed to help Conservatives only in those constituencies where a careful appraisal suggested there was a realistic chance of victory. The same strategy was adopted by Diefenbaker in his approach to Quebec in the national campaign. It was decided to curtail spending in Quebec so that the party could concentrate its effort in Ontario, the maritimes, and the western provinces where there was evidence of widespread discontent with the Liberal government.[79]

The major source of this discontent was the "feeling that the government had become too powerful, too arrogant, and careless in its relations with Parliament . . . that it had become overbearing, convinced of its infallibility and contemptuous of its critics."[80] Diefenbaker's populist style was singularly well suited to exploit this national mood. Through the leader's image the party's image was refashioned. To emphasize the point, Conservative candidates ran not under the traditional party label but as Diefenbaker candidates.

The strategy worked. The Conservative party made big gains in Ontario and the maritimes, winning 103 out of the 190 seats in the English-speaking provinces. Even in Quebec it increased its strength from four seats to nine, benefiting from the selectively applied assistance of the Union Nationale. Altogether the Conservatives won 111 seats, the Liberals 105, the CCF twenty-five, Social Credit nineteen, and Independents two. On the basis of his narrow plurality, John Diefenbaker was summoned as the first Conservative prime minister in twenty-two years.

Over the next seven months, the new administration initiated and implemented a wide range of programs which created an impression of innovation and reform. In 1958 Diefenbaker called a new election in which the party capitalized on this record and the leader's personal appeal to win an unprecedented victory. Even in Quebec, where the Union Nationale now took an open and extensive role, the Conservatives won fifty seats. It was the first time Quebec had given the Conservative party a majority since 1887. The only province the party did not win was Newfoundland. In the prairies, where the Conservatives had not had a victory since 1917, they carried forty-seven out of forty-eight seats. Altogether they won 208 out of 265 seats and 54 percent of the popular vote.

Diefenbaker had been at the centre of the campaign and the victory was widely ascribed to his personal popularity. Thus he appeared to enjoy an unchallengeable hold on the party leadership.

SUMMARY AND CONCLUSIONS

When John Diefenbaker assumed the Conservative leadership in 1956 the party had already had a long and costly experience with internal conflict. The Conservative defeats in the three critical elections of 1896, 1921, and 1935 were all in part the result of divisions within the party. No Conservative leader since Macdonald had been wholly successful in containing the strains on party unity. With the exception of Abbott, Thompson, and Tupper, no leader since Macdonald had escaped some overt challenge to his right to lead. And the career of every leader since Borden had ended with the leader under pressure to resign.

The issues which had the greatest impact on the internal politics of the party during this period were those related to the ascriptive cleavages of language and religion. The most obvious and most damaging result was the alienation of Quebec.

The confrontations over language and religious rights in education were only one dimension of the conflict arising from these cleavages. At a more general level there was a conflict between different conceptions of national identity. Most French Canadians sought their cultural fulfilment through the distinctiveness of their own society, while most English Canadians remained tied to their British connections. This difference found expression in the conflict over the country's role in the two world wars. No conflict could have been more intensely emotional or divisive for the country or for the Conservative party.

Regional cleavages also contributed to conflict in the party. There is no way to assess the influence of the emotional dimension of regionalism —defined earlier as an element of personal identity derived from regional attachments—but the impact of divergent regional economic interests is clear. Their effect was particularly important in the disagreements about economic policy which disrupted the Borden-Meighen government after World War I. At issue was the tariff which protected the manufacturing interests of central Canada at the expense of the agricultural interests of the West. Protection prevailed—at the cost of the splitting off of prairie Liberals from the coalition government in 1919. The Conservative party had to wait until Diefenbaker's victory of 1958 to restore a significant presence in the prairies. However, in a more general sense in the period under review, conflicts over economic policy were neither as intractable nor as disruptive as those involving religious and linguistic issues. The only extended doctrinal division concerned the move toward welfare-state capitalism which began during the Depression. This issue was a problem for Bennett (although, contrary to popular belief, it did not account for the defection of H. H. Stevens in 1935) and for Manion. Meighen, who had disagreed with Manion about it, himself adopted a different posture after his aborted return to the leadership in 1941. By

1942, with the election of Bracken under Meighen's sponsorship, the issue of the welfare-state was settled—despite occasional episodes of individual protest later.

The substance of policy conflict after the settlement of this issue was less clearly defined. Diefenbaker's challenge to the "Old Guard" in the party and his advocacy of the cause of "average Canadians" had a doctrinal ring, but it embraced no obviously distinctive social doctrine nor any statement of specific measures which appeared significantly different from those proposed by his rivals.

The conflicts over the party leadership before Diefenbaker's accession clearly reflected more than the divisive effect of disagreements about matters of public policy. Personal ambition and individual temperament both played their part—in some cases, such as the defection of Stevens, a very damaging part. The clash of groups in party history has been sharpened and supplemented by the clash of personalities—expressed both in terms of personal ambition and in terms of emotional responses to situations and to other personalities.

This fact supports the point made at the outset that conflict within the party cannot be adequately explained unless it takes account of the full range of motives involved in individual behaviour. At one level the party's difficulties can be explained in terms of its failure to manage the cleavages in Canadian society. But this explanation cannot account for the fact that while the Conservative party failed, the Liberal party succeeded. Thus I am arguing that the investigation of conflict within the party must go beyond such explanations. It must try to encompass a much wider range of variables which affect individual behaviour in internal party politics.

Part II

4

Conflicts Over Diefenbaker's Leadership

In the general election of 1962 John Diefenbaker's government lost its majority in Parliament. Eight months later, in February 1963, with the government in difficulty in Parliament, a group of ministers tried to depose Diefenbaker. The coup failed but the divisions it exposed left the Conservative party severely weakened. Forced into a new election, the Diefenbaker government was defeated.

Diefenbaker's leadership was soon the focus for renewed conflict within the party. This conflict grew progressively wider and more intense. It reached its climax at the annual meeting of the National Association in 1966 when, by a small majority, the delegates voted to call a leadership convention.

This chapter will discuss the factors which contributed to these conflicts over Diefenbaker's leadership. Each episode will be described and analysed separately.

THE CABINET REVOLT OF 1963

The most important factor in the background to the cabinet revolt of 1963 was the precipitous decline in popular support for the Conservative government which began in 1959. Between January 1959 and September 1960 support for the Conservatives in the Canadian Institution of Public Opinion poll fell from 59 percent to 38 percent[1] and it did not again rise above 40 percent. In the federal election of 1962 the Conservative share of the popular vote fell to 37 percent (from 54 percent in 1958) and the party lost so many seats that it was reduced to the status of a minority government. Among the factors which contributed to this dramatic change, three appear to have been particularly important.

First, the Conservatives had assumed office just as the country was entering a recession. Over the next five years the annual rate of economic growth declined, unemployment reached its highest levels since the Depression, and there was persistent pressure on the Canadian dollar. The government was slow in its attempts to deal with these problems. In part this was because it was frustrated by a conflict with the governor of the Bank of Canada, James Coyne, over the control and appropriate course of monetary policy.[2] Another cause of delay was the cautious advice it received from the officials of the Department of Finance.[3] But what was most important was the cabinet's own approach to policy-making which tended to protract the period in which every decision was taken.[4] This general proclivity to delay meant not only that policies were not approved in time to deal effectively with problems, but also that decisions had the appearance of being taken and often were taken in an atmosphere of crisis.

A good illustration was the devaluation of the Canadian dollar which was forced on the government in the middle of the 1962 election campaign. This decision became the central issue in the campaign—with damaging consequences for the government.[5]

The contrast between the promise of Diefenbaker's messianic appeal in 1958 and the performance of the government was a second factor in the government's political decline. Diefenbaker's own behaviour added to this credibility gap. In response to criticism of government economic policy the prime minister was evasive, attacking his critics or accusing privileged interests of conspiring to frustrate the government's purpose. He also resorted to the same kind of arbitrary acts for which he had so effectively criticized the Liberals in 1956 and 1957. A notable example was his personal comportment in and the government's collective handling of the dismissal of James Coyne from his position at the Bank of Canada. There was a good case to be made against Coyne's attempt to pursue a course independent of the cabinet, but the government chose instead to emphasize the charge that Coyne had acted improperly in approving an increase in his pension which had been voted by the Bank's board of directors.[6] Coyne was provoked by this tactic to resist the efforts to have him resign and the government was drawn into an extended public confrontation in which it appeared to be bullying Coyne. The government's image was further damaged by its refusal to permit Coyne to be heard before a committee of the House of Commons.[7]

Another illustration of the discrepancy between the standard Diefenbaker applied in his criticism of the former Liberal administration and his own behaviour was his response to critical evaluations of the government by journalists. Both publicly and privately he accused members of the parliamentary press gallery of partisan bias and he tried to restrict the reporting opportunities of journalists whose stories and commentaries he found particularly offensive.[8] Quite apart from its effect on his image as an advocate of popular rights, this response was a serious mistake in press relations. Whatever the original disposition of the journalists, Diefenbaker's accusations and harassments could only serve to colour their judgements and analyses. By 1962 the prime minister's relationships with members of the press gallery had "reached the breaking point"[9] and his government had been widely stigmatized in editorial comment as evasive and high-handed.

A third factor in the government's decline was its handling of Quebec. It was unfortunate for the Conservatives that they had come to office just when important social, economic, and cultural changes were taking shape in Quebec.[10] Diefenbaker was prepared to make some symbolic gestures toward the recognition of French-Canadian concerns[11] but they were not sufficient to satisfy the aspirations of a new, more liberal, and assertive French-Canadian nationalism.

Substantively and symbolically, one of Diefenbaker's biggest mistakes was his failure to give French Canada strong representation in his cabinet. French Canadians were never accorded a proportionate share of senior cabinet portfolios; in fact they held no senior portfolio at all until 1960. In addition, there was no French-Canadian minister with enough support or stature among his colleagues to assume the natural leadership of the Quebec wing of the party and Diefenbaker refused to designate a French-Canadian lieutenant. The French-Canadian presence was further weakened by Diefenbaker's refusal to permit the Quebec members to meet together as a provincial caucus to discuss their distinctive concerns.[12]

The party's dependence on the Union Nationale created another set of difficulties. For one thing the dominant faction in the Union Nationale was out of touch with the changes which were taking place in Quebec.[13] This was reflected in its defeat in the provincial election of 1960. Equally important, when the Union Nationale fell from power Conservative organization in Quebec was severely weakened. But no effort was made either to respond to appeals from the Union Nationale for help in shoring up provincial party organization[14] or to establish independent Conservative organization. As a result, the party fought the 1962 election in Quebec with an organization hardly more effective than the one it had had in 1957.

In the general election in June 1962, the Progressive Conservative party lost ninety-two seats. The government was able to retain office only because Conservative losses in Quebec had not been matched by Liberal gains, large numbers of Quebec voters having abandoned both established parties to vote for Social Credit candidates. In the new House the Conservatives held 116 seats, the Liberals ninety-eight, Social Credit thirty, and the New Democratic Party (NDP)—formed in 1961 from an alliance of trade unions and the CCF—nineteen.

The election struck a damaging blow at Diefenbaker's leadership. For one thing, it was apparent that, as public opinion polls had suggested, he no longer enjoyed the popular appeal which had made such a substantial contribution to the party's victory in 1958.[15] He was thus deprived of one of his most valuable political resources. In addition, most ministers believed the party's losses were the result of mistakes which the government could have avoided and some ascribed the blame for these mistakes to the prime minister.

The main complaint against Diefenbaker's leadership was that he was indecisive. Even ministers who were to remain loyal to him shared this view.[16] The prime minister insisted that every cabinet decision be unanimous. If there was only a small dissenting group he would still defer decisions and permit discussions to continue repetitiously. This meant not only that important problems remained unsolved but also that ministers wasted time in unnecessary meetings of the cabinet.

There had been tension in the relationship between Diefenbaker and some members of the cabinet long before 1962. Alvin Hamilton, a minister sympathetic to Diefenbaker, claimed the basis of this tension was "conservative" resistance to Diefenbaker's "progressive" policies.[17] On the face of the evidence about policy conflicts within the cabinet, it is difficult to sustain this explanation. The cabinet did not divide into consistent voting blocs which persisted from issue to issue. Moreover, even in the early conflicts over economic policy, the alignments which occurred did not conform to a simple distinction between "progressives" and "conservatives."[18] Yet there is a sense in which this explanation identifies a source of discontent within the cabinet. In seeking to make himself the advocate of "the average Canadian," Diefenbaker had cast himself as the adversary of "big interests." Some ministers were disturbed by this aspect of his political style not because of any policy in which it had resulted but because of the effect of its tone on the party's relations with big business.[19]

On balance, however, this seems to have been far less important as a source of tension than the nature of the prime minister's personal interactions with many of his ministers. Diefenbaker treated most members of the cabinet who had not supported him in 1956 with continuing mistrust;[20] he frequently expressed his disapproval of ministerial actions in outbursts of temper which humiliated the ministers concerned;[21] he sought personal credit for all of the government's achievements while blaming other members of the cabinet for its mistakes;[22] and he sometimes gossiped about the private lives of his ministers, or made unflattering personal remarks to colleagues about ministers whom he disliked.[23]

The extent of cabinet alienation immediately following the 1962 election is not wholly clear. Most of the ministers who ultimately opposed Diefenbaker have said that despite whatever misgivings they may have had at that time it was several months before they reached the conclusion that Diefenbaker should go. In any event, by February 1963 close to half the cabinet was ready to seek a change.

Four factors helped transform the discontent within the cabinet into the challenge to Diefenbaker's leadership.

First, the prime minister would not commit himself to a clear position in the discussion of a long-delayed decision about the acquisition of nuclear weapons for Canadian forces in NATO and the North American Air Defence Command. Since the Cuban missile crisis in October there had been increasing public pressure, re-enforced by pressure from the American government, for some action in this matter. The government had appeared to agree to the acquisition of nuclear weapons in 1959 when it undertook to equip Canadian forces with delivery vehicles designed to carry nuclear explosives. However, it began to hedge its position in 1961 as a result of its foreign policy commitment to act as a mediator in the negotiation of nuclear disarmament. A decision had been required for some time because Canada had begun to equip its forces with the new delivery vehicles. Most members of the cabinet wanted to proceed with the acquisition of nuclear weapons, at least for the Bomarc missiles installed in Canada as part of the continental air defence agreement.[24]

Second, no progress had been made toward the formulation of a new budget. This was a cause of particular concern in relation to the government's position in Parliament because the 1962 budget had never been formally adopted. Although a cabinet committee on economic policy had completed its work in November, the prime minister had made no effort to have its proposals presented to cabinet for discussion.

Third, the prime minister had refused to cooperate in efforts to negotiate terms with the thirty Social Credit members of Parliament for stabilizing the government's position in Parliament. Social Credit votes had kept the government in office throughout the autumn, but the Social Credit leader, Robert Thompson, had warned government representatives that his party's support would not continue without some clear indication of government attention to outstanding problems.[25]

Fourth, criticism of the government outside Parliament had spread to include its own nominal supporters, among them several Conservative newspapers and some officers of the National Association. One source of party criticism was the fact that during the Cuban missile crisis the government had delayed for forty-two hours before acceding to the American request that Canada place its armed forces on full alert. Another was the government's failure to execute an agreement with the United States for the acquisition of nuclear weapons.[26]

Rumours of cabinet dissatisfaction with the prime minister had reached the press as early as November and had prompted a number of speculative newspaper articles about a change in the party leadership. But there had been no serious discussion of attempting to force Diefenbaker to resign. In fact, the challenge to Diefenbaker occurred by accident rather than as the result of any prior plan.

The series of events which led to it began when the House of Commons met on January 21 and the opposition pressed the government for an explanation of its nuclear weapons policy. In response, on January 25, Diefenbaker made a long and ambiguous speech. On January 28, Douglas Harkness, the minister of defence, issued a statement claiming that, contrary to press interpretations of the prime minister's speech, it had been clear that Diefenbaker had confirmed the government's intention to accept nuclear weapons. In the House, Diefenbaker refused to make any further comment, either in elaboration of his speech or in confirmation of the statement of the defence minister. Two days later, the American State Department published a statement in which it offered its own clarification of and correction to the prime minister's speech. This so angered Diefenbaker that he recalled the Canadian ambassador to Washington and began to canvass the opinion of some of his closest advisers about the possibility of calling an election on the issue of American interference in Canadian affairs.

This suggestion, along with the determination of Harkness to secure acceptance of nuclear weapons, created a crisis in the cabinet. On the morning of February 3, Diefenbaker met members of the cabinet at his home.[27] The prime minister proposed that Parliament be dissolved and an election fought on the issue of relations with the United States. George Hees, the minister of trade and commerce, opposed him and raised the nuclear weapons issue. Then Harkness attacked the prime minister, asserting that he had lost the confidence of the country. Diefenbaker interrupted him to demand that those who were with him stand up. When eleven of the twenty-one ministers present remained seated, Diefenbaker announced that he would resign and left the room. After the prime minister left, several ministers said they had not stood up because they did not know whether they were being asked to vote on the question of the dissolution or on the question of Diefenbaker's leadership. A memorandum was therefore drafted, urging Diefenbaker not to resign and not to seek a dissolution. Harkness refused to sign this memorandum and declared that in any event he would have to resign.

In the Commons on the following day, Social Credit leader Robert Thompson introduced a motion of non-confidence which seemed likely to have the support of the Liberal and New Democratic parties. When the House adjourned, five ministers—George Hees, George Nowlan, Wallace McCutcheon, Pierre Sévigny, and Léon Balcer—met with

Thompson to see if it might be possible to save the government. Thompson made it clear that he would only be willing to support the Conservatives if Diefenbaker were replaced. As a result, the five ministers agreed to ask Diefenbaker to resign. On the morning of February 5, Hees presented this request to the prime minister, but Diefenbaker refused.

It was now impossible to escape defeat in the House that evening. However, the ministers who had met with Thompson believed that if they could force Diefenbaker to resign they could form a government under a new leader and avoid an election. They believed there might be as many as eleven of the remaining ministers willing to depose Diefenbaker, while he could count on only nine. They therefore decided to confront Diefenbaker at a cabinet meeting scheduled for the next morning. While the rebels knew they lacked the support of the caucus, which was to meet immediately following the cabinet meeting, they hoped to present caucus with a *fait accompli*. But Diefenbaker, having learned of their plans, advanced the time of the caucus meeting so that it took place before the cabinet meeting. He therefore ensured that the confrontation took place in a forum in which he had a substantial majority. The result was the capitulation of the rebels. Hees, who had led the attack in caucus, was chosen to announce to the press that the party was united behind its leader and ready to fight a new election.

Three days later Hees and Pierre Sévigny, the associate minister of defence, resigned—ostensibly because of the prime minister's failure to satisfy their concerns about defence policy. Hees claimed that the prime minister had repudiated a privately made promise, given during the caucus on February 6, to satisfy his objections to defence policy. Behind this public explanation there was another. After the caucus on February 6—two close friends—E. A. Goodman, a member of the national executive, and John Bassett, the publisher of the Toronto *Telegram*—pressured him to resign, arguing that by continuing in the cabinet he was humiliating himself and breaking faith with them. (Both Goodman and Bassett had given public and private support to the efforts to force Diefenbaker out and both were pledged to help Hees succeed to the leadership.) Goodman said in an interview that when he learned Hees had not resigned he went to see him and "told him he had been conned. When he found out that he had been had, he quit."[28] Sévigny has made it clear that it was not defence policy, but a personal slight he had received from Diefenbaker that led him to resign. Since the resignation of Harkness he had been acting minister of defence. On February 7 a press release issued by the Defence Department described Sévigny as the minister. When asked whether the omission of the word "acting" indicated that Sévigny had been permanently assigned to the new portfolio, Diefenbaker replied "Certainly not!" As a result, Sévigny writes: "I felt as if my face had been slapped. Something snapped in my mind. Why should I take this abuse?

It was bad enough being utterly concerned with defence principles and policies that could no longer be explained. Why should I furthermore be insulted and accept such treatment? There was only one answer and that was to resign."[29]

Together, Hees and Sévigny tried to persuade other anti-Diefenbaker ministers to join them. Their principal target was Balcer. Balcer said in an interview that Hees and Sévigny had told him that Diefenbaker was going to make a speech repudiating what they felt was an undertaking to acquire nuclear weapons. He explained his response and reaction as follows: "I said 'What are you going to tell the press?' I thought they would look foolish. I said 'Let us wait and see what [Diefenbaker] says.' I had no personal reason to resign. I was in a good position to get re-elected. I knew the government would be defeated, but I thought Diefenbaker would go after the election and that we would carry on."[30] Thus Balcer refused to participate in this further act of rebellion. Although three other anti-Diefenbaker ministers, Davie Fulton, Ernest Halpenny, and Donald Fleming, decided not to run in the election, they continued in the cabinet for the duration of the campaign. Fulton had announced in November that he planned to return to British Columbia to accept the leadership of the provincial party which was attempting to rebuild itself, while Fleming and Halpenny both announced that they wished to retire for personal reasons of a non-political nature. All three of these ministers had strained relations with Diefenbaker and both Fulton and Halpenny had been active in the efforts to force him to resign. Although Fleming had not been active, he was regarded as a potential supporter of the rebels.

It was the prime minister's refusal to make an unequivocal commitment to nuclear weapons that had led to the conflict. At a substantive level this had evoked concern about the effectiveness of the country's defences against nuclear attack, the strength of its commitment to its allies, and the state of its relations with the United States. Yet only Harkness had thought defence policy sufficiently important to stake his career on it. Other ministers, including Hees and Sévigny, had been prepared to defer a decision even longer if delay could be explained in politically credible terms. (Both of them had been among a group who tried to persuade Harkness on February 1 that he should agree to give his support to the prime minister until after the NATO foreign ministers' meeting in May, when Diefenbaker had promised to take a definitive position.)[31]

In fact, for most of the anti-Diefenbaker ministers, the substance of defence policy was less important than the political implications of the conflict it had produced. The prime minister seemed to be unable or unwilling to lead the cabinet to a decision on any question about which there existed or was likely to be disagreement. Moreover, his reaction to the pressure of the American government convinced them that he had lost his political judgement. They believed Diefenbaker's continued leadership would destroy the government. What was at stake was their political survival. If the cabinet could not be mobilized to action the government would fall. Beyond defeat in Parliament they saw defeat in a general election.

Their political analysis reflected an assessment of the situation in the metropolitan heartland of the country. It was in the densely populated industrial corridor running along Lake Ontario and the St. Lawrence River that the party had suffered its most substantial losses in 1962. It was from the press and party in this area that the most severe criticism of the government had been coming. Quite apart from its implications for the party's plurality in Parliament, a further loss in Conservative votes here threatened many of them personally. Thus, out of eleven ministers who had seats in this area, only three were clearly committed to Diefenbaker.

Undoubtedly, their own interest in the leadership influenced the behaviour of some of the rebel ministers. Fulton, Hees, Nowlan, and Fleming had all been mentioned as possible successors. As early as November, Hees had been engaged in discussions with friends outside the caucus to plan a leadership campaign, although he claims that these discussions were held in anticipation of Diefenbaker's resignation and not with the intention of forcing it. Some of the ministers sympathetic to Diefenbaker claim that Fulton participated only because he had what one of them called "an unholy ambition to be Prime Minister."[32]

The strain in their personal relations with the prime minister was a contributing factor in the estrangement of some of the anti-Diefenbaker ministers. None of them felt any bond of affection for him and some of them disliked him intensely. By his behaviour toward them he had deprived himself of a reserve of personal support which might have served to restrain their discontent when the sanctioning effect of his popular appeal had lost its potency.

On the other side of the conflict, the substance of defence policy had even less importance. Most of the ministers who supported Diefenbaker agreed with anti-Diefenbaker ministers that the country should accept nuclear weapons.[33] Their loyalty was based on a strong bond of affection, empathy with Diefenbaker's populism, and gratitude for their political success.

The emotional commitment was of over-riding importance.[34] In part, this was a personal commitment, but it was also a group commitment. Diefenbaker had created a circle of "insiders" within the cabinet. They were not all his social intimates, but they were all accorded his trust. Their affective ties to Diefenbaker as a personality were re-enforced by affective ties to the Diefenbaker group.

Paradoxically, the solidarity of this group appears to have been re-enforced by the feeling of some of its members that socially and politically they were outsiders. An interesting piece of evidence in this regard is found by using the social characteristics of members of the cabinet to rank them on a scale measuring their social distance from the centres of national power. As table 1 shows, the fewer "establishment" social characteristics a minister possessed, the more likely the minister was to be a Diefenbaker loyalist. (The characteristics used in creating the scale are explained in the table.) It seems reasonable to suppose that these ministers were attracted to Diefenbaker because his symbolic attacks on negative stereotypes of the dominant elite in the country (and the party) gave expression to their feelings of exclusion from the establishment. In any event, some of them clearly felt a special debt of gratitude to him for their political success, believing they might not have been appointed to the cabinet by another prime minister. Michael Starr, for example, was deeply conscious of the fact that, as the son of Ukrainian immigrants, he was the first person of a non-charter ethnic group to be appointed to a federal cabinet.[35] It was not just a matter of gratitude for their elevation to the cabinet which instilled loyalty; there were still sections of the electorate among whom Diefenbaker remained very popular. In fact, despite the decline in his rating in the polls, there was reason to believe

Table 1 **Percentage of "Diefenbaker loyalists" among ministers by their scores on a scale of establishment social characteristics**

	Scale of establishment characteristics[a]				
	4	3	2	1	0
Percentage loyal to Diefenbaker[b]	13	67	75	100	100
N	(8)	(6)	(4)	(2)	(1)

(a) Each minister was accorded one "point" for each of the following characteristics: representative of an Ontario or Quebec riding; representative of a wholly urban riding; in a major professional (e.g. lawyer, doctor, engineer) or corporate occupation; university-educated.

(b) A "Diefenbaker loyalist" is defined as a minister who took an unequivocal stance in support of Diefenbaker at every stage in the conflict. These ministers were Gordon Churchill, Howard Green, Alvin Hamilton, Raymond O'Hurley, Hugh John Flemming, J. Angus MacLean, Michael Starr, Walter Dinsdale, and J. Waldo Monteith. (It has been suggested that H. J. Flemming was part of the coup attempt; in an interview Flemming said he "never at any time opposed Mr. Diefenbaker's continued leadership.")

that Diefenbaker was still more appealing to voters than the Liberal leader, Lester Pearson.[36] Thus, some ministers saw his continued leadership not as a threat to their political survival but as a condition for its achievement.

THE REVOLT IN THE PARTY: 1964–66

In the 1963 election the Diefenbaker government lost an additional twenty-one seats and with them its plurality in Parliament. As a result, the Liberal party took office under the leadership of Lester Pearson.

Since there was no longer a cabinet, the institutional centre of dissatisfaction with Diefenbaker's leadership had been eliminated. The only other institution with a continuing life where the issue might be raised was the caucus and there Diefenbaker faced no immediate threat. Even before the election, as we have seen, he had the support of a substantial majority in the caucus. The election had strengthened his position because it had removed some of the members who might have been disposed to challenge him. The elected wing of the caucus now consisted predominantly of members from the prairies, the maritimes, and rural and small town sections of the central provinces (mainly Ontario)—members who had reason to have a strong sense of identification with and dependency on Diefenbaker. The shifting balance of power in the caucus is reflected in the fact that, after the 1957 election, prairie members comprised 13 percent and Ontario members 54 percent of the elected membership, and after the 1963 election, prairie members comprised 43 percent and Ontario members 28 percent.

Opinion of Diefenbaker's leadership outside the caucus was more critical, but dissidents had no national forum in which to express their views. Thus, it was not until the annual meeting of the National Association in February 1964 that any new evidence of discontent appeared. The issue was raised by a motion to conduct the normally routine vote of confidence in the leader by secret ballot. Since the vote of confidence always before had been a standing vote, Diefenbaker chose to fight the secret ballot. Although he won a substantial majority, because the decision to reject the secret ballot was itself taken by a standing vote, the true strength of opposition to him remained in doubt. The overwhelming vote of confidence he ultimately received therefore did not settle the issue.

Douglas Harkness had been the only member of Parliament to vote against Diefenbaker at the annual meeting, but by the middle of 1964 there was a small group in the caucus which had begun informally to discuss the need for a change in leadership. They were particularly concerned by the state of personal relations within the caucus. The conflict of 1963 had left a residue of bitterness which infected these relations. Diefenbaker made a direct personal contribution to the perpetuation of ill-feeling by subjecting known or suspected dissidents to personal slights and petty harassments. The intensity of his hostility and the lengths to which he was prepared to go in expressing it are reflected in his attempt during a defence policy debate in October 1963 to prevent Harkness from speaking to the House. It actually required a formal vote of the whole House to override Diefenbaker's objection to a speech on defence policy from a man who only ten months before had been the minister of defence. Such acts created serious strains among Conservatives in Parliament. Several of the new members elected in 1962 and 1963 "were shocked by the internal condition of the party . . . [and] by Diefenbaker's behaviour."[37]

The strains within the caucus were seriously aggravated in the autumn of 1964 when Diefenbaker decided to stage a parliamentary filibuster to try to block the adoption of a new national flag. Most of the eight remaining francophone members of the caucus saw Diefenbaker's opposition to a distinctive national flag—establishing more clearly Canada's independence of Britain—as one further indication that he was insensitive to the feelings of French Canadians. They already had a good deal of evidence to support this view: the conflict over his choice of nominators at the 1956 leadership convention; the win-without-Quebec strategy he adopted in the 1957 election campaign; his failure to give a senior portfolio to a French-Canadian minister before 1960; his refusal to designate a Quebec lieutenant while he was prime minister; and his constant affirmation of his conception of the country as "one Canada," a view which seemed to deny the French-Canadian claim to distinctive cultural recognition.

In 1964, in an attempt to overcome the charge that he was unsympathetic to French Canada, Diefenbaker had at last appointed a Quebec lieutenant—Léon Balcer. This act proved to be an empty gesture. Balcer was given a place of prominence seated next to the leader in the House, but Diefenbaker did not accord him any commensurate role in party decision-making. (In fact, even though they were seat-mates, Diefenbaker rarely spoke to Balcer, even to exchange a formal greeting.)[38]

The filibuster decision also struck a further blow at external support for his leadership. He was criticized in the press both because of the anti-French implication of his position and because of the effect of the filibuster in delaying other parts of the government's legislative program. It was argued that Diefenbaker was obstructing the government and undermining public confidence in the parliamentary system by abusing the right of the opposition to debate government proposals.

The criticism in the press provoked concern among leading members of the extra-parliamentary party as well as among members of the caucus.

Equally important, members of the extra-parliamentary leadership were aware that party fund raisers were finding it difficult to meet the party's financial needs and it was being made clear that this financial problem was directly related to Diefenbaker's continued leadership. When Senator Wallace McCutcheon, a key figure in the business community, tried to establish a sustaining fund for national headquarters he received more than sixty letters which said contributions would only be made if Diefenbaker were replaced.[39]

There was open criticism of Diefenbaker's leadership at a meeting of the national executive in December. A few days later Balcer called upon the government to use closure to end the flag debate. Following this open break with his leader, Balcer mobilized Quebec members of caucus behind an appeal to the national executive for the convening of a leadership convention. When the national executive met in February 1965, Diefenbaker confronted it with a challenge to its right to deal with the issue. On February 5, the day before the executive meeting, Diefenbaker had secured a vote of confidence in his Commons leadership from his loyal majority in the caucus. He had thus presented the extra-parliamentary party with the possibility of a conflict over its authority. "Decide on your convention," he reportedly told the executive, "but I'm not going to accept it. I'll have to go back to caucus. They've just given me a vote of confidence."[40]

Members of the executive were to be asked to answer two questions which had been formulated by the principal officers.[41] The first asked whether a leadership convention should be called; the second sought an assessment of Diefenbaker's leadership.

After Diefenbaker had delivered his challenge, Erik Nielsen, an MP loyal to the leader, argued that the executive should not deal with the question of confidence and moved that it not be presented to the meeting. Nielsen's amendment was passed by a majority of only two votes and the five principal officers, most of whom were anti-Diefenbaker, had abstained. Subsequently, by a larger majority, the call for a leadership convention was defeated. While the constitutional issue had been avoided, Diefenbaker had unambiguous evidence that he had lost the confidence of a large part of the national executive. Yet he chose to treat the executive's decision as a reaffirmation of support for his continued leadership, forgetting his statement to the national president that if more than 30 percent of the national executive voted against him, he would feel compelled to resign.[42]

On February 19, 1965, one of the francophone members of the caucus, Rémi Paul, left the Conservative party to become an Independent. For two months Balcer resisted pressures to follow a similar course. His resignation was ultimately provoked by a debate in caucus over Diefenbaker's opposition to government proposals which would have had the effect of permitting some provinces to develop distinctive areas of legislative and administrative jurisdiction. Diefenbaker was prepared to commit the party to another extended parliamentary battle on this issue on the ground that to permit some provinces powers which other provinces did not possess was to endanger national unity. Balcer saw in this position another attack on French-Canadian interests both because there was strong feeling in Quebec that that province would require distinctive constitutional arrangements if it were to be able to give adequate protection to its French-Canadian culture and because one of the proposed pieces of legislation touched directly upon an agreement between the federal government and the government of Quebec. For reasons that are not clear Diefenbaker agreed to moderate his position,[43] but for Balcer the acrimony and invective of the struggle had been too much. His motives and character had been impugned by crude gossip which was repeated directly and by innuendo in the virtually continuous heckling to which he was subjected whenever he spoke in caucus. Despite the pleas of several colleagues, Balcer decided to resign from the caucus because life there had become unbearable.[44]

In the fall of 1965, Prime Minister Pearson called a new election. Despite the intensity of feeling within the Progressive Conservative party, a facade of unity was created for the campaign. Two of the ministers who had resigned in 1963, Hees and Fulton, sought re-election; E. A. Goodman, a leading member of the extra-parliamentary party who had refused to take an active role in the 1963 campaign, became campaign chairman; and the four Conservative provincial premiers provided a public display of support. One reason for the return of these rebels, according to Goodman, was that there was a risk the party would fall completely into the hands of a Diefenbaker rump.[45] For Fulton and Hees there was the additional motive of personal ambition. Fulton's efforts to rebuild the electoral base of the provincial party in British Columbia had failed disastrously, while Hees had found private life "less exciting" than politics. Both aspired to succeed Diefenbaker and wished to re-establish their standing in the national party in preparation for a leadership convention which they believed would not be long in coming.[46]

For all its outward appearance of unity the party was not entirely free of inner conflict during the 1965 campaign. In some ridings, Diefenbaker partisans attempted to replace candidates whose loyalty to the leader was doubtful, among them Gordon Fairweather, a member of caucus who had supported the resolution calling for a leadership convention at the national executive meeting in February. These efforts, while not systematically organized or supported, reflected the extent to which the party was in danger of complete factional polarization. Activity of this kind at the constituency level was unprecedented in the modern history of the party.

The outcome of the 1965 election failed to alter the basic distribution of power in the Commons, each of the two major parties achieving a net gain of two seats. The complexion of the Conservative caucus was also basically unchanged which meant that Diefenbaker could still command a substantial majority there.

It was not until the following spring that the conflict over Diefenbaker's leadership was resumed.[47] The principal figure this time was Dalton Camp, the president of the National Association.

Camp's career in the party had been built upon his skills as a publicist and political strategist. Until 1963 his main interest and sphere of activity had been provincial politics. He had had an important role in provincial campaigns in Nova Scotia, New Brunswick, Newfoundland, Prince Edward Island, and Manitoba and retained a close relationship with Premier Robert Stanfield of Nova Scotia and Premier Duff Roblin of Manitoba. Camp had been chosen by Diefenbaker to manage the national campaign in 1963, and in 1964 he was elected president of the association.

Camp and Diefenbaker had had a good working relationship in the 1963 campaign but some strain began to develop when Camp, in an appraisal of the campaign, told a party meeting that the party could not afford "to make a god of its leader." In 1964 this strain was deepened by Diefenbaker's criticism of Camp's plan for a conference of intellectuals to discuss Conservative policies for the future. The leader treated the conference with public disdain and made only a token appearance. Later in the year, Camp found the relationship growing even more difficult after he advised Diefenbaker that the Conservative filibuster in the flag debate was hurting the party. In January 1965 newspaper stories implied that Camp was involved with the Balcer challenge to Diefenbaker's leadership. Apparently, in consequence, Camp was approached by a member of caucus who, to test his loyalty, tried to trap him into making critical statements about the leader. Camp was disturbed by the paranoiac atmosphere this suggested and was subsequently shocked by Diefenbaker's behaviour during a six-hour meeting in which the leader was by turns "recriminating, abusive and flattering. [He seemed to be] prepared to wreck the party . . . to avoid becoming the fall guy."[48]

But the national president was not yet prepared (in 1965) to join the fight against Diefenbaker. He believed Diefenbaker had the right to lead the party in another election and that if the party were to lose, Diefenbaker would resign—if he were given time to do so with dignity. Camp's reluctance to become a rebel in 1965 was probably also related to his own interest in becoming a candidate for the succession. He had worked hard to maintain "open lines" with all sections of the party and believed that if he could acquire some parliamentary experience he might be able to establish credibility as a leadership candidate.

In the spring of 1966 two factors convinced Camp that it would no longer do to wait for Diefenbaker to resign. One was the decision by James Johnston, the new national director, to dismiss Flora Macdonald, the senior permanent member of the staff of national headquarters, who was an experienced and well-liked figure in the party organization. This decision seemed to suggest that anyone whose loyalty to Diefenbaker was even remotely suspected might be purged, no matter what the cost to the party. The second factor was that Diefenbaker, by persistent efforts in Parliament to force another election, had made it clear that he did not intend to resign. Although "it occurred to [him] that by opposing Diefenbaker [he] would dismiss [his] own leadership chances for ten years,"[49] Camp decided to launch a campaign to get a proposal before the annual meeting of the association in the fall to hold a leadership convention before the summer of 1968. In a speech to a private meeting of Conservatives in May and in informal conversations through the spring and summer he argued that since the Liberals were also in considerable difficulty, electoral advantage would lie with the Conservatives if they were to effect an early "renewal." In September he publicly called for a reassessment of the leadership.

Camp's strategy was to cast the struggle in terms of a principle. He did not attack Diefenbaker personally nor did he even mention the leader by name. The issue, he argued, was party democracy, the right of the membership to submit its leader to some evaluation that was more than a *pro forma* or ritual exercise.

Diefenbaker's supporters responded by making an issue of the propriety of Camp's behaviour. They attacked him personally, arguing that he was abusing the prerogatives of his office as national president in using it to launch his reassessment campaign. A second element of their strategy was to evoke Conservative fears about the party's reputation for disloyalty to its leaders. They argued that, intrinsically and in the interest of party cohesion, loyalty to the leader was a principle which ought to be respected.

Inevitably, Camp's re-election as president became a critical issue. Camp decided to make this issue a test of confidence in his call for leadership review. The Diefenbaker forces chose Arthur Maloney, a popular former member of Parliament who had been an active supporter of Fleming in 1956, to run against Camp.

There was little Camp could do to secure the election of committed constituency delegates. This would have required months of intensive organization. His strategy, therefore, was to try to elect as many supporters as possible among the new provincial association executives which were to be chosen before the annual meeting. The realization of this objective had four potential benefits. First, under the rules then in force, the provincial executives controlled the appointment of a large number of delegates-at-large; second, representatives of the provincial executives were more likely than constituency delegates to attend the meeting;[50] third, their opinion-leadership might have some effect on the decisions of constituency delegates; and fourth, the representatives of the provincial executives would be members of the national executive where critical procedural questions would have to be resolved.

With the help of Flora MacDonald, who knew most of the leading activists across the country, Camp was able to develop a loose network of contacts among all the groups within the party who believed there was a need for leadership review. A national speaking tour of Young Progressive Conservative (YPC) associations and Progressive Conservative Student federations (PCSF), where there was known to be considerable anti-Diefenbaker feeling,[51] provided him a relatively uncritical forum in which to publicize his campaign. It also helped to mobilize younger party members who might otherwise have remained inactive.

Diefenbaker, through Johnston, the national director, controlled the party's national headquarters, but his advantage was of limited value. For one thing, as was pointed out earlier, the locus of power in party organization in most parts of the country is at the provincial level.[52] In addition, in the fall of 1966, communications between national headquarters and local party associations were not very effective because Johnston had had virtually no experience in national party affairs and neither knew nor was well known among provincial and local activists.

The success of Camp's strategy became apparent when the national executive assembled to give final approval to procedural arrangements for the association meeting. Johnston had prepared an agenda deferring the election of officers until the last day of the meeting. Camp challenged the agenda, believing that his advantage lay in avoiding an early debate of the reassessment resolution. If the executive election were held first, his personal victory could be symbolically influential in the vote on the resolution and he would have the authority of a renewed mandate from which to deal with procedural issues raised in the presentation of the resolution. The national executive redrew the agenda, placing the election of officers first. Among Camp's supporters on this crucial vote were most of the officers of the National Association, the YPC and PCSF representatives, the representatives of the provincial associations from Quebec, Ontario, and British Columbia, and significant proportions of the representatives of the four Atlantic provincial associations, the Manitoba association, and the Alberta association.

This defeat placed Diefenbaker on the defensive. When he addressed the formal opening of the meeting he tried to deal with the question of leadership review by attacking Camp. The result was disastrous. Camp supporters had been directed to the auditorium early and had occupied most of the seats. Thus Diefenbaker faced a hostile audience: "Diefenbaker called on the unlistening crowd to work together to build the party. He quoted at length an earlier statement by Camp that praised his leadership. He was building towards the question: why did the change take place? But he never had a chance. He was greeted by hoots and catcalls. The Old Chief lost his stride; he poked and prodded and searched for a civilized response, but could not get one."[53]

It is impossible to assess the direct influence of Diefenbaker's speech on delegate opinion, but the reception he received had a disruptive effect on his organization, as Robert Coates observes:

> The humiliating treatment by the Camp forces on the Monday evening probably cost Arthur Maloney the election as President. Members of Parliament had to immediately leave the Chateau and meet on the Hill in an effort to salvage from the ruins a foundation on which Diefenbaker could stand. The necessity for the elective wing to move immediately cost Maloney support, for the Members could not be in two places at the same time. If the Party were to be saved, it had to continue as an effective opposition in the House of Commons. It could only operate effectively if John Diefenbaker continued as leader. The time required to consolidate the leader's position was at the moment when Maloney needed active supporters the most, on the eve of the voting.[54]

The result of the presidential election revealed the seriousness of the division within the party. Camp had 564 votes and Maloney 502.

Maloney's defeat further demoralized Diefenbaker's organization with the result that it was not prepared for a procedural manoeuvre which brought the question of the leadership to an early vote during debate on resolutions on the following day. Many of Diefenbaker's supporters had left the hall to join a procession escorting the leader to the meeting when —under the guidance of E. A. Goodman, who was chairman of the resolutions committee—a motion was quickly introduced and adopted to conduct the vote on the question of confidence in the leader by secret ballot. A resolution was then presented which affirmed confidence in Diefenbaker but proposed that "in view of the present situation in the party" a leadership convention be held before January 1, 1968. Goodman succeeded in limiting debate on the resolution and bringing it to a vote before the Diefenbaker forces could respond. As a result, the resolution was adopted 563 votes to 209.

In a general sense, the motives of participants in the conflict of 1966 were very much like those of the participants in the conflict in 1963. One factor which was different was the absence of any immediate disagreement about the substance of specific policies. There was no one question of policy that brought the conflict to a head. This was not to suggest that policy motives were unimportant in the conflict. To the contrary, they were important in four ways.

First, there had been growing concern within the party about Diefenbaker's attitude toward French Canada. There were French-Canadian Conservatives who supported Diefenbaker, but they were few in number and they did not represent the prevailing attitude in the party's Quebec wing. Léon Balcer was a better representative of that attitude.[55] By his own account he was "not an ardent nationalist" but believed—intrinsically and in the interest of combating separatism—in expanding protection for French-Canadian culture and in getting more French Canadians involved in federal matters. "The main stumbling block was that Diefenbaker never trusted French-Canadians. . . . He was hostile to French-Canadians. His attitude was that the constitution gave the French Canadian everything he needed. . . . Essentially he was prejudiced."[56] Not everyone shared the view that Diefenbaker was prejudiced, but it was apparent that his conception of the role of French Canadians in Confederation did not recognize the changes which most Quebec opinion-leaders now felt essential to the survival of French-Canadian culture. This influenced not only French-speaking Conservatives but also English-speaking Conservatives who were concerned about national unity.[57]

Diefenbaker's attacks on the big economic interests of Toronto and Montreal could be seen to be a second policy-based cause of opposition to his leadership. These attacks did not embrace any specific proposals which might be seen to threaten corporate power. Indeed, if anything, Diefenbaker's policy positions were less interventionist than those of the Pearson government. But members of the corporate elite were suspicious of his rhetoric and, rightly or wrongly, they blamed him for the economic problems the country had experienced between 1960 and 1963. The fact that members of the corporate establishment were solidly arrayed against Diefenbaker was brought forcibly to the attention of members of the party's extra-parliamentary elite by the response to their appeals for financial support. Whatever their own relationships with and views of big business, they could see that Diefenbaker's continued leadership had seriously weakened the party financially.

Third, there is a sense in which criticism of Diefenbaker's personality can be said to have been policy-motivated. One of the most common complaints about his personality related to its effect on the process of making policy. There was a widely held view that his indecisiveness, obsessively suspicious nature, insensitivity to the feelings of colleagues, and unpredictable temperament were qualities which would immobilize any cabinet under his leadership. In addition, several members of Parliament were upset about the way in which policy was made in the caucus. One of them, a committee chairman, said that between 1963 and 1966 the discussion and formulation of policy grew progressively more disorganized: "I found . . . that certain stands were being taken independently, without any consultation, by people with access to Mr. Diefenbaker's ear. . . . There were some embarrassing situations. Decisions were made [in some matters] by people without any comprehension [of the issues involved]. The chairmen were consulted less and less. There was no communication at all. The people who were asked to consult were those who would reflect what Mr. Diefenbaker wanted to hear."[58]

Finally, policy disagreements had been significant in the behaviour of some of Diefenbaker's opponents in the sense that an initial disagreement about some issue had led to a strain in personal relations which continued after the original controversy passed. The mutual animus between Diefenbaker and Harkness is the best example. The ill-feeling which developed in this relationship illustrates the general point made by several members of both the caucus and the extra-parliamentary party that once they had expressed some disagreement with Diefenbaker they were never again fully trusted.

Quite apart from any feelings that they may have had about policy or policy-making, as such, members of the anti-Diefenbaker coalition shared the belief that the style of Diefenbaker's leadership and some of his opinions about issues had made him an electoral liability to the party. The view was spreading, especially among members of the extra-parliamentary party, that the Conservatives could never return to power under Diefenbaker's leadership because he could not appeal successfully to urban, middle-class, and young voters. Anti-Diefenbaker sentiment among these groups was such that in some constituencies it had become a threat to the preservation of the party's corps of activists. One member of caucus had been told by members of his constituency executive, for example, "that a number of them were going to resign or at least stand aside" if he did not support the calling of a leadership convention.[59]

The dilemma at the heart of the conflict lay here. Most members of the caucus majority which supported Diefenbaker, quite apart from any other consideration, perceived him as an electoral asset and many of them feared the consequences for the security of their own seats if he were forced to resign. These members came from the rural areas and small towns and/or the hinterland provinces in which Diefenbaker's political style and policies had had greatest appeal. Most of the anti-Diefenbaker group, which was drawn predominantly from the extra-parliamentary party, saw his continued leadership as an obstacle to their own or to the party's achievement of office precisely because he was unable to appeal beyond these areas. There was no way to resolve this dilemma if Diefenbaker did not choose to resolve it by resigning because both sides were probably right.

There were bigger career stakes for some of the participants on both sides of the conflict. Some of the more prominent figures in the anti-

Diefenbaker coalition had a direct personal interest in the leadership. Fulton had actually formed a committee to organize his leadership campaign even before he was re-elected to Parliament in 1965 and members of his committee had an active role in the anti-Diefenbaker coalition. Others could expect the benefit of positions of greater influence under a new leader. Conversely, many supporters of Diefenbaker had reason to be grateful to him for their positions of prominence and to fear the loss of these positions if he were removed. In this regard, however, Diefenbaker had contributed to the weakening of his power by becoming too generous in his promises of future cabinet appointments. One member of Parliament said that virtually every person in caucus had at one time or another been promised some portfolio. The result was that such promises had less and less credibility. Yet he still possessed institutional prerogatives which gave some buttress to his position in the caucus, particularly for those members who had little expectation or desire for ministerial careers.

Affective dispositions appear to have contributed more to the conflict in 1966 than they had in 1963. The leader evoked very strong negative feelings among some of his colleagues, if not for any intrinsic characteristic of his personality, at least for his manner in dealing with them.

One member of Parliament, a former minister, observed that "[Diefenbaker] approached MP's on a bullying basis . . . rather than trying to convince them. It was a matter of leadership style. . . . He was always looking over his shoulder. He seemed to create opposition [by suspecting it]. I don't see how anybody who professed himself to be stable can possibly have had anything but an unsatisfactory relationship with someone who is as emotionally unstable as Mr. Diefenbaker has been through all the years."[60] Another pointed out that there were some members to whom Diefenbaker never spoke and several with whom he had "very awkward personal relationships. At the same time he never seemed to appreciate those who were loyal. He couldn't manage people."[61]

David MacDonald, one of the MPs who opposed Diefenbaker, emphasized the importance of the positive affective ties Diefenbaker had created in preserving the loyalty of the caucus majority. "They didn't relate to the issue in intellectual terms; even now [1970] they relate to it in emotional terms. [They were bound to Diefenbaker] by deep-seated emotional ties, ties that were totally beyond the rational."[62] In support of this analysis, MacDonald cites the case of a former minister who told MacDonald of his concern with the chaotic process of decision-making within the Diefenbaker cabinet and caucus but explained that he could not bring himself to oppose Diefenbaker because of his strong personal attachment to the leader.[63]

One way to explain such attachments is to see them simply in terms of the emotional attraction that certain personalities appear to generate by their very nature—that is, in terms of the appeal of what is popularly called charisma. Diefenbaker was a rare public personality, a man who was widely seen to possess this charismatic quality. But there is a second less idiosyncratic way to explain the strength of personal attachments to him. As we have seen, in the cabinet revolt of 1963 the ministers who were most loyal to him were for the most part those whose social characteristics placed them outside the Canadian establishment. An analysis of the social backgrounds of members of caucus reveals a similar pattern in his support after 1963. As table 2 shows, the less similar the social characteristics of members to those of the dominant elite in the country, the more likely they were to support him. Diefenbaker's appeal to these social "outsiders" was essentially emotional. He sought to mobilize their support by attacking the "powerful interests," the sinister and anonymous "they" who were the hidden rulers of the country. The use of vague negative symbols of this kind provides an outlet for feelings of status insecurity. It provides an object on which to displace the frustration of being an "outsider."

Regardless of the role of such emotional dispositions in creating the conflict, an emotional content of its own appeared as it continued. In the caucus in particular, members found themselves increasingly isolated in relationships of suspicion and ill-feeling. As A. D. Hales observed: "It got so bad around here that you were labelled depending on who you were seen talking to. You had to be careful about whose office you were seen going into. It was a terrible situation."[64]

Robert Coates writes that at the annual meeting of the association in 1966 "emotion overcame reason and bitterness replaced composure."[65] Feeling ran so high at the annual meeting that there were occasions when physical blows were exchanged.[66] Even the most dispassionate of the

Table 2 **Percentages of members of Parliament supporting Diefenbaker, by scores on a scale of establishment social characteristics**

	Scale of establishment characteristics[a]				
	4	3	2	1	0
Percentage supporting Diefenbaker[b]	50	43	65	88	100
N	(2)	(21)	(23)	(25)	(23)

(a) For an explanation of the assignment of scores see note (a) in table 1.

(b) The members supporting Diefenbaker were identified from a caucus petition in support of Diefenbaker which was circulated immediately following the 1966 annual meeting.

leading participants admitted to succumbing in some measure to the emotional intensity of the situation. The development of these affective interactions helped divide the party elite into two factions which found their internal cohesion in common atitudes toward Diefenbaker and toward the rival faction. As I will show in the next chapter this factional split became the dominant cleavage in the internal politics of the party.

5

The National Elite in the 1967 Convention

In September 1967, a national convention of the Progressive Conservative party chose Robert Stanfield to succeed John Diefenbaker as the party's leader. This chapter will consider the behaviour of leading figures in the party in the events leading to this decision. The chapter is divided into three parts. The first part looks at the dispositions and actions of members of the party elite during the planning of the convention, the second at their approach to and the conduct of the convention campaign, and the third at the interactions among leading participants during the balloting at the convention.

THE DEVELOPMENT OF FACTIONALISM

John Diefenbaker's defeat at the annual meeting of the National Association in November 1966 brought the Conservative party very close to schism. On the evening of his speech to the annual meeting, several members of the caucus loyal to Diefenbaker, anticipating the outcome of the presidential election, began to discuss the possibility of forming a new party. By the end of the meeting this movement had gathered the support of some thirty members of the Commons. But nearly all of these members came from constituencies in Alberta and Saskatchewan where there was no deeply rooted popular attachment to the Progressive Conservative party. Most of the MPs from provinces where such a tradition did exist believed a new party could only lead to electoral disaster. Robert Coates, who was unable to attend a meeting of the loyal caucus members called to discuss the situation, made this point in a letter which he asked to have read at the meeting: "while I appreciate history has indicated, on the part of Canadians in western Canada, that a regional group can secure support from the public, this has not been the case in eastern Canada and there is no reason to believe they will break from the historic pattern of voting for either the Conservative or Liberal parties. There are also the very real problems associated with finances and organization that cannot be overlooked as far as eastern Canada is concerned."[1] In addition, Diefenbaker himself gave no encouragement to the proposal for a new party, as James Johnston reports in describing a conversation between Diefenbaker and his wife: "Jim has been telling me that some of the Members are thinking of breaking away and forming a new party, and I have said that they must not do that.' 'Why not?' Mrs. Diefenbaker asked. 'Well, they must not. That would be awful,' said the Chief."[2] Diefenbaker's supporters, therefore, abandoned the idea of a new party and contented themselves with a declaration of their loyalty to Diefenbaker in the form of a petition requesting him to continue as leader.

Seventy-one of the ninety-six Conservative members of the Commons signed this petition. Not all of them actually wanted Diefenbaker to stay. Several believed that if Diefenbaker did not have some demonstration of the support of caucus he would resign immediately and thus precipitate the fragmentation of the party. Others were concerned to protect their career interests. They believed that by signing the petition and taking no more active role they could preserve some influence with the Diefenbaker faction without alienating the anti-Diefenbaker groups. It is estimated that the hardcore of Diefenbaker's support probably consisted of no more than forty members[3] and most of this number recognized that because of his age, he would soon be compelled to retire.

Whatever the intentions or opinions of its signatories, the petition had the effect of giving Diefenbaker a broad new mandate. As Johnston observes, "no one knew exactly what the petition meant or just how far reaching it might be."[4] As a result, the issue of Diefenbaker's leadership remained unresolved.

The immediate fear of some members of the anti-Diefenbaker alliance was that Diefenbaker might use his caucus mandate to challenge the legitimacy of the decision to call a convention. It was not until January 18, nearly two months after the annual meeting, that Diefenbaker ended this threat. In a television address he called for the convening of the convention at the earliest possible date. At the same time he warned this was "no swan song," holding out the possibility he might become a candidate for re-election.

Authority to call the convention under the constitution effective in 1967 was vested in the national executive. The national executive was authorized to constitute a convention committee with the power to set the time and place for the convention, to establish rules for its conduct, to decide how delegates would be apportioned, and to adjudicate the credentials of delegates. The smaller executive committee, which consisted of the principal officers, the provincial vice-presidents, the national director, two representatives from the Commons, and one representative from the Senate, was designated as the convention committee. This committee immediately became a focus of conflict.

The committee contained an anti-Diefenbaker majority but in the national executive—partly as a result of the election of new representatives from the Commons and the Senate, which involved a deliberate attempt to purge anti-Diefenbaker members[5]—there was a fairly even balance between the two groups. Thus Diefenbaker's supporters believed his interests were protected by the implicit threat of an appeal to the parent body.[6]

Diefenbaker's representatives on the committee appear to have been concerned primarily with saving him from any further humiliation and, concomitantly, with limiting the power of Camp. Camp's presence in the role of national president was a continuing source of aggravation to Diefenbaker supporters. It is difficult to describe the passion of their hostility toward him. Among those closest to Diefenbaker, any action by Camp was likely to provoke a diametrically opposed reaction. They analysed every decision to look for his hand. Camp's name became their code-word for stigmatizing enemies. Any association with him was sufficient to rouse their suspicion. He was transformed into a symbol for everything they opposed.

The reality of Camp's power was less significant than this sentiment implied. The group which had supported him in 1966 did not see him as its leader. Indeed, once the question of leadership review had been settled, many of them had begun to think of him as a dispensable figure. He could and perhaps should be moved aside to satisfy the Diefenbaker wing and restore party unity.[7]

There was no suggestion, therefore, that Camp should be chairman of the convention committee.[8] This position was given to E. A. Goodman. Despite his role at the November meeting, he had taken no active part in organizing the anti-Diefenbaker campaign and continued to have access to Diefenbaker and key members of the Diefenbaker faction. Roger Régimbal, a francophone member of Parliament who had signed the caucus petition of support for Diefenbaker, was chosen co-chairman.

Most of the conflict within the committee was at the symbolic level. The selection of a date for the convention was a good example.

Diefenbaker had called for an early convention; Camp had proposed it not be held until November. There were practical reasons for delay, but Diefenbaker's supporters in the committee wanted to ensure that deferral of the date would not afford Camp a symbolic victory, as Johnston explains:

> Bob Coates talked with Camp and found him determined to push Diefenbaker still further by setting a late fall date. Coates phoned me in the middle of the night and the two of us concluded that we could stop Camp by suggesting a meeting between Diefenbaker and Goodman to discuss the convention date, and this would give the leader some of the respect to which he was entitled. . . . I . . . told [Goodman] that any decision setting the date in late fall as Camp had suggested would be considered an unnecessary slap at Diefenbaker. It might lead to a walkout by the pro-Diefs and, indeed, even Diefenbaker's immediate resignation, because he had taken as much abuse as he was going to take. . . . He said he had been thinking about the date himself. He felt that June was too early and November too late, but perhaps September would suit. I replied that September was earlier than November, and as the Chief wanted an early convention I thought it would be acceptable.[9]

On the basis of this accommodation the decision was made to hold the convention in Toronto in the first week of September.

Potentially more difficult decisions about the designation of types of delegates were settled in one meeting, without serious dissent. The model of past conventions served as a precedent for the committee in this respect. Three kinds of delegates were designated: ex officio delegates, delegates-at-large, and constituency delegates. In his January speech, Diefenbaker had appealed for a convention without appointed delegates-at-large from the provinces. He might have been concerned that the power to appoint such delegates would give an important advantage to his opponents who controlled the association executives in the bigger provinces. Certainly the issue had been raised at an earlier convention on his behalf,[10] but no one within the committee objected to the designation of delegates-at-large, not even the caucus representatives who were there to protect his interests. However, one of the caucus representatives, George Chatterton, did propose that delegates-at-large should be elected and not appointed.[11] This proposal was rejected, but as a partial concession to Diefenbaker it was agreed to introduce a procedure for appointment which would provide a safeguard against blatant manipulation. In the past the procedure had been left to the provincial association itself to decide. The committee's innovation provided that appointments be made by a specifically designated committee consisting of the president of the provincial association, the national vice-president from the province and the two directors from the province on the national executive.

The most serious controversy within the committee concerned procedural arrangements for an address to the convention by Diefenbaker. Party tradition called for a formal address by the retiring leader, but since Diefenbaker had not made clear his intention to retire, the anti-Diefenbaker group feared he might use the address to launch a campaign for re-election. At the April meeting it was agreed the deadline for acceptance of nominations would be the afternoon of the first day of the convention. This meant Diefenbaker would have to declare his intention before the formal opening ceremonies and, therefore, that the committee would be in a position to prevent him from speaking ex officio if he did decide to run. In a letter to Goodman, prior to the June meeting, Diefenbaker demanded that this restraint be removed and he supported his demand with a threat: "I underwent organized efforts to humiliate me at the annual meeting of the Progressive Conservative party last November. I have said nothing about it but there comes a limit to the continuance of the course of silence regarding that meeting that I have followed up to the present time."[12] Diefenbaker wanted a guarantee that he would be permitted to speak at the opening of the convention even if he were a candidate and he wanted the nomination deadline extended until the day before the balloting.

After some discussion, it was decided Diefenbaker could speak to the convention on opening night whether or not he intended to be a candidate, while the deadline for the acceptance of nominations would remain unchanged. Subsequently, in the face of Diefenbaker's persistence, Goodman agreed to get the committee to advance the nomination deadline to the day before balloting.

The arguments in the committee about these issues were always made in terms of their substantive implications, but their greater importance as symbols is apparent from the comments of members of the Diefenbaker faction. Diefenbaker's own reference to "organized efforts to humiliate" him suggests the importance of pride in his own behaviour. By winning victories on these technical questions he could regain some lost esteem—or, at least, avoid further humiliation.

At the same time these issues were symbolically important to his followers in the caucus. Their commitment to Diefenbaker represented an investment of their own prestige. To the extent he suffered further defeats so too did they.

Some members of Parliament on both sides were anxious to find a means to close the breach. As early as December, Coates had taken an important initiative in this regard, proposing and helping to organize a caucus policy conference. The first conference was so successful that a second was held in January. There were differences among the participants in these conferences about the specifics of policy, but these differences cut across the cleavage over Diefenbaker's leadership and agreement was reached on a series of policy resolutions at the conclusion of the discussions. Both Johnston and Coates emphasized the value of these conferences in abating the conflict within the caucus.[13]

The success of these conferences suggests two points. First, whatever its original causes, the conflict after the annual meeting of 1966 had little or no policy content. Second, there was a basic consensus on policy which could help give members a sense of solidarity when they took the time to consider it. These are points to which I shall return later in this chapter.

The two policy conferences may have helped prevent a schism at the time they were held but, as we have seen, they did not bring an end to the conflict within the party. The conflict continued to be kept alive by the persistence of an active Diefenbaker faction.

Diefenbaker himself had to bear the main burden of responsibility. After the annual meeting of 1966, it was clear that he had lost the confidence of too large a section of the party to continue in the leadership. Yet he took two months to acknowledge the legitimacy of the decision of the annual meeting and then kept open the possibility that he would be a candidate for re-election. The effect of his persistence was to contribute to the development of factionalism within the party.

All intra-party conflicts involve factions, that is, groups which establish independent organizational structure, formal or informal, for the purpose of seeking some allocation from the party.[14] Factions, as such, constitute no special threat to the cohesion of the party. But this threat will emerge when these groups persist from conflict to conflict, seeking or finding new common purposes even after the purpose for which they were originally organized has been achieved or is no longer a matter to be decided. This condition is factionalism. The danger in factionalism is the creation of subgroup loyalties which compete with members' loyalties to the party as a whole. It weakens the consciousness of common interest and diverts energies which would normally be applied to the pursuit of collective purposes.

Factionalism may have other causes, but it is likely to be re-enforced by emotional bonds and the development of negative emotional responses toward adversaries.[15] This dimension of it is all the more likely to develop when the conflict from which it emerges already has a substantial emotional content. This was certainly the case in the conflict over Diefenbaker's leadership. The bitterness of anti-Camp feeling in the Diefenbaker faction is not easily described.[16] Camp had come to personify the "they" against whom Diefenbaker had fought throughout his career. Even after the question of Diefenbaker's leadership had been finally put to rest and Camp himself had ceased to have a central role in the party, Camp's name continued to be used as a negative symbol to rally opposition to the party "establishment."

This point will be developed more fully later.

THE CONVENTION CAMPAIGN

Diefenbaker's uncertain intentions created a special problem for his supporters. Without some indication of his plans they were reluctant to endorse or seek another candidate. They feared, however, that if they did not act they would lose the opportunity to have any influence in the choice of a successor, because other candidates were quickly in the field. Fulton was the first to declare—within a few days of the announcement that the convention would proceed. He had canvassed his prospects before returning to federal politics in 1965 and had formed a national committee soon after the election.

Fulton was unacceptable to the Diefenbaker faction. Hostility toward him could be traced back to his relationship with Diefenbaker when the party was in power. He was stigmatized as a man whose own excessive ambition for the leadership had made him a disloyal lieutenant. This reputation was re-inforced by his support of the leadership review campaign in 1966 and by his refusal to sign the caucus petition of confidence in Diefenbaker.

George Hees announced his candidacy in mid-February. Hees had stayed out of the 1966 conflict but he still suffered among the Diefenbaker loyalists for his role in the events of 1963. In addition, there was a feeling that his position in 1966 had been opportunistic. Staying out was not good enough. If he had wanted Diefenbaker to endorse him he should have given Diefenbaker open support at the annual meeting.[17] The fact that Hees had signed the caucus petition served only to strengthen the impression that he was playing an opportunistic role.

Two members of Parliament who remained loyal to Diefenbaker announced their candidacies in May. The first, Michael Starr, was a former minister of labour. The second, Alvin Hamilton, had been Diefenbaker's minister of agriculture. Both had been encouraged by Diefenbaker to run and assumed therefore that Diefenbaker would not be a candidate.[18] Starr had also assumed that Diefenbaker's encouragement implied Diefenbaker's support, but it was soon clear to him that he had been mistaken.[19] None of the members of the caucus numbered among Diefenbaker's most intimate friends made any move to support either of these ostensible Diefenbaker candidates and they found little evidence of support from other caucus members.

Gordon Churchill, Diefenbaker's closest caucus friend and effective leader of his caucus faction, was among those who remained uncertain of Diefenbaker's plans: "He wouldn't give any of us any indication of what he intended to do. I suspect that he did not know himself. It made my position very difficult."[20]

However, it was not just for this reason that the Diefenbaker wing withheld its support from Starr and Hamilton. In the words of one of its members, "Starr was viewed as a lightweight and Hamilton was thought of simply as a Diefenbaker man."[21] It was believed that if a candidate were to have any prospect of winning he would have to appeal beyond hard-core Diefenbaker loyalists.

With this in mind, as early as January, Churchill had approached Donald Fleming, who had not had an active role in the party since his retirement from the cabinet in 1963. Fleming's interest in the leadership was whetted by assurances of widespread caucus support and by the direct personal encouragement of Diefenbaker. Fleming pressed Diefenbaker for a clear commitment about his intentions and he became convinced that Diefenbaker would not run.[22] Among the other inducements Fleming received was an invitation signed by sixty members of the caucus. In June, after a good deal of hesitation and further conversation with Diefenbaker, Fleming announced his candidacy.

Diefenbaker's plans were also a factor in the considerations of those around Camp. Some of Camp's allies of the fall had had candidates in mind long before the annual meeting. Two of them, Fulton and Senator Wallace McCutcheon, had themselves become candidates, but Camp remained uncommitted.

The main consideration for Camp was to ensure that there was a strong alternative to Diefenbaker because he feared that without such an alternative, Diefenbaker could declare his candidacy even at the last moment and carry the convention. Some of the younger members of the party who had joined Camp's leadership review campaign were pressing him to run himself, but he had few illusions about the prospects for his own candidacy. He believed he might be able to win but only at the cost of a split in the party. He was prepared to run only if he could find no other candidates who could stop Diefenbaker.[23]

Camp doubted the strength of the candidates who had already declared. He therefore looked for an alternative among the three provincial premiers—John Robarts in Ontario, Duff Roblin in Manitoba, and Robert Stanfield in Nova Scotia—who had achieved some recognition in the national press.

Robarts told Camp early in 1967 that there was no circumstance under which he would run. Thus the choice had to fall on Stanfield or Roblin. Camp had had long personal associations with both men, having had an important part in the campaigns that brought them to power. Both were interested but both were reluctant to move.

Stanfield, with a provincial election in May, was absorbed in provincial affairs. Moreover, before running he wanted to be assured of a broad national interest in his candidacy and that had not been evident.

Three different explanations have been offered for Roblin's hesitancy. A theory advanced by some leading figures in the party who had contacts with him during this period is that he wanted to have the leadership "bestowed" on him, presumably by Diefenbaker. Another theory is that he did not want to run as the candidate of some apparent broker (Camp) and that he wanted to avoid the danger of a conflict with Diefenbaker which he feared would be the result if he were to run as Camp's candidate.[24] Roblin's own explanation is that he had not really decided whether he wanted to run.[25]

It was not the first time Roblin had played the role of reluctant candidate. In 1965 Alvin Hamilton had approached both Roblin and Stanfield with an offer of caucus support and Roblin had given a favourable response. Subsequently, Hamilton had presented Roblin with a letter signed by sixty members of the caucus inviting him to run for Parliament. After the 1965 election had been called, Roblin had held a meeting with Diefenbaker at Winnipeg airport in which it was believed Diefenbaker had promised Roblin support for the succession if he would enter Parliament. Roblin says Diefenbaker never made the offer.[26] In any event, he did not seek a federal seat.

Partly with this incident in mind, Camp told Roblin in June that if he wished to have Camp's help he must make his decision by July 10. After that date, Camp said, his offer would no longer hold. When the deadline passed without a response, Camp again talked to Stanfield. For the first time, the Nova Scotia premier indicated he would be willing to run, but within twenty-four hours, under pressure from cabinet colleagues who warned him of impending financial difficulties for the province, he changed his mind again.[27]

Camp now turned to planning his own campaign. He called a small group to his summer home in New Brunswick to make the initial preparations. Meanwhile friends of Stanfield had persuaded him that the situation in Nova Scotia was not so serious as to prevent him from running. Thus two days after refusing Camp he telephoned him to say he was about to announce his candidacy. Camp immediately abandoned his own plans and the group he had assembled was dispatched to Halifax to work for Stanfield.

Two weeks later Duff Roblin announced that he, too, would become a candidate.

The factional split created by the conflict over Diefenbaker's leadership posed a problem for all of the candidates. Most of them tried to build support across this cleavage. For Fulton and McCutcheon this was difficult because both had given open support to Camp's campaign in 1966. It also presented a problem for Stanfield and Roblin because of their close association with Camp.

Stanfield dealt with this problem by giving key appointments in his campaign committee, including the chairmanship, to Diefenbaker loyalists from Nova Scotia. If these appointees had reservations about Stanfield's relationship with Camp they were in no position to question it. Stanfield exercised unchallengeable authority over the provincial party and the provincial party controlled federal organization in Nova Scotia.[28] As

Coates observed, for the eight Nova Scotia members of Parliament who were loyalists "there was no choice" but to support Stanfield.[29]

Roblin's position was quite different. Because he did not have the same control over the party in his province he could not be sure, if he accepted Camp's offer of help, that any loyalists would support him. Roblin's hold on the provincial party was weaker for two reasons. First, federal constituency organization in Manitoba is relatively independent of provincial control and, second, Roblin had announced that he would resign the premiership regardless of the outcome of the convention which cast him in the role of a "lame-duck" leader. It may have been, therefore, that his only option was to try to free himself of the Camp connection. Whatever the truth of the claim that he deliberately delayed his entry for this purpose, Roblin's organizers made a point of emphasizing that he was not Camp's candidate.

Most of the candidates did their best in the campaign not to be drawn into discussion of the Diefenbaker conflict. Starr, whose strategy was to mobilize Diefenbaker's supporters, was the only exception. When Stanfield announced his candidacy, Starr attacked him as a front for Camp. The only other public reference to the subject, in the context of the campaign, was Roblin's comment to reporters in Toronto that he believed Camp "already [had] another candidate."[30]

Roblin had hoped for Diefenbaker's support but it did not come. Johnston claims this was because Diefenbaker believed Camp was behind Roblin's candidacy. Johnston pressed Diefenbaker to try to draft the mayor of Montreal, Jean Drapeau. Diefenbaker finally agreed to a meeting with Drapeau but it did not achieve the result that Johnson had hoped. "What went on that morning . . . remains for others to tell, but the Chief was convinced that the combination now could not be worked."[31]

When the convention began, Diefenbaker still had not announced a decision. The other candidates called on him in his hotel suite and he told them nothing. Not even his most intimate friends knew what he intended.

In his address to the opening meeting of the convention, Diefenbaker still left the question unanswered. But the speech was a challenge to the party. Its major thrust was an impassioned attack on the "deux nations" theory of Canadian federalism. This theory holds that Confederation rests on a union between "two founding peoples"; that Quebec, because of its unique cultural and linguistic character, is the representative of one of these two founding groups; and therefore that the provincial government of Quebec is entitled to certain distinctive constitutional powers or "special status." In preparation for policy discussions at the convention, the convention committee had arranged for a conference of academics, experts from business, and party intellectuals to discuss policy papers which would be brought before the convention's resolutions committee. This conference at Montmorency, Quebec, in August, had endorsed the "deux nations" principle and the resolutions committee of the convention had proposed that the convention also endorse it.

Diefenbaker's conflict with Léon Balcer in 1965 had touched on the same issue. Diefenbaker had also been critical of the Liberal government's measures to create more flexible arrangements with the provincial governments in areas of joint or contested federal-provincial jurisdiction.[32] Although the pressures for these changes had come from other provinces as well, Diefenbaker focused his criticism on the implication of special concessions for Quebec. In his speech he developed this theme:

> You may not agree with me, but the theory that Canada is two nations can only lead to division and dissension and finally to de-confederation. If you bring it into effect, what about the six million Canadians of racial origin other than the parent races? Are they to have second-class citizenship? I shall never agree with that. Are we to have degrees of citizenship? Through the years (and it is fifty years since I first spoke on this subject), I had just come out of the armed forces and was proud of the Canada badge on my shoulder strap—I asked, 'Let us be Canadians.' That has been the course I have followed throughout the years. Are we to have degrees of citizenship? Are we to have one or two degrees of citizenship in the two Canadas? . . . from the earliest day when it was unpopular I raised the standard of equality in this country. Let us be Canadians. Let us not deny equality to those whose surnames are not of the parent races. I don't believe that the true heart of French Canada wants the two nation idea. . . . I must tell you, in all frankness and without equivocation, I cannot accept the two nation policy. I implore you. You make the decision for me when you decide on that policy because I cannot and shall not accept it. I am not going to go back 100 years and more to borrow a policy that has proven to be wrong, to get votes in 1967. The sub-committee and committee on policy has accepted the two nations principle. I hope that the convention will repudiate it before we leave here. I cannot be interested in the question of leadership in this party under a policy that is borrowed Liberalism.[33]

The next morning, minutes before the deadline for the filing of nominations, Diefenbaker announced his candidacy.

Ostensibly he intervened to prevent the party from adopting the "deux nations" policy, but it is hard to believe this was the real reason, since, on the morning of the balloting, Churchill, acting for Diefenbaker, secured an agreement from Goodman to have the resolutions committee report tabled without bringing it to a vote. As Diefenbaker himself argued, this decision effectively cast the offensive "deux nations" resolution into limbo, at least insofar as the convention was concerned. Thus, once again as he argued himself, he had achieved his purpose. Yet, when he was asked whether he would now withdraw his candidacy he explained that, to the contrary, since the party had freed itself of the deux nations policy, he was free to run.

The explanation for Diefenbaker's candidacy seems to lie in his obsession with Camp. Senator David Walker, one of his close friends in Ottawa, says Diefenbaker had retained the air of mystery about his plans through the spring and summer because he wanted to be free to run against Camp if Camp were to become a candidate.[34] Camp did not become a candidate, but his presence was still an important factor at the convention and this presence, Johnston argues, was a persistent aggravation to Diefenbaker:

> He came to Toronto, still looking for an honourable way out but wherever he turned he was thwarted. There was no gesture, nothing that would let John Diefenbaker step out with dignity. It seemed that the party establishment was in the hands of those who were deliberately trying to humiliate him. A few moves by the party executive to give the leader the respect he deserved, a few attempts to cooperate with him, and a great number of shattering incidents would never have taken place. Camp, despite what he had done, would not stay out of sight. If he could not be king, he would settle for king-maker. While Goodman had pushed him as far into the background as he could during the pre-convention months, Camp was now appearing, and his people were openly and blatantly taking over the Stanfield organization.[35]

If this was Diefenbaker's perception of the situation he may have concluded that he could only defeat Camp and restore his own prestige by becoming a candidate, demonstrating his continued popularity, and, perhaps, by himself becoming the king-maker. Both Walker and Churchill warned Diefenbaker "he would be massacred"[36] if he were to run, but Johnston told him he could expect to have the support of 600 of the 2,250 delegates, enough to give him the lead on the first ballot. It would also be enough if his delegates would follow his direction to give him a good chance of dictating the choice of his successor.

Although Johnston's estimate was to prove to be excessively optimistic, it was not unreasonable for him to assume that Diefenbaker might do well because, when the convention met, no candidate appeared to have established a clear lead and there were still many delegates who evidently had not decided for whom to vote. It was a situation in which the drama of the opportunity presented by Diefenbaker's speech might well be effective in mobilizing the convention.

The effect of Diefenbaker's speech was enhanced by the fact that it was delivered in the context of a campaign which had been notably free of issue conflict. On most of the issues there appeared to be widespread agreement among the candidates.[37] All except Stanfield opposed the introduction of a capital gains tax; they all agreed that there should be no restrictions on American investment in Canada; they all endorsed Canada's existing defence and foreign policy commitments to NATO and the North American Air Defence agreement; they all proposed more substantial government expenditures on education and urban problems; they all agreed in principle to the need for some form of constitutional reform to accommodate changes in the social and economic responsibilities of the federal and provincial governments.

There were differences over two aspects of welfare policy; the level of expenditure and the maintenance of the principle of universality. Fleming and Hees called for government fiscal restraint, Fleming explicitly and Hees implicitly rejecting further increases in welfare expenditures. Hees at the same time joined Fulton and Roblin in attacking the principle of universality, urging reform of social security programs to relate benefits to need. In contrast, Stanfield urged support for universal programs and, in the one notable exception to a common practice of avoiding open conflict with other candidates, made it a point at a press conference to express his disagreement with Roblin's call for a selective medical-care plan.

The main differences among the candidates lay in their choices of approach and emphasis. Most of the candidates used their public statements to try to demonstrate personal qualities: their competence to govern, their leadership style, or their vote-winning ability. The exceptions were McCutcheon and Hamilton, both of whom ran campaigns which emphasized their ideas. McCutcheon appealed in ideological language for a commitment to the principles of traditional economic liberalism, arguing that the party could achieve electoral advantage by establishing itself to the right of the Liberal party. Hamilton, in contrast, proposed a plan for national economic development in which government would have an activist role. Comparisons of their positions over the spectrum of issues discussed in the campaign suggest that the differences between McCutcheon and Hamilton were more related to points of emphasis than to fundamentals, but they presented themselves and were perceived as ideological alternatives.[38] The other candidates sought positions between these polar stereotypes.

The public response to Diefenbaker's televised address was exactly what he must have hoped. Telegrams poured in, including one from the Social Credit premier of Alberta, declaring enthusiastic support for his attack on the "deux nations" theory. Diefenbaker had captured the attention of the country and delegates in a way which no other candidate had been able to do. All of the other candidates appeared to be in a position in which they would have to respond to Diefenbaker's initiative.

For Roblin it posed a special problem because a key element in his strategy for winning the convention was his ability to appeal to Quebec. Before deciding to run he had courted and won the support of Daniel Johnson, the Union Nationale premier of Quebec,[39] and Johnson was a leading advocate of the "deux nations" theory. Roblin was faced with the choice of weakening his appeal in Quebec or risking a public denunciation by Diefenbaker which could seriously hurt him in his effort to attract regional support in the West.

In their main addresses to the convention on the night following Diefenbaker's speech, Hamilton and Starr joined Diefenbaker in rejecting the theory that Canada was comprised of "two nations." Roblin tried to deal with the problem by focusing on the distinction in meaning between the English "two nations" and the French "deux nations."

> We must not let words divide us. We must make their meaning clear so they become a source of strength. When we hear the words "two nations," let Canadians of both languages mean the same thing. In the political sense and in the constitutional sense we are one nation. It cannot be otherwise, if we are true to the Fathers of Confederation, if Canada is to stand and if our independence is to survive. All Canadians agree on this. But there is another more limited sense in which the words "two nations" can help us to understand Canada better. In the cultural and sociological sense there are two nations based on the simple fact that we have two great language groups in this country—French and English. This does not divide Canada. This does not mean separatism, this does not mean associate states, this does not mean the perversion or subversion of our constitution.[40]

Roblin was alone in responding directly and at length to Diefenbaker's challenge. McCutcheon said bluntly, if enigmatically, that he was "not afraid to say 'deux nations'," while Fleming, Fulton, Hees, and Stanfield, avoiding the semantic issue, reaffirmed their support for measures which would help make French Canadians feel more secure in Confederation.[41]

The "deux nations" issue had served its purpose for Diefenbaker. As one of his closest associates put it in an interview, "I didn't put much in that. It was just a means for him to rally his supporters."[42] Evidently it wasn't a critical matter for his adversaries either. Roblin alone had felt compelled to defend his position but even he did not resist the proposal that the "deux nations" resolution be tabled. To most of the participants, the tabling of the resolution was a minor concession to appease Diefenbaker.

The handling of this issue illustrates an important general point. The conflict was not a policy-centred conflict. There are two other pieces of evidence which relate to this point.

First, most of the candidates took an instrumental approach to policy in their appeals for delegate support. Policy references were usually designed to fit the thematic emphasis on personal qualities which, as I have already mentioned, was a common strategy. The extreme case was the Hees campaign. Hees published detailed statements about policy in a

Table 3 **Reasons given by leading participants for voting choices on the first ballot**

	Number of participants who mentioned reason
Friendship for candidate	25
Friendship for person working for candidate	7
Attractive personality of candidate	3
(Total who mentioned at least one "affective" reason)[a]	(34)[c]
Unspecified personal characteristics	6
"Patronage"[b]	12
Policy	6
Party unity	4

(a) Affective reasons included an affective response to the personality of the candidate (or an intermediary), perceived either negatively or positively, leadership style, friendship, and a sense of personal loyalty (as distinct from obligation based on a past or anticipated favour).

(b) Reasons which are categorized as patronage reasons included a sense of obligation to the candidate (or an intermediary) for some past favour and a desire for some personal advantage.

(c) This is the number who gave one of the first three reasons. The total (34) is less than the sum of the three "affective" reasons because some of the participants gave more than one response.

series of papers proposing specific solutions to a broad range of social and economic problems. But he made little use of these papers in his speeches and had difficulty explaining them in his press conferences. The papers had in fact been drafted under the direction of his campaign chairman for the wholly instrumental purpose of combating a common view of Hees as a man who lacked the intellectual depth or the command of issues needed in a prime minister.[43]

Second, in interviews, few of the leading participants gave policy reasons for their choice of candidates. As table 3 shows, by far the most important factor in the recruitment of people to key roles in candidate organizations was personal friendship. Of the forty-nine members of candidate organizations interviewed, thirty-two mentioned friendship—either for the candidate or for another person working for the candidate—as a reason for their involvement. Twenty-one of these people gave this as the only reason. Another thirteen gave patronage as a motive and, of these, eight mentioned no other inducement. Altogether, there were only six references to policy as a contributing factor, and all six of the people who mentioned it also named other reasons.

THE SEARCH FOR SECONDARY SUPPORT

It took the convention five ballots to choose Robert Stanfield as the new Conservative leader. On the first ballot Diefenbaker's hold on the leadership was finally broken. He placed fifth with the support of just 12 percent of the delegates. Stanfield led with 519 votes. Roblin had 349, Fulton 343, Hees 295, Diefenbaker 271, McCutcheon 137, Hamilton 136, Fleming 128, and Starr forty-five. Two token candidates, John McLean and Mary Sawka, accounted for the other twelve votes.[44]

Most of the candidates had anticipated that it would require several ballots to make a final choice and most of them assumed that the opinions of key figures in the party might influence the voting choices of other delegates. For this reason they attached considerable importance to their ability to win support from other candidates and the workers of other candidates as the balloting progressed. In the remaining section of this chapter, I shall examine the interactions among leading participants involved in this process of seeking secondary support.

The progress of the balloting is shown in table 4. The nomination of McLean and Mrs. Sawka had ensured that none of the other candidates would be eliminated on the first ballot. As a result, it was not until after the second ballot that the search for secondary support seriously began. On the second ballot both Stanfield and Roblin made gains, while Fulton remained in virtually the same position and the other candidates all suffered losses. After the second ballot, most of the participants believed the final choice would lie between Stanfield and Roblin.

At the end of the second ballot, under a rule which forced out the person standing last on each ballot, Starr was eliminated and McCutcheon decided to withdraw. Starr was not approached by other candidates for support and he made no effort to indicate an alternative preference.[45] McCutcheon announced that he would support Stanfield. McCutcheon "knew [Stanfield] extremely well and regarded him as being entirely capable and a conservative."[46] But his choice had not been finally determined until the last day of the convention. He had been angry with Stanfield because, before deciding to run himself, he had tried to persuade Stanfield to do so and he felt Stanfield had acted in bad faith and hurt his candidacy by subsequently entering.[47] To repair the damage, McCutcheon's son-in-law had arranged with a friend in the Stanfield organization to have Stanfield telephone McCutcheon.[48] When this conversation took place there was no discussion of any exchange of favours; in

Table 4 **Distribution of votes for each candidate for each ballot**

	Ballot One	Ballot Two	Ballot Three	Ballot Four	Ballot Five
Stanfield	519	613	717	865	1,150
Roblin	349	430	541	771	969
Fulton	343	346	361	357	—
Hees	295	299	277	—	—
Diefenbaker	271	172	114	—	—
McCutcheon	137	76	—	—	—
Hamilton	136	127	106	167	—
Fleming	126	115	76	—	—
Starr	45	34	—	—	—
Others	12	—	—	—	—
Total votes cast[a]	2,233	2,212	2,192	2,060	2,119

(a) The total number of votes cast was different for each ballot. One possible explanation is that some delegates lost interest once the candidate of their first choice was eliminated. Another is that the procedure of voting by machine, with which the delegates were not familiar, produced mistakes in the recording of the votes. A third is that many delegates were overcome by fatigue because the balloting occurred over several hours under uncomfortable conditions.

fact, there was no reference of any kind to what might happen during the balloting. The call was a symbolic act by Stanfield intended to restore McCutcheon's goodwill by indicating Stanfield's regard for him.

Roblin used a more explicit bargaining approach. Even before the balloting began, he had authorized his organization to send emissaries to Hamilton, Hees, Fulton, McCutcheon, and Churchill (who had switched from Fleming to Diefenbaker).[49] These contacts had done Roblin some harm because they were made on the assumption that the other candidates would have to choose between him and Stanfield. The reaction it elicited is suggested by Fulton's reported response: "Will he support me?"[50]

Both the style of Roblin's approach and his personality had an influence on the decision by Hees to support Stanfield when Hees decided to withdraw at the end of the third ballot.

Key advisers to Hees urged him to support Stanfield. One, E. A. Goodman, the convention chairman, who was a close personal friend, had not had a high opinion of Roblin since Roblin's refusal to accept Diefenbaker's invitation to run for Parliament in 1965. When Goodman had discussed the invitation with Roblin, "Roblin behaved badly. He said he wasn't going to sit as a backbencher."[51] Roblin's attitude created an impression which was ultimately to convince Goodman that Roblin "had too many of the qualities of Diefenbaker" to be entrusted with the leadership.[52]

Lionel Schipper, delegate chairman in the Hees organization, believed Stanfield was the more able of the two men, but he was also influenced by his distaste for the Roblin organization. He had been told by Gene Rheaume, the convention secretary, that the Roblin people "had been obnoxious in dealing with the headquarters staff" and he had heard a Roblin organizer for Ontario making "the most untruthful statements about Hees. I felt I couldn't have any confidence in Roblin if these were the kind of people he picked to work for him."[53]

According to his campaign manager,[54] Hees himself disliked Roblin. This is a view which is supported by Goodman's account of how the decision was finally made: "I said to him: 'Who do you want to serve under?' Hees said: 'No contest—Bob!' "[55]

The third ballot had also ended the candidacies of Fleming and Diefenbaker. Fleming was forced out and Diefenbaker decided to withdraw.

Fleming had been deeply shocked by the result of the first ballot. R. A. Bell, the co-manager of his campaign, had advised him to withdraw immediately but he persisted, apparently in the hope that the votes he had lost to Diefenbaker might yet return. There was no consensus among members of the Fleming organization on any alternative.[56] Bell was approached by Fulton workers and pledged them his personal support, but some other members of the group favoured Stanfield and some favoured Roblin. Despite his own commitment, Bell advised Fleming to make no commitment.[57]

Senator Walker said that Diefenbaker too was shocked by the outcome of the first ballot.[58] This may account for his failure to withdraw immediately. The delay destroyed what little hope he may have retained that he could control the choice of his successor, since he was left with the support of less than 5 percent of the delegates. Churchill tried to persuade him to direct his remaining support to Roblin, but Diefenbaker refused. Johnston claims that, despite his personal silence, Diefenbaker actually gave his organization an unspoken direction to work for Roblin:

> "I will not name anyone," said Diefenbaker "You can work for whomever you please."
> "All right then, you are going to know who we're working for," I said and turned to Gordon Churchill and asked how his vote would go.
> "Roblin," he replied.
> And around the room it went, one after another, "Roblin," . . . I told Diefenbaker that . . . we would try to get Roblin elected, and that we took his knowledge of the situation as a sort of tacit approval."[59]

This was not an obvious choice since Roblin had been the only candidate who had advocated anything approximating a "deux nations" policy. In effect, Diefenbaker's "tacit approval" of Roblin was an endorsement of the only candidate who had directly challenged the views on which Diefenbaker had based his candidacy. This casts further doubt on the credibility of the argument that Diefenbaker's candidacy was based on his concern about the "deux nations" issue. There is nothing in Johnston's account of this meeting to explain the common preference for Roblin, but it seems reasonable to suggest that it was the fact that Roblin had managed to maintain some distance from Camp. There is some corroborative evidence for this explanation in interviews with other figures close to Diefenbaker.[60] Another factor mentioned by Churchill was the feeling that Roblin was owed support as a regional candidate.

At the end of the fourth ballot, Hamilton was eliminated and Fulton withdrew. Fulton decided to support Stanfield, but Hamilton made no commitment.

Fulton said he had personal reasons for supporting Stanfield, but he did not explain them. Among members of his organization, however, there was widespread anti-Roblin feeling. One reason was Roblin's comment at a press conference that he had felt free to become a candidate only after Stanfield entered because Stanfield had "made the race respectable. That turned people off. Then they tried to raid [our organization]. Everything seemed to be on an even keel until Roblin came in.

Then it became more personal. Perhaps it was a coincidence, but that is how it happened."[61]

In addition, there were close personal ties between some members of the Fulton organization and members of the Stanfield organization. These included associations which had been formed in the leadership review campaign in 1966 and friendships with deeper roots. Fulton's campaign manager, Lowell Murray, for example, had worked closely with Camp in the leadership review campaign and had worked for Stanfield in Nova Scotia.

Sterling Lyon, a Manitoba cabinet minister, argued vigorously with Murray that Roblin would win Quebec. Murray told him "I'm from Nova Scotia," and Lyon replied "sentiment doesn't win elections."[62] Fulton's own attitude is illustrated by his refusal to have a meeting with Roblin. As he was about to leave the room where he made his decision, Brian Mulroney, one of Fulton's Quebec organizers, conveying a message from Lyon, told him "Duff says you can have anything you want," but Fulton said it was too late.[63]

The Roblin organization used the same approach with Hamilton. Ralph Hedlin was sent to offer him his choice of positions in a Roblin cabinet,[64] but Hamilton wasn't interested: "I wanted no deals with anyone. There was nothing I wanted and there was nothing I was prepared to give."[65]

His decision came as a shock to the Roblin organization,[66] for Hamilton was both a westerner and a Diefenbaker loyalist. But Hamilton was convinced that the convention had to avoid the appearance of polarization on the issue of loyalty to Diefenbaker and he did not want to offend the large number of his workers who, he believed, favoured Stanfield.[67]

Moreover, Hamilton had reason to resent Roblin's presumption. In 1964 it was Hamilton who had launched the movement to make Roblin Diefenbaker's successor. In the spring of 1965, with Roblin's encouragement, he and Churchill had persuaded sixty leading members of caucus to sign a letter urging Roblin to run for Parliament but then Roblin had refused to run. In summing up his reaction to Roblin's behaviour, Hamilton said: "We could have won the election in '65 with Duff. My popularity and usefulness in caucus were literally ended [because of Roblin's decision]."[68]

Twelve months later Hamilton had another meeting with Roblin to discuss the situation and to tell him of his own plans to run if there were no alternatives to Fulton and Hees. At a subsequent meeting Hamilton asked Roblin if he would accept an appointment in a Hamilton cabinet. Roblin declined, giving him no reasons. Roy Faibish observed that "[those] meetings had a great bearing on Hamilton's decision not to support [Roblin] on the last ballot. . . . As much as Hamilton thought that

Roblin was the better man, he felt that after the way Roblin had conducted himself he just couldn't vote for him."[69]

It was widely believed that Roblin's failure to win endorsement from other candidates cost him the convention. This view can be challenged, as will be shown later,[70] but the fact remains that among the leading participants, Roblin did fail to win the secondary support he believed he needed.

Information already adduced from interviews suggests that one reason for this failure was his insensitivity to the importance of the affective dimension of relations among the leading participants. A summary of data from interviews with key members of the Diefenbaker, Fleming, Fulton, Hamilton, Hees, McCutcheon, and Starr organizations emphasizes the significance of affective relations in their choices. Among the thirty-two who gave reasons for their final choices, twenty-seven mentioned affective reasons, only two mentioned considerations of power and patronage, and only two mentioned policy[71] (see table 5). But in their approaches to other organizations, the Roblin strategists had emphasized patronage considerations—often at the cost of offending those whose support they sought. In the words of McCutcheon's son-in-law, they "were trying to twist arms . . . and they weren't very tactful."[72]

In contrast, contact between Stanfield workers and those of other organizations was always of a low-key nature. Stanfield workers had been instructed to open lines of communications, but never to try to pressure other workers or delegates. The Stanfield organization sought no prior commitments and it offered no bargains. It operated on the assumption that natural alliances would form on the basis of past associations and that in the end these alliances would add up to the bigger total. The one concern was to avoid any action or word which might obstruct this natural movement towards Stanfield.[73]

It is a measure of the success of the Stanfield strategy that personal comments about him were free of the ambivalence which seemed to characterize attitudes toward Roblin. Where Stanfield suffered was through his association with Camp. The concomitant of personal loyalty to Diefenbaker was hostility toward Camp, and Roblin gained secondary support among leading participants on the strength of this feeling.

It is particularly interesting that of the thirty-two leading participants who explained their second choices, only two gave reasons of policy. Sterling Lyon, the attorney general of Manitoba, made the general observation that "doctrine and ideology [were] totally unimportant in this whole struggle."[74] This comment would appear to require qualification in only one respect. Policy stances had the negative effect of denying credibility to certain candidacies. Thus, McCutcheon and Fleming were

Table 5 **Reasons given for second choices by leading participants who had to change**

	Number of participants who mentioned reason
Appealing personal characteristics	4
Friendship for candidate	1
Friendship for person working for candidate	8
Dislike of other candidate or person working for other candidate	8
(Total who mentioned at least one "affective" reason)[a]	(21)[c]
Policy	2
"Patronage"[b]	1
Regional loyalty	1
Would not say	1
Unspecified personal characteristics	8

(a) Affective reasons included an affective response to the personality of the candidate (or an intermediary) perceived either negatively or positively, leadership style, friendship, and a sense of personal loyalty (as distinct from obligation based on a past or anticipated favour).

(b) Reasons which are categorized as patronage reasons including a sense of obligation to the candidate (or an intermediary) for some past favour and a desire for some personal advantage.

(c) The total giving "affective" reasons is the sum of the first four reasons.

frequently described as "too right wing" and Hamilton as "too radical."

Within these limits, even when they experienced conflicts between their policy preferences and other considerations, leading participants made their choices for non-policy reasons. Churchill, for example, said he ultimately supported Roblin despite a profound disagreement with him on the "deux nations" issue.[75] In fact, as Johnston points out, most of the Diefenbaker group turned to Roblin after Diefenbaker was eliminated. And on the other side, McCutcheon, the free enterprise ideologue, endorsed Stanfield, the only candidate who advocated a capital gains tax.

These comments suggest one of the more important general points to be drawn from the discussion in this chapter. The conflict over the leadership in 1967 was not policy-centred. The evidence on this point is quite compelling.

1. When members of Parliament wanted to reduce tension within the caucus they sought to engage their colleagues in a discussion of policy. This process brought members together in cooperative interaction and resulted in a set of resolutions which demonstrated that they had enough in common to reach accommodation on most dimensions of policy.

2. The existence of an underlying consensus was apparent in the approach to issues in the convention campaign. The campaign did not produce sharp clashes over policy, even when Diefenbaker introduced the "deux nations" issue. Not even the apparent "ideological" divergence between McCutcheon and Hamilton was so fundamental as to prevent them from agreeing about the basic principles and many of the specifics of policy.

3. Most of the candidates took an instrumental approach to policy in making their appeals for delegate support.

4. Very few of the leading participants said policy motives were a significant factor in their choice of candidates, either on the first ballot or, for those who had to switch, on subsequent ballots.

5. Several leading participants acted in a manner which was inconsistent with their stated policy preferences.

A second general point relates to the nature and significance of the factional split which developed within the party from the conflict over Diefenbaker's leadership. In a sense there was only one faction, the "Diefenbaker" faction. Although it was the "Diefenbaker" faction, its members were motivated less and less by their desire to keep Diefenbaker in the leadership and increasingly by their opposition to Camp. The number of them who believed Diefenbaker could continue in the leadership was relatively small; many of them, in fact, were unwilling to wait for Diefenbaker to decide whether to run and sought other candidates. Camp became the symbol for all the frustrations and anger they felt from their defeat in 1966. Their first objective was to purge him from his position of power in the party and, if they could not achieve this objective, to prevent him from extending or consolidating his power.

While there was only one faction, as such, ties among members of the anti-Diefenbaker groups did influence the movement toward Stanfield as other candidates dropped out. The friendships which had been formed or strengthened among people who had supported Camp in the leadership review campaign in 1966 drew members of other candidate organizations toward the Stanfield group.

This leads to one further point: the important role of responses at the affective level in the interactions and decisions of leading participants. Affective dispositions were the operative factor in the pattern of choices along the factional split and they were important outside the context of factionalism. Friendships were more important than any other factor in the formation of initial choices; and the personal insensitivity of Roblin and some of his workers generated feelings of dislike which worked against him when he needed secondary support.

6

Conflicts During Stanfield's Tenure

Robert Stanfield's biggest problem when he assumed the Conservative leadership in September 1967 was the persistent effect of the factional cleavage generated by the conflict over John Diefenbaker's leadership. This problem had its most serious implications for his relationship with the parliamentary caucus. Only twenty-four of the ninety-six members of caucus had supported Dalton Camp's campaign for leadership review in 1966. Among the remainder there were some who had backed Diefenbaker for other reasons, but a majority were members who had been personally committed to him. Stanfield was closely identified with Camp. Although he had succeeded in winning some support from the Diefenbaker faction in the convention, Camp had publicly endorsed him and, perhaps most important, Camp had been given widespread credit in newspaper, television, and radio accounts of the convention for putting together the organization which elected him. Stanfield himself had had no public role in the anti-Diefenbaker campaign in 1966, but he had given Camp quiet assistance at a critical moment during the 1966 annual meeting. Furthermore, in his acceptance speech at the convention he had made a point of acknowledging his association with Camp by "promising to try to get along with that fellow Camp." All of these circumstances made many members of the caucus deeply suspicious of Stanfield.

To add to these difficulties there was the fact that the caucus included five of the men Stanfield had defeated for the leadership: Diefenbaker, Fulton, Hamilton, Hees, and Starr. Not only did Stanfield have the problem of securing the loyalty of his rivals; he had also to meet the challenge of comparisons between their performance and his, comparisons which were unlikely to be to his advantage since he did not hold a seat in Parliament and had had no previous experience there.

Diefenbaker's continued presence in the caucus obviously posed special difficulties. If Diefenbaker chose to try to prove that the party had made a mistake in dismissing him, he might seek to establish the contrast between his own strengths and Stanfield's weaknesses and he might attempt to give active leadership to a recalcitrant opposition within the caucus.

The new leader's resources consisted first in the constraints upon those who might wish to challenge him. At the most basic level the party could hardly survive another early leadership crisis. So long as they were committed to the party as such, Stanfield's potential foes could not risk any manifest effort to obstruct him. This practical consideration was buttressed by the moral constraint of Stanfield's legitimacy. At the root of the conflict over Diefenbaker's leadership was the question of his right to lead the party. In a speech at the conclusion of the convention in which he accepted Stanfield's election, Diefenbaker had recognized that legitimacy lay in the convention. While the question of when a leader might be called to account remained unsettled, it had been clearly established that it was to the party as a whole that the leader owed his office. An additional constraint on potential rebels was the dramatic rise in the party's popular support which followed the convention. In national opinion polls, the Conservatives had moved from third place in June, their worst position since 1945, to first place in October. A threat to Stanfield might jeopardize the achievement of power. Equally important, because Stanfield appeared likely to become prime minister, the sanctions and rewards inherent in that office effectively served him even though he did not yet possess them. While he had few tangible rewards to bestow in the fall of 1967, he could make appointments and symbolic awards which bore promise of tangible fulfilment.

His ability to make such appointments constituted Stanfield's second resource. Under Diefenbaker the authority to make appointments of caucus committee chairmen, that is, shadow ministerial appointments, lay nominally with the committees. In practice, this meant that the leader would communicate his wishes on these appointments and the appropriate committees would validate them. Thus, the committee chairmanships were within the leader's prerogative. In addition, he had the authority to appoint the House leaders of the Commons and the Senate, the Commons whip, the national director of the party members of the party headquarters staff, a personal staff in the office of the leader of the opposition, and members of ad hoc committees with special organizational responsibilities.

The strategies available to a leader in using this kind of resource embrace three basic options: to deprive all former rivals and their supporters of power and status; to share power and status selectively with former rivals and their supporters; or to afford a representative share of power and status to all former rivals and their supporters. The choice among these strategies is likely to be influenced by a variety of factors: the importance of preserving the image of unity; myths about the appropriate form of conduct toward losers; the inherent strength of the leader's personal political base; the leader's personal resources for expanding his base; and the leader's conception of his role.

All of these factors weighed against the choice of the first option, but three were particularly important. First, Stanfield had emerged from the convention with a qualified mandate, the ultimate choice of only 54 percent of the delegates, and the first choice of fewer than one-quarter of them. He did not have a strong independent base outside the caucus. Second, Stanfield did not have the kind of personal resources which could be used to create such a base. He was not an effective public speaker, being competent in debate only when armed with a text. In conversation, his speaking style was halting and ponderous, a characteristic which created an unfortunate impression on television. Third, Stanfield was by temperament and conviction a consensus politician. In part, this probably reflected his need to compensate for his inability to impose his authority by force of personality. But it was also a result of his analysis of the nature of politics. At the core of his thought was the pluralist conception of government as the conciliator and harmonizer of interests. He believed that the art of politics lay in the patient search for compromise.[1]

Camp urged Stanfield to choose the second option, to create a coalition which would exclude the recalcitrant Diefenbaker partisans. He argued that the party could only achieve electoral success by presenting a more credible image to urban, middle-class, and young voters and this required a complete break with the image created for it in the last years of Diefenbaker's tenure. Obviously this could only be done if Stanfield were prepared to risk trouble in the caucus. Camp's solution was for Stanfield to concentrate his activity in the country and not in Parliament. In effect, he proposed that Stanfield deal with his caucus problem by building a popular base which would produce a new, more sympathetic caucus in the next election.

Stanfield feared a new public conflict and defections from the party. These fears were fed by the hostile and suspicious mood of his first meeting with caucus. One Saskatchewan member, Jack McIntosh, put the issue directly, demanding as a condition of remaining in the party that Camp not be allowed to run the party and that the "deux nations" theory be repudiated. The general atmosphere of this meeting confirmed for Stanfield that the only course available to him was to attempt to conciliate the Diefenbaker wing.[2]

Nearly three-quarters of the new leader's first caucus appointments went to members who had signed the petition urging Diefenbaker to remain in the leadership after the annual meeting of 1966. Of the most senior appointments, only one, a new position called general chairman of caucus, went to a Diefenbaker opponent, Fulton. Starr became House leader and Reynold Rapp, who supported Diefenbaker at the convention, became chief whip. Two other general appointments in caucus were given to Waldo Monteith and Théogène Ricard, both Diefenbaker loyalists in 1966 who had been active in the Fleming campaign in 1967. Most of the committee chairmanships—that is, the shadow cabinet appointments—remained virtually as Diefenbaker had made them.

For Diefenbaker himself there was no special place apart from a prominent front-bench seat in the House, but Stanfield treated him warily. In their first conversation after the convention, Diefenbaker complained to Stanfield of the reference to Camp in his acceptance speech, apparently signalling a warning to Stanfield to move carefully.[3] Shortly afterward, Diefenbaker implied in a speech to a private dinner of the parliamentary press gallery that he planned to retire.

Among the other defeated candidates, only Roblin proved difficult to deal with. The shock of defeat had been accompanied by some bitterness in the Roblin group and Roblin was personally offended because he believed Stanfield had been slow in contacting him after the convention. In October, Stanfield flew to Manitoba for his first meeting with Roblin, a gesture which was intended to symbolize the importance he attached to Roblin's future role in the party. Roblin declined an offer to have a seat opened in Parliament but he did agree to accept the chairmanship of an important ad hoc committee on policy development.[4]

Stanfield was also careful to consult regularly with Hamilton, Hees, and McCutcheon. None of them was given any new appointment, although McCutcheon had an unofficial role as special adviser in economic matters. Fleming, who had been badly shaken by the magnitude of his defeat, withdrew from politics to accept an executive appointment with a bank.

A concomitant of Stanfield's decision to conciliate the Diefenbaker faction was a decision to limit Camp's role in the party. In a meeting shortly after the convention, Camp asked Stanfield for a mandate to rebuild the party but Stanfield insisted that Camp should not have a prominent public role, arguing first that as leader he had to prove that he was "his own man" and, second, that if Camp were to take too active a public part he might become a focus for renewed conflict.[5] Camp was personally affronted by this decision and withdrew to a position of private as well as public inactivity. Although he remained as national president, he felt himself "more and more estranged from the party . . . and the people who were loyal to [him] became very disaffected."[6]

Generally, Stanfield chose the same approach in dealing with all of his own supporters. He sought their advice but he gave them few formal positions of influence. The major appointments on his personal staff were filled by Fulton workers. Lowell Murray, Fulton's campaign manager, became Stanfield's principal assistant and Joe Clark, who had had a leading role in the Fulton constituency campaign in the West became his chief speech writer. The office of national director was also filled by a Fulton supporter, Malcolm Wickson, who had been president of the provincial association in British Columbia. There was some criticism of these appointments in caucus where Fulton had few friends, but the connection to Fulton was largely coincidental. Murray, a Nova Scotian, was already well known to Stanfield and was recommended by both Camp and Flora MacDonald. MacDonald also recommended Clark, while E. A. Goodman, whom Stanfield had appointed to the new position of national chairman of organization, recommended Wickson.

The success of Stanfield's strategy of conciliation rested on his ability to establish a unifying focus for the potentially fractious groups which the coalition embraced. At first Stanfield was able to provide that focus himself, but his personal credibility in caucus soon eroded.

One reason was his performance in the House of Commons (which he entered in a by-election in October). Stanfield did not possess the kind of personality which would permit him to influence the House simply by the force of his presence, as Diefenbaker had been able to do. At the same time, his lack of experience in the federal Parliament led him into tactical errors which cost him the confidence of some of his colleagues.[7]

A second reason was his parliamentary strategy, which was too conciliatory for MPs attuned to Diefenbaker's aggressive concept of the role of the opposition. In February 1968, Gordon Churchill—the House leader during the last years of Diefenbaker's tenure—resigned from the Conservative caucus because he could not accept Stanfield's "capitulation" to the government in a heated debate over what constituted a vote of non-confidence by the House.[8] Churchill's resignation expressed the feelings of many other Conservative MPs.[9]

A third reason was Stanfield's failure to have any personal impact on the country. By early 1968, it had become apparent—particularly from the reaction of journalists—that the personal characteristics Stanfield displayed in his public appearances were not those popularly sought in a political leader at that time.

A fourth reason was that in April 1968 the Liberal party chose a new leader, Pierre Elliott Trudeau, whose personality and political style evoked a far more enthusiastic popular response. With Trudeau's emergence, as one of Stanfield's assistants remarked, those Conservatives who thought the party could win in the next election were "whistling past the graveyard."[10] Thus, the buttress of anticipated victory, which was an important support for Stanfield's leadership, was removed.

Trudeau wasted no time in calling an election, acting just a few days after his new cabinet was sworn in. The result of the election both reflected and contributed to the weakness of Stanfield's position in his party.

One problem for Stanfield in the 1968 election was that party organization had fallen into disarray as a result of the neglect and conflict of the previous five years. A complete rebuilding job was necessary to get the party ready for a general election campaign, but when the election was called, this process had only just begun. Another problem was that Trudeau made Quebec's position in Confederation a central issue in the campaign. Trudeau was a French Canadian who rejected the concept of special status for Quebec, favouring instead a centralized form of federal system in which French Canadians would take a fuller part. Stanfield was more willing to make changes to accord greater powers to the provinces. Although he had not directly committed himself to special status, he had given the leadership of the Quebec wing of the party to Marcel Faribault, one of its most outspoken advocates. This was the issue Diefenbaker had raised at the convention in September and Trudeau raised it in the election. In choosing this approach Trudeau was able to exploit the divisions within the Conservative party, divisions which were quickly made apparent in an open controversy over Faribault's views and whether Stanfield shared them. Outside Quebec Stanfield suffered because of his identification with Faribault, while inside Quebec Faribault proved no match for Trudeau.

The election produced a Conservative defeat far more serious in its implications than the net loss of twenty-five seats might suggest. In Quebec the party was reduced from eight seats to four, in Ontario from twenty-five to seventeen, and in British Columbia from three to none. Thus, in the three most populous provinces the Conservative party held only twenty-one out of 185 seats. Among the defeated Conservatives were Fulton, Hamilton, McCutcheon, Roblin, Starr, Camp, and Faribault.

Stanfield was left with a severely weakened front bench, many of his potential allies defeated, and a caucus even less representative of the urban and industrialized parts of the country than the one he had inherited from Diefenbaker. At the same time, his personal standing in the party had suffered a serious blow.

In this situation, some members of the Diefenbaker faction began to adopt a more aggressive stance in party affairs. The first open signs of their continuing discontent appeared at the party's annual meeting in March 1969. One indication was their decision to run their own candidate for the party presidency, Dr. Lewis Brand, a defeated Saskatchewan MP. There was no "Camp" candidate to oppose Brand. Camp himself had resigned the presidency several months before, while the group he had organized to fight the leadership review campaign in 1966 had long since ceased to act cohesively. Some members of this old anti-Diefenbaker coalition supported the candidacy of Frank Moores, a Newfoundland MP who had not been active in the party before 1968. Others supported Heward Grafftey, another defeated MP who had been one of the caucus opponents of Diefenbaker's leadership. Moores was the stronger of these two candidates both because he could claim to have been a neutral in the old conflict and because he had the backing of key figures in the Ontario provincial party. Brand sought to mobilize Diefenbaker's constituency in the party by attacking Moores as a "man . . . controlled by the Ontario wing of the party,"[11] but it was to no avail. Moores carried 652 votes, Grafftey 187, and Brand 112.

The Diefenbaker loyalists, however, did win a significant symbolic victory at the annual meeting when they succeeded in amending a leadership review clause in a new draft constitution. The clause, providing that a secret ballot on the desirability of a leadership convention be held at every biennial meeting of the association, was intended to prevent a recurrence of the institutional difficulties which had arisen in the conflict over Diefenbaker's leadership. The draft constitution had been prepared by a committee whose members had all been part of the anti-Diefenbaker campaign in 1966 and Stanfield had given it his private backing. The attack on the controversial clause was led by Jack Horner, the member of Parliament from Crowfoot, Alberta, who had been among Diefenbaker's most outspoken caucus supporters. After a heated debate the meeting adopted an amendment moved by Horner that severely restricted the terms of the clause, rendering it virtually useless. This result was widely attributed to the support given the amendment by one of Stanfield's closest allies, G. I. Smith, his successor as premier of Nova Scotia. One explanation for Smith's intervention was that Stanfield had not made his private views clear to him. Camp took a different view, commenting in a newspaper column that Stanfield to "placate the Western-Diefenbaker wing of the party had felt obliged to rally his own Maritime strength to support them."[12]

A more direct challenge to Stanfield came in June 1969, when a large bloc of western MPs, one from the maritimes and a few from rural Ontario, opposed the Official Languages Act, a government measure to strengthen French-Canadian language rights. Stanfield wanted the caucus to support the government legislation on the grounds that it was essential to the maintenance of French-Canadian confidence in Confederation. When the vote was taken, seventeen of the sixty-five Conservative members present in the House voted against the bill. Among them was John Diefenbaker who was accused in the press of leading the revolt. Caucus sources say that the leadership came from other members, notably

Horner. But Diefenbaker had certainly given encouragement to the rebels.

While this open defiance of his leadership could be considered a serious blow to Stanfield's prestige, in one way it led to a strengthening of his authority in the caucus. It had been the rebels who had asked that the vote in the House be recorded on division, a point which Stanfield emphasized in a subsequent speech to caucus. To seek a formal vote, he said, was not essential if they had only wished to take a position on a matter of principle. And the effect of their demand for a division had been to draw more attention to the split within the caucus and make the task of building party unity that much more difficult. He was, therefore, able to shift responsibility onto the rebels for the criticism of the party which resulted from the vote and to place them in the implied position of violating the very principle that they had accused Camp of violating, the principle of loyalty to the leader.

Despite the harassment of his leadership, Stanfield continued to pursue a strategy of reconciliation in his distribution of caucus appointments. Signers of the 1966 petition of support for Diefenbaker continued to hold a majority of the principal appointments in revisions made following the 1968 election, although their proportional strength declined. The major changes were the appointment of Gerald Baldwin, an Alberta MP who had supported Stanfield for the leadership, as House leader and T. M. Bell, a Fulton supporter from New Brunswick, as chief whip. Both men had advocated leadership review in 1966 and had refused to sign the petition of support for Diefenbaker. Review advocates were also given more senior committee chairmanships: External Affairs, Justice, Finance, and Trade and Commerce. The situation did not change significantly when further revisions were made in the fall of 1969. There was no manifest effort to punish the rebels, with one exception. Robert Coates, a Nova Scotia MP who had published a book attacking the influence accorded Camp and criticizing Stanfield's leadership—by implication and by comparison with Diefenbaker—was dropped from the revised list.

Even if Stanfield had wanted to give a larger number of prominent positions to members who had supported him or to those who had supported leadership review, it would have been difficult because there were relatively so few of them. Altogether they comprised little more than one-fifth of the total membership of the caucus. In addition, Stanfield in making his appointments had to bear in mind such factors as the maintenance of a proper regional balance and the need to have experienced members in sensitive roles.[13] His overriding concern, regardless of the attacks on him personally, remained the reestablishment of party unity and the strengthening of the party's electoral credibility.

To facilitate the achievement of these purposes Stanfield launched an extended process of policy revision, embracing all levels and elements of the party. This process was intended to serve the party's electoral interests by creating a policy with greater appeal, by attracting favourable attention from journalists, and by recruiting new members to activist roles, particularly from the academic, professional, and corporate communities. It was to serve the end of unifying the party by finding a consensus through which all groups in the party might recognize their shared interests.

As a first step, in 1968 Stanfield created a Policy Advisory Committee under the chairmanship of T. H. B. Symons, the president of Trent University. In 1969 Symons was given the task of organizing a national policy conference, embracing members of the caucus, representatives of all elements in the extra-parliamentary party, and resource people recruited mostly from the universities.

Some members of caucus were critical of the conference, arguing that it would intrude upon the caucus role in policy-making. There were complaints that the parliamentary party would constitute less than 10 percent of the delegates and that constituency associations were underrepresented. In the face of threats of a boycott, Stanfield was compelled to write each member of Parliament, urging the importance of attendance. At the same time, assurances were given that the conference was not to define policy, but to discuss it.

Diefenbaker attacked the conference from another perspective, claiming that the financial arrangements for registration would discriminate against delegates from the prairie provinces. The former leader used this issue to make another attack on Camp, whose hidden hand he alleged was directing the affairs of the party. Diefenbaker did not attend the conference.

Despite these preliminary difficulties, the conference was reasonably successful. The only sign of factional conflict was an attack by Horner on a proposal with which Stanfield had been publicly identified for the establishment of a guaranteed minimum income program to combat poverty. But debate on this issue cut across factional lines and could not be construed simply or exclusively as a challenge to Stanfield's leadership. The debate ended in a compromise which affirmed the principle of reform but accepted the need to maintain income incentives, and left the specifics to be worked out in committee. Far from having a divisive effect, therefore, it helped establish at least the appearance of an accommodation among the factions and helped to fulfil one of the objectives of the conference. In addition, the conference approved the creation of a Policy Coordinating Committee to coordinate the work of the association and the caucus in policy development. This committee was intended to provide a mechanism both for policy development as such and for the more effective resolution of policy disagreements. Its membership was carefully balanced between the caucus and the extra-parliamentary party to try to reduce institutional tensions. Stanfield himself assumed its chairmanship.

The limitations of this approach as a general technique for dealing with conflict were soon apparent. Oblique attacks on Stanfield continued in the form of criticisms of his associates and aides. Diefenbaker was among the critics, going so far on one occasion that Stanfield felt compelled to meet with him to ask that he stop.[14] Aggravating the situation were the tensions in relations between some members of caucus and Malcolm Wickson, the national director, who was accused of taking a high-handed attitude toward MPs. In addition, although he had ceased to have an active role in the party, Camp remained a source of controversy. The state of feeling among members of the Diefenbaker faction is reflected in the fact that Liam O'Brian, soon after he succeeded Wickson as national director in 1970, was criticized in caucus for having permitted the party's newsletter *Communique* to publish a review of a book by Camp.[15]

In the summer of 1970 the issue of Stanfield's leadership was raised directly when he was excluded from the list of those invited to attend a conference of delegates from the western provinces which had been convened to discuss party policy. In contrast, Diefenbaker, ostensibly as a western MP, had an active and prominent role. This symbolic message was re-enforced by widespread publicity given conference criticism of both party policy and Stanfield. Stanfield struck back with another tough speech to caucus in which he told the conference organizers that they had committed a serious breach of party discipline.

The crucial test of Stanfield's position came at a second conference of western delegates in Saskatchewan in the following year. Horner and at least a dozen other delegates met privately while the conference was in progress to discuss the leadership, but this time Stanfield had been invited to speak and had an opportunity to defend himself: "Stolid Bob Stanfield rose to the occasion. In rare form he delivered a sensitive well-written speech with a winning blend of wit and force that appeared to endear him to even his most vocal critics. While a standing ovation at a public meeting is hardly a guarantee of solidarity, even the Diefenbaker die-hards stood up and politely applauded."[16]

While the success of this speech settled the question of a direct challenge to Stanfield's leadership, the rebels continued their harassment. Just before the annual meeting in December 1971, some members of the anti-Stanfield group in caucus objected to the form of several policy resolutions drafted by the Policy Coordinating Committee (PCC) for presentation to the delegates. Their objections were met by adding a number of supplementary resolutions which they had drafted. In fact, few delegates seemed to take the resolutions very seriously because barely one-third of them bothered to complete and return their resolution ballots. Despite this low participation rate, the outcome of the balloting was satisfactory to Stanfield because, in virtually every essential, it endorsed the positions adopted in the resolutions drafted by the PCC.

More serious difficulties arose over the election of a new national president. The problem was created by the candidacy of Donald Matthews, an Ontario delegate who ran in defiance of the wishes of the provincial party organization of Premier William Davis. The Davis organization had decided to support Roy Deyell, the national treasurer, an Albertan who had backed Camp in 1966. Complicating the situation was the fact that Camp's brother-in-law, Norman Atkins, had become one of the principal figures in the Davis organization. Camp himself had close ties to Davis and many former associates of Camp had acquired leading roles in the Ontario provincial party. Thus, members of the Diefenbaker faction decided to support Matthews.

Matthews was elected on a second ballot after two other candidates failed to win sufficient support to continue. The reason appears to have been the failure of the Ontario provincial leadership to anticipate the Matthews candidacy and the failure of Stanfield's supporters to grasp its factional significance.

Whatever the explanation for the Matthews victory, as several newspaper accounts observed, it provided the Diefenbaker faction with a symbolic success. The fact that he had not been personally involved spared Stanfield any direct loss of prestige, but the episode was further evidence that the old factional cleavage was still a serious source of stress on party unity.

With the issue of Stanfield's leadership more or less suppressed, the party was able to concentrate its energies on preparations for the general election of 1972. Of paramount importance in these preparations was the commitment to Stanfield of Premier Davis. The Davis commitment was more than pro forma; the complete resources of the Ontario provincial organization were put at the disposal of the federal party. In December Malcolm Wickson,[17] who had close ties with the Davis organization and had been a key figure in the Ontario provincial campaign in 1971, was appointed by Stanfield to be director of operations for the 1972 election. Wickson recruited his organization from his associates in the Davis campaign and established his headquarters in offices adjacent to those of the provincial party in Toronto. Paid staff from the provincial party were seconded to the federal campaign and provincial fund raisers and donor lists were put at Wickson's disposal. With these resources and an extended planning period, the party was able to establish a strong campaign organization.

The Conservatives, therefore, were in a good position to take advantage of the declining popularity of the Trudeau administration. But there were problems. First, Stanfield as a political personality had failed to generate any public enthusiasm. Public opinion surveys showed that even with Trudeau's personal popularity seriously in decline, Stanfield still was less favourably perceived than the prime minister. Second, while there was criticism in the press of Liberal handling of a number of issues, uncertainty was expressed about the ability of the Conservatives to do better. Ironically, the elaborate policy-making process through which Stanfield had led the party had failed to produce a clear definition of party policy. In seeking a consensus to unify the party, Stanfield had left himself with statements couched in such general terms that they could not easily be translated into specific proposals. Third, despite Stanfield's vigorous efforts, the Conservatives had failed to establish themselves as a credible force in Quebec. One reason was the strong French-Canadian presence established by the Trudeau government in Ottawa. Another undoubtedly was the split in the Conservative caucus over the Official Languages Act.

The election ended in a virtual stalemate. The Liberals won 109 seats, the Conservatives 107, the New Democrats thirty-one, Social Credit fifteen, and Independents (including the Speaker) two.

The biggest disappointment for Stanfield was his party's failure to break the Liberal hegemony in Quebec. Conservative hopes for success there had been raised by the recruitment as Stanfield's Quebec lieutenant of Claude Wagner, a provincial judge who had been a provincial Liberal minister and runner-up at the provincial Liberal leadership convention in 1969. A survey conducted for the party had been interpreted as indicating that Wagner's personal popularity could swing a substantial number of Quebec seats. Stanfield was sufficiently impressed to authorize the establishment of a $300,000 trust fund in Wagner's interest to induce him to run.[18] But the party's interpretation of its survey had exaggerated Wagner's appeal. He was hard-pressed to win his own riding and the Conservatives elected only one other Quebec member.

Although his party had failed to win enough seats to form a government, Stanfield emerged from the election with increased prestige and a renewed opportunity. The base of the caucus had been broadened by the addition of representatives from urban centres in British Columbia and Ontario and it had been joined by several new members whose personal reputations immediately enhanced the party's image. For the first time since 1968, the party appeared to be within striking distance of office.

When Parliament met in January 1973, Conservative strategists believed it would not be long before the weakened Liberal government would be overcome in the House and forced to resign or to call a new election. This expectation rested on the assumption that the New Democratic Party, which held the voting balance in the House, would share the Conservative desire to bring an early end to the Trudeau government.

But the New Democrats were wary of precipitous action.[19] The Liberals responded to this opportunity by undertaking a series of policy shifts designed to accommodate the position of the NDP. Thus, Parliament settled down to an extended period of minority Liberal government.

For a brief time the Conservatives preserved a united front behind Stanfield's leadership, but there were signs of the underlying tensions within the party. Even before debate had begun on the Throne Speech, Diefenbaker publicly attacked Stanfield's position on language policy[20] and at the Easter recess he criticized the party's strategy in two confidence debates in the House, suggesting its comportment had damaged public confidence in Parliament.[21]

It was on the language question that the fragile unity of the caucus finally shattered. In June, in a move calculated at least in part for the very purpose of embarrassing the Conservatives,[22] the government introduced a resolution affirming commitment to the basic principles of bilingualism in the federal public service. Stanfield insisted that the Conservative party support the government resolution, but some members of the caucus, led by Horner and Diefenbaker, urged the party to oppose it.

Diefenbaker took a particularly active role. He made an impassioned speech to the caucus, attacking the resolution, those in the party who had been disloyal to him, and, implicitly, Stanfield's leadership. More than that, he personally tried to pressure a number of western members into backing him by attempting to call in debts for past campaign support or by threatening to withhold such support in future.

The issue was put clearly to caucus as a test of confidence in Stanfield's leadership, notably by Robert Coates, who had been among the members who voted against the Official Languages Act in 1969. Coates announced that he would support Stanfield precisely because the main question for the Conservative party was the question of loyalty to the leader. Another member who had voted against the Official Languages Act, Walter Dinsdale, a former Diefenbaker minister, took the same position. Stanfield himself put the case in terms of the party's credibility as a national party. Whatever the particular defects of the Official Languages policy, he argued, the vote on the resolution was a symbolic test of the party's attitude toward French Canada. These appeals evidently had some effect. Although a considerably larger number of Conservative members had indicated their dissatisfaction with elements of language policy, only sixteen (including Diefenbaker) defied the whip and voted against the resolution.

Yet the split in the party was a serious one. The depth of ill-feeling it had created was apparent shortly after the vote when a Conservative member made a personal attack on Diefenbaker on the floor of the House. This attack prompted a journalist to observe that "the Conservative party, which eight months ago came within an ace of being the government of Canada, and which has had every opportunity to establish itself as a plausible and desirable alternative to the Trudeau government, now looks more and more like a motley band of individuals with little cohesion and less sense of direction. . . . Perhaps what it needs is a leader."[23]

Over the next several months there were recurring reminders of the party's internal instability. In a vote on capital punishment in the summer, a majority of the Conservative caucus voted for retention while Stanfield voted for abolition. In one sense this should not have been an embarrassment to Stanfield since it was a division on which all parties had ostensibly removed the whip, but Stanfield was the only party leader whose position was not adopted by most of his colleagues. In the fall, when rising oil prices precipitated a national debate on energy policy, some Conservatives proposed measures which involved increasing government intervention in the oil industry, while others—mainly members with close personal or constituency ties to the industry—took the view that further government intervention should be vigorously opposed. This split in the caucus provoked the Montreal *Star* to comment that "the Conservative party becomes less and less credible."[24] The *Star's* reaction was reflected in public opinion polls. By the end of 1973, both their own polls and published polls showed the Conservatives had lost most of the support they had picked up in the 1972 election.

It was in this context that the old factional conflict was publicly resumed. The focus was the presidential election at the annual meeting of the National Association in March 1974. The incumbent president, Don Matthews, believing he had the encouragement of Stanfield,[25] decided to seek re-election. But he found himself opposed by Michael Meighen who had been a prominent member of the anti-Diefenbaker group in 1966 and had the backing of the provincial party organization of Premier Davis of Ontario in which the central figure was Norman Atkins, Dalton Camp's brother-in-law and business partner. Meighen was seen by members of the Diefenbaker faction to be running on behalf of the "Camp" wing of the party. His candidacy was particularly menacing because of the involvement of the Davis organization.

There were close ties between the Davis organization and Malcolm Wickson whom Stanfield had appointed as chairman of campaign planning with control over the whole of the party apparatus. The scope of Wickson's power had become a source of growing concern to some members of caucus, both within and outside the Diefenbaker faction. Stanfield had approved terms of reference for Wickson—which Wickson had drafted—providing the chairman of campaign planning unprecedented power. These terms of reference interposed Wickson between the leader and every other staff and support structure in the party, including for some purposes the personal staff of the leader and the party's parliamentary research office. He was made responsible for all campaign-related functions, including the "overall election plan," the appointment of personnel, the preparation and administration of the campaign budget, the direction of "the operations aspect of . . . provincial campaign organizations," and candidate recruitment. He was also empowered to "advise and be advised on matters that relate to Policy and Issue Development, Programming and Scheduling, and Speech Content [*sic*]" for the leader.[26] In this context, the Ontario party's intervention in the presidential election was seen by members of the Diefenbaker faction to be a further step by the rival faction to achieve complete mastery of the party.

There is no doubt that the support accorded Meighen by the Ontario party organization at least in part reflected Wickson's influence. There had been conflict between Wickson and Matthews because of Matthews' criticism of the management of the party's finances. Wickson claimed that Matthews was interfering with his efforts to build a strong campaign organization,[27] Matthews insisted that tighter financial controls were needed to prevent the party from running up a huge deficit.[28] The effect of this disagreement was aggravated by tension in the personal relationships between Matthews and members of the Wickson-Ontario group. For some of them this dated back to the 1971 annual meeting when Matthews had, in effect, stolen the presidency from them. They had not anticipated his candidacy and had not been able to mobilize effectively to elect their own candidate. His election had been a blow to their prestige for which they had not forgiven him. This had created a disposition of group hostility toward Matthews which had been re-enforced by subsequent disagreements.

With a big bloc of caucus support—extending well beyond the Diefenbaker faction—Matthews ran a strong campaign. Many MPs were unaware of the factional implications of the conflict and simply took the view that Matthews, having served competently, deserved another term.[29] But Matthews' support in caucus was not sufficient to overcome the advantage enjoyed by Meighen as a result of the backing of the Ontario party organization. The outcome was a narrow victory for Meighen.

The campaign created new bitterness in the party. It was alleged that the Ontario party organization had used "strong-arm" tactics, that delegate appointments had been rigged, and that personnel of national headquarters, including the national director, had worked for Meighen. On national television, Horner attacked what he called Dalton Camp's attempt to take over the party. Privately he told Stanfield he might leave the party to run as an independent candidate in the next election and news of this threat reached the press. Once again the party seemed to be obsessed with the fighting out of its old internal feuds.

Six weeks later the Conservatives and New Democrats combined in Parliament to defeat the government's budget and force a new election. In the campaign the Liberal party quickly made an issue of the Conservative proposal to apply prices and incomes controls as a method to deal with inflation.[30] There were two problems with the policy. First, its details had not been worked out and when the party leader and candidates were asked by journalists to explain it they did not have the kinds of answers that were demanded. Second, some members of Parliament and some of the party's candidates were themselves opposed to the policy and let their disagreements become known. Stanfield was confronted on the issue in mid-campaign at private meetings with the party's candidates in Toronto and Montreal. Some candidates pressed him to abandon the policy—even at that late stage—and news of their dissent leaked to the press. Diefenbaker added to the confusion when he made a speech proposing price controls without income controls. The result of these episodes was to re-enforce the image of the party's internal divisiveness and to call into question the competence of Stanfield's leadership.

The divisions within the party were also emphasized by the conflict which developed over the selection of Leonard Jones, the mayor of Moncton, New Brunswick, as the party's candidate in Moncton. Jones had refused to permit the use of French in the municipal government in Moncton—although 30 percent of the city's population was French-speaking—and he had become identified as an outspoken critic of the Official Languages Act, challenging it in the Supreme Court of Canada. When Jones won the party nomination from the sitting Conservative member of Parliament, Stanfield refused to accept him as the party's candidate. This was an unprecedented move made possible only by recent amendments to the electoral laws which required national parties to certify their candidates. It created considerable controversy within the party because it constituted an abrogation of the principle of constituency autonomy. At the same time, the fact that Jones had been able to win the party's nomination in the first place served to emphasize that there were many Conservatives who did not agree with Stanfield's support for the extension of French language rights. When Jones ran as an independent, he received public encouragement and financial contributions from many Conservatives in other parts of the country.

These conflicts in the Conservative party helped the Liberal party which had built its campaign around the theme of strong leadership. The disunity among the Conservatives served to emphasize the weakness of Stanfield's leadership. In their speeches Prime Minister Trudeau and other Liberals drew attention to each new episode of conflict in the Conservative party to keep the campaign focused on the issue of leadership. Stanfield appeared as a leader unable to manage the affairs of his party.

The election resulted in a return to Liberal majority government. The Conservatives made no gains in Quebec and lost fifteen of the forty seats they held in Ontario. The Conservative caucus was left virtually as it had been when Stanfield assumed the leadership, consisting of ninety-five members drawn mainly from rural parts of the country, from the prairies, and from the Atlantic provinces.

This third successive electoral defeat was immediately seized by Stanfield's opponents as cause for raising the issue of his leadership. The number of Stanfield's personal followers in caucus had always been relatively small, being made up almost entirely of a handful of members who had led the fight against Diefenbaker in 1966. His ability to command a majority depended on the support he could muster from members who had not been involved in the conflicts of the period between 1962 and 1966. The members in this group—whose numbers grew as the elections of 1968 and 1972 brought changes in the caucus—were compliant in Stanfield's leadership but had no special commitment to him. Their support was contingent on his effectiveness. It was quickly apparent that in view of the outcome of the election, many of these members would be prepared to join in pressing for a review of his leadership. Although some of his supporters urged him to stay, Stanfield felt he could only do so at the cost of considerable internal party strife. Faced with this prospect, in August, at the first post-election caucus, Stanfield announced that he would resign before the next election.

CAUSES OF CONFLICT: AN ANALYTICAL OVERVIEW

Ultimately, it was his failure to lead the party to victory that forced Stanfield to resign. But the party's electoral defeats during his tenure could at least in part be ascribed to the conflicts that attended his leadership. The effect of these conflicts, as reflected in the commentaries of journalists, was to contribute to the popular image of Stanfield as a weak leader, to create confusion about the nature of the party's policies, to leave the impression that a Conservative government might be unstable and ineffectual, to confirm the French-Canadian suspicion that there was a considerable body of Conservative opinion insensitive to and hostile toward French Canadians and Quebec, and to create the impression in other parts of the country that the party could not deal with the threat to national unity posed by the French-Canadian concern for cultural survival.

The source of the conflict which disrupted Stanfield's leadership was the persistence of factional cleavage from the earlier conflict over Diefenbaker's leadership. Despite his efforts at reconciliation, Stanfield was condemned by some members of caucus because of his association with Dalton Camp and the people who had supported Camp's campaign for leadership review in 1966. Diefenbaker played a principal role in keeping this issue before the party. Every alleged mistake in Stanfield's conduct of party affairs was used to imply that Camp remained the hidden master of the party and few opportunities to allege mistakes seemed to escape Diefenbaker's attention. As Stanfield observed in an interview, "Despite his assertions that he remained silent, I had the impression that he rarely hesitated to speak out."[31]

Diefenbaker's feelings are perhaps more easily understood than those of the other members of caucus who continued to see the politics of the party in terms of the old conflict. Their behaviour was certainly not consistent with the motive of personal ambition. Stanfield's strategy for managing conflict was to offer opportunities for advancement to all members of caucus, regardless of their past associations or actions. Thus, members of the Diefenbaker faction were given the chance to fulfil whatever career ambitions they might have had. Yet they chose to oppose Stanfield's leadership. There appear to be three reasons.

First, they shared the bitterness of Diefenbaker's defeat because of the strength of their emotional attachment to him. For some this was not simply a matter of their disposition toward a particular man; it reflected a psychological need for the style of leadership Diefenbaker had provided. This was a style of leadership which, as Horner pointed out, Stanfield did not provide: "Stanfield is a nice man but he is not a leader of men. I can get along with the Red Tories. I like strong opinion. Stanfield never argues back. Trudeau makes decisions. He exercises power well. Everybody must know the limits. Stanfield isn't a leader. . . . The leader should be a gigantic figure."[32]

Second, the process of conflict itself had created feelings of hostility—made all the more intense because the Diefenbaker faction had lost—which reappeared and regenerated themselves with each new episode of conflict. This effect is illustrated by the case of Sean O'Sullivan who was elected to Parliament in 1972. Although he had been only fifteen in 1967, O'Sullivan had taken an active part in Diefenbaker's efforts to win re-election to the leadership. Subsequently he became one of the key figures in a faction of the Ontario student Conservative association which regarded itself as part of an anti-establishment group within the party. O'Sullivan's definition of his role in the politics of the caucus was formed by these experiences. He thought of himself as a member of a faction which had been the "losers" in a long series of struggles for control of the party.[33]

Third, they disagreed with Stanfield about the direction in which he was leading the party. The most serious blows to Stanfield's leadership were the caucus revolts against his support of the government's bilingualism policy in 1969 and 1973. Some party members believed these revolts were just one manifestation of a more general disagreement about policy; they described their discontent with Stanfield in ideological terms. For example, out of thirteen MPs interviewed in 1973 and 1974 who had

Table 6 **Positions on bilingualism in 1969 and 1973 of members of caucus who supported, opposed, or took no public position on leadership review in 1966**[a]

	Position on Leadership Review			
		Percentages of		
	All	Supported	Opposed	Had no public position
1969				
Bilingualism vote				
For	56	89	39	65
Against	23	—	36	20
Abstained	21	11	25	15
N =	(73)	(17)	(36)	(20)
1973				
Bilingualism vote				
For	72	93	41	77
Against	15	—	36	11
Abstained	13	7	23	11
N =	(107)	(15)	(22)	(70)

(a) The calculations are based on published sources, party documents (including the caucus petition of support for Diefenbaker in 1966), and interviews.

voted against the official languages policy, eleven called themselves "conservatives" and out of this number nine identified Stanfield as a "progressive," "liberal," or "red tory." It would be wrong to infer from this that ideology was a general basis of cleavage in the caucus. Altogether, out of eighty members of the caucus who were interviewed, only thirty identified themselves as ideological conservatives and out of this number only twelve had ever engaged in any act of dissent. Moreover, if the conflict had been ideologically based, one would expect it to have been expressed in more frequent breaches of party discipline over a larger number of issues. In fact, it was only in the votes on bilingualism that there was any collective effort to defy the whip in the House. In other divisions—with the exception of those on capital punishment for which the whip was not imposed—accommodations were found which could embrace both Stanfield and his critics.

The use of ideological terms to describe cleavages in the party is a subject which will be explored more fully later. In passing, we may suggest three hypotheses to account for their use in this case.

First, the "conservatives" who rebelled on official languages policy may have been those who felt most strongly about their ideological commitment as "conservatives." If this were the case, even if differences did not exist on other issues, as "true believers" they might ascribe a different ideological position to anyone with whom they disagreed on *any* issue.

Second, ideological symbols may have been used to identify positions on issues other than those related to social and economic policy. Thus some members may have defined their "conservative" ideological stance in terms of their position on the language issue itself or in terms of their position on some moral issue such as capital punishment.

Third, it may be that the rebels used ideological language to express differences which could not be articulated in policy terms. O'Sullivan suggested this kind of explanation when he commented in an interview that the conservatives in the party had an approach to politics that was "closer to the people" while the political style of the "progressives" was impersonal, and technocratic.[34]

O'Sullivan's comment identifies an important dimension of the conflict. Stanfield's political style was very different from that of Diefenbaker. Diefenbaker was a populist. He had built his career by attacking the dominant elites in the country and asserting his identity with "the average Canadian." Stanfield was unable both by temperament and by conviction to adopt this style. Indeed, his approach to politics was distinctly technocratic. He sought to manage disagreements in the party by channeling them through a process of decision-making by committees and he turned control of the party organization over to professionals in communications technology. This difference in approaches was emphasized by the institutional cleavage between the caucus and the extra-parliamentary party. There was a shift in power away from the elective wing to the new party bureaucracy, a shift which included an intrusion—or an attempt to intrude—on the caucus prerogative in the crucial area of policy-making. The tensions thus generated were aggravated by the fact that key figures in the party apparatus adopted a patronizing and arrogant attitude toward "the yahoos" and "Diefenbaker's cowboys" in the caucus.

Underlying the conflict was a social cleavage between the dominant elites in the country and party members who did not belong to these elites. Diefenbaker's leadership had given political efficacy and enhanced self-esteem to members of Parliament whose social backgrounds gave them reason to feel excluded from the centres of power and influence in the country—members from the hinterland provinces, from rural areas and smaller communities, from small business or minor professional

Table 7 **Distribution of members of caucus voting against bilingualism, by their score on a scale of social characteristics associated with membership in the Canadian establishment**

Number of establishment characteristics[a]	Percentage voting against bilingualism			
	in 1969	N	in 1973	N[b]
4	—	(3)	—	(13)
3	—	(9)	—	(10)
2	17	(24)	14	(35)
1	18	(19)	22	(23)
0	56	(18)	41	(12)

(a) Data on the social background of members were derived from the *Canadian Parliamentary Guide* and interviews.

(b) Background information was not available on four members.

backgrounds, without advanced education. Chapter 4 showed that the more of these characteristics a member of Parliament possessed, the more likely he was to have been a Diefenbaker loyalist. The same pattern was apparent in the opposition to Stanfield. For example, as table 7 indicates, the more socially remote a member of the caucus was from the dominant national elite, the more likely he was to have voted against the policy of official bilingualism.

In attempting to discover the motivational basis of the discontent of these members, it is important to observe that their rhetoric and behaviour were almost always negative. They advocated no coherent program of social or economic policy; they did not propose positive alternatives to Stanfield's course. Even their opposition to language policy lacked a clear focus. Their speeches in the debate in the House were discursive, uncoordinated, and devoid of a clear positive theme. Their position in conflicts over the national presidency was equally negative. The object was to inflict a defeat on "the Camp group." They did not so much advocate a candidacy for its own merit as seek to defeat a candidacy because of its source, evident sponsorship, or connections.

We may hypothesize on the basis of this evidence that, for many or most of the rebel members, dissident behaviour was an emotional expression of resentment at their status as outsiders. In this view, they acted from feelings of hostility toward others which reflected their frustration at their own situation. One object of their hostility was the group within the party whom they associated with the dominant social interests in the country. French Canadians were a second. This disposition toward French Canadians may be explained by the widely observed tendency of socially pressured groups to seek ascriptively defined scapegoats on which to displace their feelings of insecurity. French Canadians were the obvious target, given the history of French-Canadian conflict in Canada and the fact that they appeared to be looking for and to be receiving privileged treatment.

Not all members who had the characteristics of outsiders were rebels. Indeed, this was hardly to be expected. For one thing, people with feelings of status insecurity may respond to these feelings in different ways. One is to act negatively by seeking objects on which to displace their anger; another is to act positively by seeking to change their status. We may suppose that many party members who were outsiders had chosen political careers for this second reason. They might therefore be expected to be more responsive to the norms of party discipline. Furthermore, possession of the characteristics of an outsider do not necessarily lead to feelings of status insecurity. Social characteristics of this kind should not be viewed as the ultimate determinants of behaviour but as constraints that have certain effects depending on each individual's distinctive experiences.

CONCLUDING NOTE

In concluding this series of chapters on elite-level politics it may be useful to repeat the point made earlier that, in using the concept of motivation to explain the behaviour of individual party members, my ultimate purpose is to link motives to constraints which inhere in distinctive characteristics of the party. The discussion of these chapters suggests a number of conclusions in this regard. Before setting them out, however, we need to examine the dispositions and behaviour of party members outside the arena of day-to-day conflict to see to what extent they are similar to the dispositions and behaviour of the national elite. The inferences to be drawn from this analysis of elite-level politics will be developed in chapter 10 in the context of an overall discussion of the party's problems with internal conflict.

Part III

7

Structural Cleavages and Delegate Behaviour at the 1967 Leadership Convention

Previous chapters have discussed leadership politics in the party mainly as a process involving a relatively small national party elite. Participation by other members of the party has been considered only as part of the context in which this national elite acted. In fact, despite the development of mechanisms for mass participation, leadership politics has continued to be a process which primarily involves people at the apex of the party. But the institutionalization of leadership selection by convention and the recognition of the legitimacy of the National Association took the final choices of the party out of the hands of the small circle at the top. The role of the larger membership is intermittent, yet it is of considerable importance. Members of the elite must submit their internal conflicts to the final adjudication of the institutions of the mass membership; in effect, these institutions embrace an electorate to which the members of the elite must refer their disputes.

This chapter is the first of three that will be concerned with politics in the party at large. This, and the following chapter, will examine factors that influence the attitudes and decisions of the larger party membership by analysing the behaviour of delegates at the 1967 leadership convention. The main data source is a mail survey of delegates conducted after the convention.

It is very important to observe that the shift in focus from elite to mass behaviour requires a shift to a broader and more inferential line of argument. I have already emphasized the difficulty of attempting to apprehend motives from the study of individual statements and actions. It is a much more speculative and tentative exercise when these statements and actions are measurable only through the application of the mass research technique of sample surveys.

THE INSTITUTIONAL CONTEXT OF CONVENTION POLITICS

Delegate behaviour at American conventions is typically explained in terms of a model in which delegates are seen not as independent actors freely exercising their own judgements, but as members of subgroups bound to act together in response to directions from various factional leaders.[1] These subgroup leaders who act as brokers of blocs of votes, are usually key figures in state parties: a senator, a governor, the mayor of a big city, a state party chairman or a county party chairman. Their power resides in the relatively elaborate, professionally staffed organization which is to be found at all levels of the party—state, county, and local. It is re-enforced by convention rules which apportion delegates by state and require that votes at the convention be cast en bloc through a roll-call of state delegations. This model emphasizes the role of patronage motives in delegate behaviour.

The style of convention politics in the Progressive Conservative party has been influenced by a very different set of constraints.[2]

To deal first with convention structure, while provincial elites are strategically well placed to act as brokers, the rules do not give them the same control over the selection of delegates or the same ability to control delegate behaviour in the convention. The system of apportionment, as we have seen, distributes delegates among *all* of the constituent elements of the party, not to the provinces. One large block of delegates—in 1967, 23 percent—is determined ex officio and, therefore, lies outside the selection process, while delegates to represent the mass membership are chosen not on a province-wide basis, but in separate meetings in each of the constituency associations at a time and place and under procedures which the constituency associations themselves decide. A difference in voting procedure at the convention is also important. Voting is not mediated through the provinces, but is done by individual secret ballot. Thus, the provincial delegation does not of necessity become the focus for delegate decision-making at the convention.

Party structure in Canada is also different from the United States in that linkages below the provincial level are generally weaker than linkages below the state level in American parties—because of the absence of professional organization, the relatively small and inactive nature of constituency membership, and the separation in Canada of federal and provincial constituency organizations. In any province when the party is out of office these linkages are likely to be intermittent and uncertain. In provinces where the party has not held office for a long time or where it is not an effective competitor for provincial office, they are tenuous or non-existent.

Even when provincial elites have the capacity to intervene in the selection of a national leader they have often been reluctant to do so—at least in a collective and concerted way. The costs of intervention include the diversion of the energies of provincial organization from its main tasks and the risk of involvement in federal conflicts which may create strains within and disrupt the provincial party. The benefits are a good deal less substantial than those which can accrue to state parties in the United States. The fortunes of the state parties are closely tied to the selection of a presidential candidate by the system of joint federal, state, and local elections with its common ballot; by the overwhelming power (and patronage) of federal office; and by the national orientation of the American political culture which gives the image of the presidential candidate considerable force as a mobilizing agent in state and local elections. In Canada provincial parties have less at stake in the national leadership because federal and provincial elections are conducted independently of one another; because there is greater provincial autonomy within the federal system and, therefore, less dependence for patronage and policy allocations on the federal government; and because the Canadian political culture emphasizes provincial rather than national orientations.

In 1967 the Nova Scotia and Manitoba parties were the only provincial parties to make an open commitment—to their respective provincial leaders—Premier Stanfield and Premier Roblin. Roblin also had the unannounced support of the Union Nationale in Quebec. In keeping with his party's official posture of indifference to federal politics, Premier Johnson did not publicly declare his commitment to Roblin. But key figures from the Union Nationale assumed the leading roles in Roblin's Quebec campaign, establishing what was effectively an autonomous Quebec campaign committee under Union Nationale control.[3] In other provinces, while many individual members of the provincial elite took sides, there were no collective party commitments.

Thus, candidates had to try to build their own organizations in each province. But no candidate had either enough money or a sufficiently strong network of personal contacts across the country to employ the large full-time staff needed to create and manage effective organization on a nation-wide scale. The financial obstacles are best illustrated by pointing out that the federal party as a whole has never been able to afford professional organization on a nation-wide scale. As we saw earlier, even the maintenance of a minimally effective national headquarters has been a continuing financial problem for the party. The development of organization through personal networks is inhibited by the fact that the networks of national party figures tend to overlap. Such networks are normally developed through contacts on formal occasions at national meetings or during brief local visits for speaking engagements, with the result that they are limited to the same relatively small circles of provincial and constituency elites.

Table 8 **Percentage of the delegates approached by each of the candidates and/or his workers**

	Candidate and worker	Candidate only	Worker only	Total approached
Diefenbaker	1	1	5	7
Fleming	4	6	7	17
Fulton	8	13	12	33
Hamilton	3	5	8	16
Hees	6	10	12	28
McCutcheon	3	5	9	17
Roblin	7	8	17	31
Stanfield	6	6	18	30
		(N = 1091)		

Without strong organization across the country, candidates were unable to have any significant effect on the selection of constituency delegates, even though in many constituencies it would have been a relatively easy matter to "pack" the delegate selection meeting. Fulton was the only candidate whose organization made an extensive effort to do this, but this effort was successful only in a relatively few constituencies.[4] Their inability to organize effectively on a nation-wide scale also meant that candidates had considerable difficulty in reaching delegates to make personal approaches for support. Data from the delegate survey show that the largest number of delegates personally approached for support by any candidate organization was only 33 percent. (See table 8.)

Thus, the mobilization of delegate support took place under conditions very different from those which prevail in American party conventions. There was no structure of intermediate leadership to fill the brokerage role and candidates had to rely on forms of mass communication to appeal for support.[5]

We may hypothesize therefore that Conservative delegate behaviour will be less likely to reflect the influence of patronage motives than their American counterparts.

There are two pieces of evidence about delegate voting behaviour which relate to this hypothesis.

Table 9 **Percentages of delegates (by candidate supported) who continued to support their first ballot choices on succeeding ballots**

Candidate	Ballot 2	Ballot 3	Ballot 4	Ballot 5[a]	N
Diefenbaker	61	39	—	—	(133)
Fleming	69	—	—	—	(52)
Fulton	89	84	71	—	(164)
Hamilton	73	57	38	—	(60)
Hees	78	52	—	—	(124)
McCutcheon	42	—	—	—	(83)
Roblin	92	91	89	82	(167)
Stanfield	87	88	87	84	(259)
Starr	48	—	—	—	(33)

(a) It should be noted that 14 percent of the sample did not report their behaviour on ballot 5. It should not be assumed therefore that 16 percent of Stanfield's supporters shifted to Roblin or that 18 percent of Roblin's supporters shifted to Stanfield. Roblin's reported loss to Stanfield was 5 percent and Stanfield's reported loss to Roblin was 1 percent. Some of the remaining loss is to be accounted for by non-voting and, of course, as was noted earlier, some of the Roblin vote appears not to have been reported.

First, a majority of the delegates in the survey said they had not entered into agreements committing their support. Among the sample as a whole, the number of delegates who had made such commitments was only 44 percent. Among constituency delegates, it was only 38 percent. In American conventions, nearly all of the delegates have commitments—either to candidates or to state or county leaders.

Second, there was evidence in delegate voting behaviour that candidates did not have much control over their delegates. For one thing, there was a good deal of vote switching as the balloting progressed. Excluding those who voted for the two leading candidates—Stanfield and Roblin—only 55 percent of the delegates continued to support the candidate for whom they voted on the first ballot until that candidate dropped out. (See table 9.) In addition, the three candidates—McCutcheon, Hees, and Fulton—who tried to transfer their support when they withdrew were not very successful. Fulton delivered a majority of his delegates—64 percent—but both the other candidates each delivered only 41 percent. (See table 10.)

Table 10 **Distribution of McCutcheon, Hees, and Fulton delegates from the last ballot contested by these candidates on the ballot following their candidate's withdrawal**

	Percentages from previous ballot who voted for							
	Stanfield	Roblin	Fulton	Hamilton	Hees	Diefenbaker	Did not vote	N
McCutcheon delegates on ballot 3	41	18	26	3	10	—	3	(39)
All delegates on ballot 3	33	24	16	6	8	5	8	(1082)
Hees delegates on ballot 4	41	35	5	8	—	—	11	(83)
All delegates on ballot 4	41	30	14	6	—	—	9	(1078)
Fulton delegates on ballot 5	64	29	—	—	—	—	7	(154)
All delegates on ballot 5	52	34	—	—	—	—	14	(1074)

If there had been extensive networks of patronage linkages within the convention, delegates would be expected to have made commitments of support. They would also be expected to have been loyal to the candidates to whom they first gave their support. These data therefore provide inferential support for the hypothesis. They show that large numbers of delegates did not behave as they would be expected to behave if they were acting under the constraints of patronage ties.

In summary, in this section of the chapter I have tried to show that distinctive characteristics of party and convention structures in the Conservative party create conditions unlike those of the American patronage-brokerage model of convention politics:

1. Provincial parties do not usually have either incentive or the resources to influence the selection of delegates or to control delegate behaviour.

2. In the absence of intervention by provincial elites, there is no structure of intermediate leadership which might be used to mobilize and direct delegate support.

3. The wide dispersal of delegates across the country, together with the candidates' limited networks of personal contacts, makes it impossible for candidates to make direct personal approaches to more than a very limited number of delegates.

4. With only limited opportunities for personal contacts between candidate organizations and delegates and in the absence of structures of intermediate leadership, the mobilization of support through patronage agreements is unlikely to be extensive.

5. Candidates have to rely heavily on forms of mass communication to appeal for support.

SOCIAL CLEAVAGE

Institutional constraints have also influenced the effect of social cleavage on Conservative politics. Since party conventions have been designed to reflect the federal nature of the country, they have ensured full representation for those areas where the party has been electorally weak. Thus in 1967, although the party held few seats in Quebec and in the metro-

Table 11 **Selected demographic characteristics of members of the 1967 caucus and delegates to the 1967 convention**

Size of community of residence			Caucus	Convention
Farm or rural area			26	14
Community from	1,000–9,999		32	21
	10,000–99,999		30	22
	100,000–249,999		12	12
	250,000 or more		0	30
		N =	(95)	(1021)
Region				
Atlantic			19	15
Quebec			8	17
Ontario			29	37
Prairies			40	20
British Columbia			3	9
Territories			3	9
		N =	(95)	(1091)

politan centres of the country, the convention accorded full representation to both. The significance of this fact will be apparent in table 11 which compares the composition of the 1967 convention with that of the 1967 caucus on the dimensions of community size and province.

While more or less accurately reflecting the social composition of the country on these dimensions—as chapter 2 pointed out—the convention was distinctively unrepresentative of the Canadian population on dimensions of socio-economic status. Its members were almost exclusively in middle-class occupations or from middle-class backgrounds. This does not mean the convention might not produce behaviour based on status cleavages. In the analysis of elite-level politics, we have seen the effect on Conservative politics of status differentiation within the middle class.

Table 12 **Percentages of delegates (by their score on a scale of establishment characteristics) who supported or opposed leadership review**

	0	1	2	3	4	Percentage of sample
Supported review	45	56	68	74	82	65
Opposed review	46	33	25	21	12	28
DNA	9	10	7	5	6	8
N =	(138)	(296)	(319)	(207)	(131)	(1091)

chi square significant at .0000
V = .12

In particular, we have observed a relationship between behaviour and a scale ranking caucus members by their social distance from a dominant national elite, described as university-educated, professional or corporate executives, who live in the major urban areas of the central provinces. In the conflict over Diefenbaker's leadership it was the members of the party caucus who were most remote—in terms of their social characteristics—from this dominant national elite who were most likely to be loyal to Diefenbaker. The same pattern can be observed in the extra-parliamentary party as reflected in the reported attitudes of delegates toward leadership review in 1966. As table 12 shows, the greater the social distance of a delegate from the dominant elite, the more likely he was to oppose leadership review, that is, to be loyal to Diefenbaker. Among those delegates who were most remote from the establishment—that is, those who possessed none of the social characteristics of the dominant elite—51 percent had been Diefenbaker loyalists, while among those who were closest to the establishment, only 13 percent had been Diefenbaker loyalists.

Table 13 **Percentages of delegates (by their score on a scale of establishment characteristics) voting for each candidate on the first ballot**

	0	1	2	3	4	Percentage of sample
Diefenbaker	21	15	11	7	8	12
Hamilton	12	5	3	7	5	6
Fleming	4	3	7	3	7	5
Fulton	12	15	15	17	15	15
Hees	3	10	14	13	15	11
McCutcheon	1	6	10	10	8	8
Roblin	12	14	14	20	18	15
Stanfield	31	26	23	22	15	24
DNA	2	3	3	1	5	4
N =	(138)	(296)	(319)	(207)	(131)	(1091)

chi square significant at .0000
V = .16

There was an association between this variable and voting behaviour on the first ballot at the 1967 convention but it was relatively weak and Diefenbaker did not retain the level of support among social outsiders that he had had in 1966. As table 13 shows, only 21 percent of this group continued to support him in 1967. Clearly, some other influences were at work in 1967. Diefenbaker's personal conduct might have been one factor in the sense that, because he delayed his decision to run for so long, he forced potential supporters to make other choices. Another factor might have been that his age made him an improbable candidate even to those people in the party who had backed him in 1966; they might have sought a candidate with a more realistic chance of winning. But neither Hamilton nor Starr—the two candidates most closely identified with Diefenbaker—picked up many of Diefenbaker's lost votes from "outsiders." The candidate who did best among the outsiders and the candidate whose support generally was most closely associated with the social distance scale was Stanfield.

Table 14 **Distribution of first ballot votes by province**

	Percentage who voted for								
Province	Diefen-baker	Fleming	Fulton	Hamilton	Hees	Mc-Cutcheon	Roblin	Stanfield	N
Newfoundland	23	—	—	—	—	—	—	77	(13)
Nova Scotia	3	1	—	—	—	—	1	95	(80)
New Brunswick	8	—	11	2	6	8	4	62	(53)
Prince Edward Island	24	—	29	—	—	6	—	41	(17)
Quebec	6	12	19	2	23	6	25	8	(173)
Ontario	12	6	10	7	17	14	12	23	(382)
Manitoba	15	1	1	—	—	—	82	—	(67)
Saskatchewan	51	—	3	27	8	3	5	2	(59)
Alberta	17	1	26	4	6	12	5	29	(77)
British Columbia	10	5	61	5	3	1	10	5	(88)
All	13	5	16	5	12	8	16	25	(1009)[a]

chi square significant at .001

V = .32

(a) Not included are 17 delegates who voted for Starr, 7 who voted for McLean, and 58 who did not report their vote.

Stanfield's strength among social outsiders was related to his regional strength in the Atlantic provinces; none of the other components of the scale had the same effect on his vote as the variable "province of residence." This reflected a general pattern in the relationship between social cleavage and first ballot voting behaviour.

Table 15 **Strength of association between selected group variables and voting choices on the first and fifth ballots using Cramer's V**

	Ballot 1	Ballot 5
Size of community of residence	.14	.11
Province of residence	.32[a]	.44[a]
Age	.12	.06
Religion	.13[a]	.11
Ethnic origin	.15	.16[a]
Income	.09	.07
Education	.11	.10
Occupation	.12	.11

(a) Indicates chi square was significant at .001

On the first ballot, the only social group characteristics associated with voting choice at an acceptable level of statistical significance (using chi square values of .001)[6] were province of residence, size of community of residence, religion, and ethnic origin. The strongest association (using Cramer's V)[7] was between voting choice and province of residence. Wherever there was a native candidate, with the exception of Ontario, he won or led his province. In Saskatchewan, where there were two native candidates, Diefenbaker and Hamilton, between them they took 77 percent of the vote. There was a broader regional cleavage in the vote in that Stanfield did well not just in Nova Scotia but in the other Atlantic provinces, while the collective western candidacies of Diefenbaker, Fulton, Hamilton, and Roblin carried a preponderance of delegates in the prairies and British Columbia. The deviant cases were Prince Edward Island, among the Atlantic provinces, giving Stanfield only 41 percent, and Alberta among the western provinces, giving the collective regional candidacies just over 50 percent.

The associations between the voting choices of delegates and the size of the communities in which they lived, their religious attributes, and their ethnic attributes were very weak.[8]

Stanfield, Diefenbaker, and Hamilton did slightly better than average among rural delegates; Stanfield did better among delegates from small towns; Stanfield and Diefenbaker did better among delegates from towns and cities in the population range 10,000 to 100,000; and Roblin, Fulton, and Hees did better among delegates in cities with populations of 250,000 or more. Roblin, Fulton, Hees, and Fleming had greater than average support among Roman Catholics, and Stanfield had greater than average support among the smaller Protestant groups. Roblin, Hees, and Fleming did better among persons of French extraction; Stanfield among those of Scottish descent; and Roblin among those of non-British, non-French European descent.

There are obvious elements of interdependence among these three variables and province. In fact, when voting choices are related to them within, instead of across provincial boundaries, most of the distinctions disappear. For example, Stanfield's rural, small town, and small city strength seems to reflect not general rural, small town, and small city strength, but his strength in the Atlantic provinces where these are the major patterns of population distribution. In Alberta, by contrast, he did best in the two large cities, Calgary and Edmonton. Both religion and ethnic origin did seem to exercise some independent effect: Fulton's support among Roman Catholics cuts across both ethnic differences and provincial boundaries, and Stanfield's support among Scots and the

Table 16 **Distribution of fifth ballot votes by province**

	Percentage who voted for		
Province	Roblin	Stanfield	N
Newfoundland	9	91	(111)
Nova Scotia	1	99	(69)
New Brunswick	9	91	(44)
Prince Edward Island	21	79	(14)
Quebec	53	47	(154)
Ontario	34	67	(343)
Manitoba	96	4	(55)
Saskatchewan	70	30	(50)
Alberta	35	65	(75)
British Columbia	44	56	(79)
All	40	60	(894)[a]

chi square significant at .001

V = .44

(a) Excluded are those who did not report their votes and/or did not vote.

smaller Protestant groups persisted from province to province. Still, it is clear that province is the variable with the greatest degree of independent association with vote.

One of the most striking features of the relationship between social cleavage and voting choice on the fifth ballot was the disappearance of the association between vote and the scale measuring social distance from the dominant national elite. Stanfield and Roblin drew approximately the same support across all of the divisions on this scale. But there was again a strong association between voting choice and the variable province of residence. Indeed the association on the fifth ballot is stronger than on the first ballot. As table 16 shows, Stanfield strengthened his base in the Atlantic provinces and carried majorities in Ontario, Alberta, and British Columbia. Roblin won Quebec, Manitoba, and Saskatchewan.

The association of vote preference with ethnic origin and religion also persisted but at a very weak level.[9] Roblin did better among the French-speaking, people of non-British and non-French European extraction, and Roman Catholics; while Stanfield did better among people of Scottish and English extraction and Protestants. Roblin's strength among francophones was the strongest of this group of associations.

These data on social cleavages suggest some hypotheses about the motivational basis of politics in the 1967 convention.

First, since the effect of the status cleavage based on social distance from the dominant elite was relatively weak on the first ballot and was not apparent on the fifth ballot, it evidently had little substance independent of the conflict over Diefenbaker's leadership. We may hypothesize, therefore, that its focus was primarily on the personality of Diefenbaker and, accordingly, that it had a high affective content.

Second, since the effect of this cleavage lay primarily in its territorial components (the cleavages between major urban centres and smaller communities and between the central and hinterland provinces) and there was no independent association between any socio-economic variable and voting choice, it is unlikely that many delegates could have made their choices on the basis of issues of social or economic policy.

Third, patronage ties may explain part of the native-son support for Roblin, Stanfield, Fulton, Hamilton, and Diefenbaker and they also probably explain some of Roblin's strength in Quebec, because his support was greatest there among delegates who said they were active members of the Union Nationale. But the regional pattern in the vote was more extensive than an explanation based solely on patronage linkages could account for. And such an explanation could not account for the greater strength of the association of province and vote on the final ballot.

Fourth, the association of religious and ethnic cleavages with vote suggests the significance of issues with a high affective content—or the mobilization of support through responses based on feelings of group affinity. There are two pieces of evidence which indicate the significance of the latter effect: Fulton's support among Roman Catholics and Stanfield's support among Scots. There were no issues of a religious nature in the campaign but Fulton was the only Catholic candidate and many of the key figures in his campaign organization were Catholics. The support of Scots for Stanfield is equally without explanation in any manifest question of policy, but his campaign made extensive use of the provincial symbols of Nova Scotia all of which have a strong Scottish motif.

THE FACTIONAL CLEAVAGE OVER DIEFENBAKER'S LEADERSHIP

In discussing the actions and interactions of people in elite roles in the party we have observed the importance of the factional cleavage over

Table 17 **Distribution of first ballot votes of delegates who in 1966 actively worked for or against leadership review, and of other delegates who supported or opposed leadership review**

	Actively worked for review	Actively worked against review	Supported review	Opposed review
Diefenbaker	2	45	5	29
Fleming	4	4	5	7
Fulton	21	4	15	13
Hamilton	4	4	7	10
Hees	13	13	14	4
McCutcheon	9	3	10	5
Roblin	18	4	15	13
Stanfield	28	18	28	15
Starr	1	3	1	4
N[a] =	(314)	(65)	(346)	(205)

chi square significant at .001

V = .28

(a) Excluded from the table are non-voters, delegates who voted for McLean or Walker-Sawka, and those who indicated no position on leadership review.

Diefenbaker's leadership. We have seen its influence both in relations within the party generally, in the strategy and conduct of the convention campaign, and in the secondary voting choices made by leading participants. Although Diefenbaker did not have the votes in 1967 he might have expected from his supporters in 1966, the effect of this cleavage was still apparent in the behaviour of the delegates.

On the first ballot, of the delegates who had actively opposed leadership review, 45 percent voted for Diefenbaker and 8 percent voted for Hamilton and Starr, the two other candidates who had vigorously opposed review. In comparison, only 23 percent of these delegates voted for Stanfield, Fulton, and McCutcheon, the three candidates identified with support for review or with Camp, its principal advocate. Conversely, of the delegates who had actively supported leadership review, 58 percent voted for Stanfield, Fulton, and McCutcheon, while only 7 percent voted for Diefenbaker, Hamilton, and Starr.

Among all delegates who said they had taken sides in the 1966 conflict—that is, not just those who were actively engaged in it—a similar pattern occurred, although it was less clearly defined.

The effect of this cleavage persisted on the fifth ballot, although the statistical association was not as strong as on the first ballot. (See Table 18.) Supporters of review were more likely to vote for Stanfield, while opponents were more likely to vote for Roblin.

The fact that Diefenbaker did not do better among those who were loyal to him in 1966 seems to support the argument that after the annual

Table 18 **Distribution of fifth ballot votes of delegates who in 1966 actively worked for or against leadership review, and of all delegates who supported or opposed review**

	Actively worked for review	Actively worked against review	Supported review	Opposed review
Stanfield	67	48	67	47
Roblin	33	52	33	54
N[a] =	(217)	(62)	(313)	(187)

chi square significant at .001

V = .19

(a) Excluded from the table are non-voters and those who indicated no position on leadership review.

Table 19 **Percentages of respondents supporting or opposing leadership review in 1966 in each province who voted on the fifth ballot for Stanfield or Roblin**

	Percentages who voted		
	Roblin	Stanfield	Number[a]
Quebec			
Supported review	49	51	(88)
Opposed review	50	50	(38)
Ontario			
Supported review	27	73	(243)
Opposed review	53	47	(72)
Manitoba			
Supported review	97	3	(31)
Opposed review	95	5	(20)
Saskatchewan			
Supported review	50	50	(14)
Opposed review	79	21	(33)
Alberta			
Supported review	22	78	(49)
Opposed review	52	48	(21)
British Columbia			
Supported review	39	61	(55)
Opposed review	61	39	(18)
Newfoundland			
Supported review	14	86	(7)
Opposed review	—	100	(3)
Nova Scotia			
Supported review	—	100	(38)
Opposed review	4	96	(24)
New Brunswick			
Supported review	1	99	(25)
Opposed review	—	100	(10)
Prince Edward Island			
Supported review	15	85	(13)
Opposed review	100	—	(1)

(a) Total numbers will not necessarily correspond to the numbers for each province in other tables because respondents who did not answer the review questions or who did not indicate a fifth ballot vote preference have not been included.

meeting of 1966 the significance of the conflict at that meeting lay less in the substance of the conflict—the issue of Diefenbaker's continued leadership—and more in the factional cleavage it had created. It was the pattern of relationships which the conflict had created and not the issue itself which was reflected in the voting choices of delegates.

The effect of this cleavage was moderated only by the cross-cutting effect of regional ties. On the fifth ballot, Stanfield carried the Atlantic provinces and Roblin carried Quebec and Manitoba, regardless of the dispositions of delegates in the 1966 conflict. In other provinces, however, Stanfield benefited from his support among delegates who had sided with Camp in 1966. (See table 19.) The support he received from these delegates accounted for his victories in Alberta (the only prairie province which did not give a majority to Roblin), in British Columba, and in Ontario.

CONCLUSION

In this chapter we have considered the implications for delegate behaviour of three kinds of structural variables: the institutional context of the convention, social cleavage, and the factional cleavage from the conflict in 1966 over John Diefenbaker's leadership.

It has been shown that the patronage-brokerage model of convention politics—emphasizing the bloc manipulation of votes and operating through networks of patronage linkages—at best could have only very limited application to the behaviour of delegates at the 1967 Conservative Convention.

The behaviour of most delegates would seem to be better explained in terms of a model of mass politics which would emphasize the autonomy of individual delegate choice and the mobilization of support through techniques of mass persuasion similar to those used in popular elections. Under these conditions, we would expect patronage motives to be relatively less important, and the other types of motives to be relatively more important in delegate behaviour.

Analysis of the effects of social cleavage suggested several points:

1. The status cleavage based on social distance from the dominant national elite was largely limited in its effect to attitudes toward Diefenbaker personally, which seems to support the interpretation that this cleavage had high affective content.

2. The effect of the social distance scale lay primarily in the cleavages between metropolitan and hinterland communities and provinces.

3. The absence of any independent association between voting behaviour and the socio-economic characteristics of delegates indicated that

issues of social and economic policy were unlikely to have been very important.

4. The dimension of social cleavage most strongly associated with voting choice was province of residence. While this probably in part reflected the mobilization of support through access to provincial party resources and the patron-client networks developed by native-son candidates, it extended beyond any pattern that could be explained solely by the operation of factors of this kind.

5. The association of ethnic and religious characteristics of delegates with their voting choices suggests the significance of issues with an intrinsically affective content and/or the influence of stimuli mobilizing affective group feelings.

Finally, the factional cleavage over Diefenbaker's leadership had a significantly independent effect on the vote. Since Diefenbaker himself carried less than half his 1966 supporters, it may be inferred that at least in part the effect of this cleavage reflected the relationships formed in factional interactions as distinct from concern with Diefenbaker's continued leadership. This inference is supported by the fact that the cleavage persisted on the fifth ballot—that is, after the question of Diefenbaker's leadership itself was no longer at issue. This implies that there was a significant affective element in the effect of this cleavage as well.

8

Motivational Patterns in Delegate Behaviour

Chapter 6 has suggested certain propositions about the motives of delegates at the 1967 convention. But motives cannot be imputed simply on the basis of structural observations. Such evidence is helpful but not conclusive. We can only say that given the observed conditions, a certain pattern of motivation would seem more likely. This chapter will extend the analysis of delegate motives by discussing the reasons the delegates gave for their voting choices and the relationships between their choices and their attitudes on certain issues.

DELEGATE EXPLANATIONS FOR THEIR VOTING CHOICES

One question in the 1967 survey asked delegates to give the reasons for their voting choices on the first ballot and—if they changed their votes on subsequent ballots—the reasons for their secondary choices.[1] Their responses for the first ballot are shown in table 20. For purposes of analysis, these responses have been assigned—where it was possible—to one of the three basic types of motives which were defined in chapter one. Not all of the explanations delegates gave can be assigned to the categories of the typology. In part, this is a problem of ambiguities in the language used. In part, as well, it is a problem which resides in the fact that explanations for actions may lie at different levels. There is one level which relates to the situation in which the action occurs and there

Table 20 **Percentage of delegates mentioning each of a given set of reasons for first ballot voting choice[a]**

	Percentage mentioning each reason
I agreed with his views on policy matters	73
His personal characteristics were more appealing to me	58
I liked his political style	50
I thought he would be the best vote-getter for the party	44
He understands my part of the country better	35
I knew him better than the other candidates	33
He has helped the party in my community in the past	25
A person prominent in the party whose judgement I respect was supporting him	21
I thought my own position in the party would be stronger if he were the leader	9
I thought he was going to win the leadership and I wanted to be on the winning side	8
He has helped me personally in the past	7
I was asked to vote for him by a person prominent in the party who has helped me in the past or may be able to help me	6
Personal loyalty[b]	6
One of his workers approached me and those of the other candidates did not	5
Personality (affective responses)[b]	4
Policy (general)[b]	2
Patronage (general)[b]	2
Other (unclassifiable)[b]	6
N	(1091)

(a) These data are derived from responses to question 32: "On the first ballot, which of these reasons were most important to you in helping you to decide for whom you would vote. . . ." Delegates were allowed to mention any number of reasons.

(b) These categories were created from response to the option "Other (please specify)."

is another level which relates to basic motives. Explanation at the first level need contain no indication of the underlying motives. There are two reasons which were frequently mentioned that cannot be assigned to one of the categories. One was "I thought he would be the best vote-getter for the party" and the other was "He understands my part of the country better." The significance of both these explanations will be discussed later. The discussion which follows will focus on the explanations delegates gave for their first ballot choices. Analysis of the explanations for second choices revealed the same patterns observed for first choices. The list of reasons given for second choices is reported in Appendix B, table 42.

In striking contrast to the leading participants, most of the delegates who explained their choices gave policy as a reason. Of the delegates who explained their choices on the first ballot, 73 percent gave a policy reason. But most other delegates also gave other reasons. In fact, 68 percent of the delegates who explained their first ballot choices mentioned at least three reasons and 50 percent at least four reasons.

This pattern of multiple responses is a reminder of the complexity of motivational influences on political actions. Any attempt at explanation must take this complexity into account. Thus, while it may be possible to assign greater or lesser importance to particular motives, it is necessary always to bear in mind the relative character of such assignments.

There is no inherent measure of the relative importance of the reasons the delegates gave for their choices because, although they were asked to rank their responses, very few of them did. But there is an a priori reason for questioning the extent to which policy motives were the determinative factor. As I have already pointed out, there is a strong moral imperative to articulate or rationalize political choices in terms of policy motives, since the morally approved purpose of politics is to make decisions in the collective interest. Confronted with a statement expressing motives in this legitimate way, many delegates may have felt constrained to mention it.

This need not imply that a policy response was untruthful. If a delegate did not profoundly disagree with a candidate's policy views or if he agreed with him on most matters he could well say that policy was a factor in his choice. Since the area of disagreement among the candidates was relatively limited, it would be reasonable to assume on a wide range of issues that if one candidate's views were acceptable to a delegate, the views of most of the candidates would also be acceptable to him. The delegate, therefore, could say that agreement with the candidate's policy views was a factor in his choice, regardless of the choice he made. But this factor would not explain why he chose one candidate in preference to another. And for this analysis, the crucial question is whether policy reasons explained such preferences.

Table 21 **Distribution of delegate responses to 32 issue statements for those issues on which dissenting opinion exceeded 20 percent of the total sample**[a]

	Percentage who	
	Agreed	Disagreed[b,c]
Issues on which dissenting opinion exceeded 40 percent		
French Canadians should have no more privileges than other ethnic groups	52	43
Quebec's position in Confederation should receive special recognition	42	52
Soviet Communism is no longer a threat to Canada	41	47
Issues on which dissenting opinion exceeded 30 percent, but was less than 40 percent		
Canada ought to devote much more effort and money to aiding the underdeveloped countries	51	36
There should be special laws to regulate foreign (mostly U.S.) investment in Canada	58	35
Canada must take steps to reduce American influence on its culture and mass media	53	35
Central Canada has too much say in Canadian politics	35	53
French-speaking Canadians outside Quebec should be able to use French when they deal with their own governments	58	34
Wealthy people have too much say in politics	35	53
Provincial governments should have more power	32	58
Governments spend too much money on social welfare	59	32
The monarchy is an essential part of the Canadian constitution	57	32
We ought to seek greater American investment in Canada	58	30

Issues on which dissenting opinion exceeded 20 percent but was less than 30 percent		
Old age pensions and baby bonuses should only be paid to people who need them	66	29
Canada should spend less on defence	59	29
We should pay no special attention to the demands of Quebec	27	68
The federal government should give more money to the provinces	55	26
Government ought to interfere less with business	61	26
Farmers should have more say in determining the policy of the Conservative party	26	56
The Commonwealth connection is no longer important for Canada	25	67
The workers' right to strike should not be restricted	23	68
More government planning is needed to develop the Canadian economy	72	21
Canada should take steps to bring its foreign policy more closely into line with that of the United States	20	69

(a) These data are derived from responses to question 31: "Please indicate whether you agree, disagree or have no opinion on the following statements."

(b) For the sake of clarity in the table, "No Opinion" responses are excluded. Their exclusion accounts for the difference between the sum of the agree and disagree distributions and 100.

(c) Individual numbers of cases are not included for each distribution, since for each distribution the N = 1091.

Delegate opinion was in fact divided on a number of issues, as is shown by analysis of responses to thirty-two issue statements with which delegates were asked to agree or disagree. There were thirteen statements on which the level of dissent from the prevailing opinion in the sample exceeded 30 percent and another ten on which it was between 20 and 30 percent. (See table 21.)

However, direct tests for associations between issue positions and voting choice cast some doubt upon the significance of these differences in delegate behaviour. There were only twelve of the thirty-two issue statements which were associated with first ballot choice at the .001 level using chi square—that is, at a level which, for this sample size, could conservatively be held to be more than a chance occurrence—and in none of these cases was the association very strong. Thus, there is good reason from evidence in the data to question whether delegates, in citing policy motives as a factor in their choices, were actually explaining why they chose one candidate in preference to others.

To explore this matter further, a test was devised relating delegate issue positions to delegate perceptions of candidate issue positions. Delegates had been asked which of the candidates was most favourable and which most unfavourable to each of fourteen items expressing sympathy for a specific issue position: "social welfare," "free enterprise," "French Canada," "Canadian independence of the United States," "a deux nations policy," "a strong stand against Communism," "more aid to underdeveloped countries," "loyalty to the monarchy," "the farmer," "less spending on defence," "the poorer provinces," "trade unions," "a strong central government," and "restricting Medicare to those who need it." For each of the statements the delegates were asked to choose the candidate who was "most favourable," the candidate who was "next most favourable," the candidate who was "most unfavourable," and the candidate who was "next most unfavourable." For the purposes of the test, rankings were dichotomized as favourable and unfavourable. A delegate, therefore, could rank two candidates as favourable and two as unfavourable to each issue statement. The test consisted in relating the delegate's ranking of the candidates, his own issue positions, and his vote to see if he voted for the candidate whose issue positions he perceived to accord most closely with his own.[2]

The method used to apply this test requires some explanation. Neither of the questions used in the test asked delegates to say what importance they ascribed to an issue. One approach to the problem of interpretation that this poses would be to assume that a policy motive had been proved if a delegate voted for any candidate with whom he agreed on any issue, even if he had agreed with some other candidate on a larger number of issues. Another approach would be to assume that a policy motive had been proved only if a delegate voted for the candidate with whom he had agreed on the largest number of issues. Since, as a simple matter of chance, there was a strong probability that a delegate would mention each candidate at least once over the whole range of issues, the second procedure seemed more reasonable to adopt. Of course, there was still the possibility that one issue might mean more to a delegate than all of the rest separately or together. It was, therefore, decided to use external criteria to try to build some measure of the likely importance of issues into the test.

One criterion which was chosen was the amount of attention issues received in press coverage of the campaign. It was assumed that press coverage would reflect the importance attached to issues by the candidates and—since the delegates had to rely on the mass media for much of their information about the campaign—that it would fairly accurately reflect the issues about which the delegates had heard and read the most. There were six issues which were identified from content analysis of newspaper coverage as receiving somewhat more attention than other issues. "Free enterprise," "French Canada," "a deux nations policy," "welfare spending," "loyalty to the monarchy," and "restricting Medicare to those who need it."[3] These issues were treated as one subgroup which might have greater importance to a delegate than the whole set considered collectively.

A second subgroup was chosen by looking at the distribution of delegate opinion on each of the issues. If there was substantial disagreement among the delegates about an issue, it was assumed that that issue would be more important in the choice of a leadership candidate than an issue about which most of the delegates agreed. If 30 percent or more of the delegates dissented from the prevailing opinion on an issue, it was designated as an issue about which there was "substantial" disagreement.[4] There were eleven issues which fell into this category. They included, in addition to those used in the press test, "Canadian independence of the United States," "more aid to underdeveloped countries," "sympathy for the farmer," "less spending on defence," and "sympathy toward trade unions."[5]

The dramatic emphasis given the "deux nations" issue by Diefenbaker suggested that it might have a distinctively important status and should be treated not just as a component of these groups but on its own. Thus it was chosen for separate treatment.

The test was run in four stages. In the first stage a delegate's vote was said to be policy-motivated if he voted for one of the two candidates whom he said was closest to his own position on the "deux nations" policy. In the second stage a delegate was said to be policy-motivated if he voted for the candidate whom he ranked closest to himself on the six issues mentioned most frequently in press reports of the convention campaign. (A delegate would be said to have ranked a candidate closest even if he only mentioned that candidate on two issues and other candidates on one issue.) In the third stage a delegate was said to be policy-motivated if he voted for the candidate whom he ranked closest to himself on the eleven issues on which there was substantial disagreement. In the final stage, a delegate was said to be policy-motivated if he voted for the candidate he ranked closest to himself over all the issues for which respondents were asked to rank the candidates.[6] As the test progressed, delegates who met the standard of policy motivation for any stage were said to be policy-motivated and excluded from the further stage or stages.

Table 22 **Percentages of delegates voting for candidates to whom they perceived themselves closest on four policy tests**

	Voted for candidate perceived closest	Voted for another candidate	Did not answer[a]	Accorded same ranking to more than one candidate	Voted for candidate perceived closest on previous test (tests)	Not included in the test[b]
A "deux nations" policy	21	29	45	—	—	5
The five issues mentioned most often in the press	10	22	23	21	21	5
The eleven issues on which dissenting opinion exceeded 20 percent	4	24	21	16	31	5
All thirteen issues	3	24	20	13	35	5
For all four tests	38	24	20	13	38	5

(a) Did not answer includes those who did not rank a candidate and/or did not give an issue position. In the case of the second, third, and fourth tests, it includes those who did not rank a candidate and/or did not give an issue position on *any* of the issues used in the test.

(b) Those not included in the test were non-voters and delegates who voted for Starr and McLean.

As table 22 shows, 38 percent of the delegates voted for a candidate they had ranked closest to themselves. Five percent of the delegates were not included in the test, 13 percent accorded the same ranking to more than one candidate over all stages, and 20 percent did not answer either the issue question or that asking them to rank the candidates.

The purpose of the test was to determine whether a policy motive explained the delegate's choice of one candidate *in preference to others.* In these terms, the behaviour of the 13 percent who gave equal ranking to more than one candidate cannot be explained by a policy motive. Thus, the total number of delegates whose behaviour cannot be explained by a policy motive is 37 percent of the sample, while the total number whose behaviour can be explained by a policy motive is 38 percent.

Given the assumptions on which the test is based, these figures need to be interpreted with some caution. The effect of the test is not to *prove or disprove,* but to indicate the *probability* that choices were policy-based. The data may be interpreted to show that while most delegates mentioned policy as a reason for their choices, it is probable that policy was the *decisive* factor in the choices of a good deal less than half of the sample.

Evaluation of the importance of other reasons the delegates gave for their voting choices is complicated by the fact that not all of the reasons mentioned by the delegates can be assigned to one of the basic motivational categories. Analysis of the responses that *can* be assigned in this way shows 79 percent of the sample gave one or more affective reasons and 37 percent gave one or more patronage reasons. Since such a large number of delegates gave at least one affective reason, it is useful to look just at those who gave two or more affective reasons. They constitute 49 percent of the sample and therefore still make up a larger proportion

Table 23 **Percentages of delegates giving none, one, two, or three or more affective and patronage reasons for first ballot choice**

Percentage who gave	None	One	Two	Three or more	Did not vote or gave no reasons of any kind	N
Affective reasons[a]	19	30	30	19	1	(1091)
Patronage reasons[b]	62	26	5	6	1	(1091)

than the number whose behaviour was consistent with a policy motive. (See tables 23 and 24.)

Table 24 **Percentages of delegates consistent on policy tests and percentages giving affective or patronage reasons for first ballot vote**

	Percentage	N
Consistent on policy tests	38	(1091)
Gave one or more affective reasons[a]	77	(1091)
Gave one or more patronage reasons[b]	35	(1091)
Gave no reasons of any kind	5	(1091)

(a) Reasons which were called "affective" were: "His personal characteristics were more appealing to me"; "I knew him better than the other candidates"; "I liked his political style"; "Loyalty" (a volunteered answer); and "Other affective" (an answer compiled from the "Other (Please specify)" category).

(b) Reasons which were called "patronage" were: "I thought my own position in the party would be stronger if he were the leader"; "I was asked to vote for him by a person prominent in the party who has helped me in the past or may be able to help me"; "He has helped the party in my community in the past"; "He has helped me personally in the past"; "I thought he was going to win the leadership and I wanted to be on the winning side"; "Other patronage" (an answer compiled from the "Other (Please specify)" category).

Table 25 **Distribution of delegates by policy, affective, and patronage motives, based on articulated affective and patronage motives, and consistency on policy tests**

	Percentage
Policy only	5
Affective only	31
Patronage only	5
Policy and affective	20
Policy and patronage	2
Affective and patronage	17
Policy, affective, and patronage	13
None of these	8
	(N = 1032)

Table 25 shows the number of delegates who gave reasons of only one kind. Altogether 41 percent of the sample explained their motives exclusively in terms of only one kind of motive. Of these, 31 percent gave only an affective reason, 5 percent only a policy reason, and 5 percent only a patronage reason.

To the extent that the reasons the delegates gave can be assigned to one of the three basic types of motivational categories, this evidence seems to suggest that affective types of reasons were somewhat more important in delegate behaviour. However, the pattern is by no means as clear as it was among leading participants. (See chapter 5.) And it is certainly the case that policy motives were a good deal more important in the behaviour of delegates considered as a whole than they were in the behaviour of the leading participants.

THE SIGNIFICANCE OF PATRONAGE MOTIVES

Among the reasons delegates mentioned which could not be classified within the categories of the basic typology of motives was the statement "I thought he would be the best vote-getter for the party." This explanation could be related to motives of any one of the three basic types. A delegate might want to have a leader who could help the party win because he hoped to achieve some policy goal, because he sought some patronage reward, or because he had an affective commitment to the party, as such, and wanted it to succeed in its organizational purposes. However, there is reason to suppose that a leader's vote-winning ability would be of special interest to a delegate who is patronage-motivated. The achievement of power is a necessary condition for the fulfilment of aspirations of this kind. The fact that a delegate cited vote-winning ability as a reason for his choice would not prove that he had been patronage-motivated, but if he did *not* cite it there would be ground to suspect that patronage motives were not a primary influence in his behaviour. Analysis of responses to this statement may therefore help identify more clearly the role of patronage motives in delegate behaviour.

The number of delegates who mentioned this statement amounted to 44 percent of the total sample. This suggests that patronage motives were of low priority for a majority of the delegates. Moreover, further analysis indicated this reason was not a strong influence in the choices of most of those delegates who did mention it.

Delegates had been asked to rank the candidates they thought best and worst on a number of characteristics, among them vote-winning ability. It was assumed that if vote-winning ability had a strong influence in a delegate's choice he would vote for one of the candidates he ranked best on this characteristic. In fact, of the delegates who gave vote-winning ability as a reason, only 56 percent actually voted for one of the candidates they had ranked best as a vote-getter.

An additional refinement to this test is provided by extending it to incorporate responses to a question which asked the delegate to name prominent party members who could help win votes in the delegate's constituency. Of the delegates who mentioned vote-winning ability as a reason, less than one-quarter voted for a candidate they both ranked highest on this characteristic and whom they said would help win votes for the party in their constituencies.

Perhaps one of the most telling pieces of evidence about the significance of this factor in delegate choices is the low ranking Stanfield received as a vote-getter. Of the eight candidates who were thought to be desirable campaigners, Stanfield was ranked first by only 3 percent of the sample, giving him fewer first place rankings than any of the others. (See table 26.) When all of the choices of delegates—that is their first, second, third, and fourth preferences—are taken together, Stanfield ranked fifth behind Roblin, Fulton, Hamilton, and Hees. Even more striking is the fact that while Stanfield received the fifth ballot votes of more than 56 percent of the delegates in the sample, only 17 percent thought he would be useful to them in winning votes in a local campaign.

Table 26 **Percentages of delegates mentioning each candidate as a person who would help in a local campaign**[a]

	First choice	All choices
Stanfield	3	17
Fulton	17	28
Hamilton	15	26
Diefenbaker	6	11
McCutcheon	3	8
Roblin	3	31
Hees	12	22
Fleming	not mentioned	
Starr	4	10

(a) The analysis is based on responses to the question: "List at least five nationally known party members who would be of most help in a campaign in your constituency – choose at least one from each of these groups.

1. Former ministers in Mr. Diefenbaker's government.
2. Members of Parliament other than former ministers.
3. Provincial leaders or former provincial leaders.
4. Other prominent party people."

Looked at another way, of the delegates who voted for Stanfield on the first ballot, only 27 percent mentioned his vote-winning ability; only 14 percent of the Stanfield voters gave this reason and also ranked him first or second among the candidates as a vote-getter; and only 7 percent gave his vote-winning ability as a reason, ranked him first or second among the candidates as a vote-getter, and also thought him a desirable person to help win votes in a constituency campaign. These data seem to discount the theory that the overriding concern for delegates was to find a leader who could help the party win. Certainly their motives for choosing Stanfield seem to have had little to do with his perceived ability as a vote-winner.

On balance, the evidence we have seen suggests patronage motives were not a primary factor in the choices of delegates. How is this to be explained?

One part of the explanation would appear to lie in the party's long experience without office. The fact that a party does not hold office and seems to have relatively little prospect for achieving it will be a deterrent to participation for those people who seek party roles for patronage reasons. This is a point with which I will deal more extensively later.

Another part of the explanation is probably the fact that most delegates are relatively remote from the centre of politics in the party. This can be understood in two senses. First, a majority of the delegates have relatively little involvement in party affairs generally. Their participation is as occasional activists at the provincial or constituency levels. They are, therefore, less likely to place value on outcomes in terms of patronage benefits than a person whose whole career is bound up with his party role. Second, if the party does win office, most delegates have less to gain than the central participants. The potential spoils for a person at the periphery are a good deal less substantial than those available to people at the centre.

There is some evidence to test this interpretation from answers to questions which measured the delegates' involvement in the convention and the extent to which they perceived participation in the party to have career and financial costs or benefits. Table 27 shows that the more active the role assumed by the delegate in the convention conflict, the more likely he was to perceive party work to have material costs and benefits. It was also found that the more active the delegate's role, the more likely he was to give a patronage reason.

Although the extent to which delegates may act from patronage motives appears to be related in this way to the degree of their involvement in the convention, it should be noted that, at each level of involvement, the number of delegates giving a patronage reason was a good deal less than half. Among all delegates—regardless of their proximity to the centre of the conflict—patronage reasons were mentioned much less frequently than those of the other two types.

Table 27 **Measures of personal costs and benefits from participation in the party by degree of involvement in the convention**

Degree of involvement	Percentage who perceived costs and benefits from participation in active party role		
	Financial costs and benefits	Career costs and benefits	(N)
Was a member of a candidate's organization	34	19	(287)
Supported a candidate without being a member of his organization	23	16	(496)
Did not engage in any activity to support a candidate	17	12	(308)

THE NATURE OF POLICY CLEAVAGES

In discussing the significance of policy motives in delegate behaviour, I did not deal with the nature of the issues that divided delegates. Two questions are particularly important in this regard: to what extent did issue cleavages reflect ideological differences among the delegates and to what extent did they reflect disagreement at the affective level?

If there were ideological differences of the conventionally understood "left/right" type one might expect some consistency in delegate attitudes on the issue statements relating to government interference with business, government planning of the economy, welfare spending, the adoption of medicare, trade unions, and communism. In fact, not one pair of statements within this set was strongly associated (using the statistic Yule's Q).[7] This does not mean there were not some delegates who had consistent "left" or "right" positions from issue to issue, but it does mean that such "left/right" distinctions did not constitute a substantial basis of differentiation among the delegates considered as a whole.

Analysis of the relationships among responses to all thirty-two of the issue statements about which the delegates were asked to express their opinions shows there were only eleven out of 496 possible pairs of correlations in which responses were strongly associated. It appears, therefore, that there were few delegates whose attitudes were linked by underlying general properties. That is, within the context of the range of issues discussed within the party at that time, opinion was characterized by pragmatic rather than ideological differences.

The only linkages which involved more than one pair of statements consisted of those among attitudes on the statements related to French-Canadian rights and the position of Quebec in Confederation. On the four questions which dealt with these subjects there was a tendency for attitudes to separate into consistent positions on a dimension which might be called sympathy for French-Canadian claims to special recognition. (See table 28.)

The analysis of social cleavages in chapter 7 suggested that to the extent that there were policy cleavages in delegate behaviour they would involve issues of this kind. Measures of the association between issue positions and voting choices show this was substantially correct. It was noted earlier in this chapter that out of thirty-two issue statements, there were only twelve which were associated with voting choices on the first ballot at a statistically significant level. Of these, five were issues relating to cultural cleavages and four were issues relating to regional and/or federal/provincial institutional cleavages. (See table 29.) The others were "wealthy people have too much say in politics," "more government planning is needed to develop the Canadian economy," and "farmers should have more say in determining the policy of the Conservative party."

The significance of the statements about the influence of "wealthy people" and the need for "more government planning" suggests some delegates did make choices from "left/right" dispositions. However, examination of the distribution of votes on these issues indicates the number of delegates acting in this way was probably very small. Indeed, the basis of the association lay primarily in the lack of support for McCutcheon's candidacy among people who took the "left" position on these issues. This evidence is consistent with the explanation suggested for the role of policy motives in the behaviour of leading participants. It was suggested in that case that the "ideological" stances of McCutcheon and Hamilton were less important in attracting support than in repelling it. That is, the leading participants were unwilling to support a candidate who took an extremist position. McCutcheon's lack of support among people who took the "left" or, more accurately, the "non-right" position would appear to be a manifestation of the same disposition.

REGIONALISM

As table 29 shows, 35 percent of the delegates gave as a reason for voting for a candidate the statement "He understands my part of the country better." There is no way to determine from the statement itself the under-

Table 28 **Distribution of the delegates on eleven groups of issue statements associated at the .6 level or better using Yule's Q**

	Percentage whose responses were				
	Positive	Negative	Inconsistent	Percentage who did not answer or expressed no opinion	Yule's Q[a]
Support for the British connection (Questions 12 and 23)	49	18	18	15	.85
Support for special status for Quebec (Questions 1 and 27)	39	24	27	9	.89
Support for special language rights for French Canadians (Questions 15 and 30)	33	25	31	11	.63
Support for special attention to Quebec demands and special privileges for French Canadians (Questions 27 and 30)	40	24	28	8	.86

Support for special status for Quebec and language rights for French Canadians (Questions 1 and 15)	32	26	30	12	.66
Support for special status for Quebec and special privileges for French Canadians (Questions 1 and 30)	31	40	20	9	.85
Support for French-Canadian language rights and special attention to Quebec demads (Questions 15 and 27)	46	16	26	12	.63
Support for strengthening of provincial governments (Questions 7 and 18)	26	21	30	23	.70
Perceive Communism as threat (Questions 10 and 17)	19	34	28	19	.72
Support for measures to control American influence in Canada (Questions 16 and 25)	39	19	26	16	.62
Support for farmers (Questions 5 and 26)	24	13	39	25	.69

(a) This statistic is explained in note 3 to this chapter.

Table 29 **Distribution of first ballot vote choices of delegates, differentiated by agreement or disagreement with the issue statements associated with voting preferences at the .001 level of significance using chi square**

		Percentage who voted for								
		Diefen-baker	Fleming	Fulton	Hamilton	Hees	Mc-Cutcheon	Roblin	Stan-field	N
Quebec's position in Confederation should receive special recognition	Agree	6	5	18	3	14	8	19	27	445
	Disagree	19	4	14	8	11	8	14	23	535
We should pay no special attention to the demand of Quebec	Agree	20	5	12	8	13	7	12	23	283
	Disagree	9	5	18	5	12	8	18	26	687
French Canadians should have no more privileges than other ethnic groups	Agree	18	4	12	7	11	8	14	27	535
	Disagree	7	5	21	5	13	7	20	23	459
Provincial governments should have more power	Agree	7	7	15	3	17	9	20	22	340
	Disagree	15	4	17	7	9	7	15	26	600
Canada needs a strong central government	Agree	14	5	15	6	12	7	15	26	896
	Disagree	3	9	18	6	11	12	25	16	105

More federal government money should be used to develop the economies of the poorer provinces	Agree	13	5	16	6	11	7	16	27	876
	Disagree	7	6	15	5	16	19	19	14	88
Central Canada has too much say in Canadian politics	Agree	17	2	16	8	6	5	16	30	362
	Disagree	10	7	16	5	17	9	17	20	550
The Commonwealth connection is no longer important for Canada	Agree	9	7	17	4	17	7	21	19	260
	Disagree	15	4	15	6	10	10	15	26	700
The monarchy is an essential part of the Canadian constitution	Agree	17	5	14	7	10	8	14	26	594
	Disagree	6	6	20	2	14	7	22	23	329
Wealthy people have too much say in politics	Agree	14	6	16	8	13	3	18	22	353
	Disagree	12	5	16	4	12	10	16	26	558
More government is needed to develop the Canadian economy	Agree	13	5	16	6	12	6	16	27	747
	Disagree	11	3	19	6	12	14	16	18	225
Farmers should have more say in determining the policy of the Conservative party	Agree	22	5	11	7	14	5	18	19	275
	Disagree	9	5	19	5	11	8	17	26	577
All delegates		12	5	15	6	12	8	16	24	1042

lying motivational basis of this explanation. However, there is good reason to assume its importance, given the regional cleavages in voting behaviour identified in chapter 7. Regional ties were clearly a significant factor in delegate voting behaviour.

The nature of the issues about which the delegates disagreed and which were associated at a significant level with delegate voting behaviour indicates one dimension of this factor. The main line of issue cleavage was between Quebec delegates and delegates from the other provinces. This pattern appeared (with some individual variations among the other provinces) in responses to the questions dealing with French-Canadian rights, special status for Quebec, increasing the power of provincial governments (which was related to the principle of special status), the importance of Canadian ties to the monarchy and Commonwealth, and resistance to American cultural penetration of Canada. There were also some regional variations, although in differing patterns, in the distribution of opinion on the other issues significantly associated with voting choice.

A second factor which influenced the regional distribution of the vote, as we might expect, was control of a provincial party. Sixty-eight percent of the delegates from Saskatchewan, 65 percent of the delegates from Nova Scotia, and 58 percent of the delegates from Manitoba—compared to 35 percent for the whole sample—mentioned at least one patronage reason in accounting for their first ballot choices.

A third factor was the affective response of delegates to native-son candidates in provinces where such candidates had had a long established provincial role—that is, Stanfield in Nova Scotia, Roblin in Manitoba, and Fulton (still nominally the provincial leader) in British Columbia. Among voters for each of these candidates in their own provinces more than 60 percent gave *three* or more affective reasons, compared to a sample average (giving three or more affective reasons) of 19 percent. The explanation for this probably lies in the formation of affective ties which normally results from extended participation in cooperative activity.

Each of these three variables—provincial differences in attitudes on particular issues, the control of provincial resources, and affective responses to native-son candidates—can account for some but not all of the provincial variations in support. Among other things, they do not account for the strong regional pattern in the voting choices of delegates on the fifth ballot. In this regard, it is particularly interesting to note that *not one issue was significantly associated with voting choices on the fifth ballot*. Stanfield and Roblin attracted support in roughly the same proportions on both sides of all the issues.

There is apparently a residual effect in the distribution of the vote which inheres in the fact of provincial cleavage itself. A similar effect has been observed in attitudes on dimensions of political culture in studies of mass opinion in Canada. Regionalism appears to embrace a dimension which is independent of the cumulative effect of obvious causal variables. It would seem reasonable to suppose that this relates to attachments to community as such. These attachments operate in political choice through feelings of affinity for other people from the same community or, in this case, for other people from the same province or region.

SUMMARY AND CONCLUSIONS

In this chapter, the motivational factors in delegate behaviour at the 1967 convention have been examined through an analysis of the reasons the delegates gave for their voting choices. The fact that most of the delegates mentioned several reasons for their choices emphasizes the complexities of analysis using the concept of motivation. The interpretation of the data considered in this chapter must be viewed in this context.

The main points of the analysis may be summarized as follows.

1. Policy motives were more important in the behaviour of delegates than in the behaviour of leading participants. The behaviour of about 38 percent of the delegates was found to be consistent with a policy motive.

2. Most delegates gave explanations which emphasized affective responses to the personalities of candidates. This kind of explanation was mentioned by 77 percent of the delegates. The number who mentioned two or more reasons of this kind was 49 percent and the number who mentioned three or more was 19 percent.

3. Patronage reasons were mentioned by smaller numbers of delegates than were either affective or policy reasons.

4. The vote-winning ability of the candidates, although mentioned by 44 percent of the delegates, actually did not appear to be the decisive factor for very many of them. This seemed to support the finding that patronage motives were not a significant factor in the choices of most of the delegates.

5. Some evidence was presented to support the proposition that the extent to which delegates were patronage-motivated was related to the degree of their involvement in the convention: the more active the delegate, the more likely he was to express a patronage motive.

6. Analysis of the issue positions of the delegates and the relationships between their issue positions and their voting choices suggested four points: (*a*) As anticipated from observations about the nature of the social structure of the convention, differences on socio-economic issues were not related to one another in ideologically distinctive patterns. (*b*) However, there was one piece of evidence which seemed to be consistent with the argument made earlier in respect to leading participants that

there was some aversion to McCutcheon because of his overtly "ideological" stance. (*c*) Of the twelve (out of thirty-two) issue statements on which delegate opinion was significantly associated with voting choice on the first ballot, only three touched on socio-economic questions. (*d*) And, the issues which were most strongly associated with voting choice were those related to the historical cleavages within the party on the dimensions of cultural identity.

7. There was additional evidence to support the finding in chapter 7 that regional ties were an important factor in delegate behaviour.

8. Part of the effect of regional ties is to be explained by regional differences in policy views, part by the patronage linkages within provincial parties, and part by affective feelings for native-son candidates. But there is still a substantial residual effect which can only be explained by some attachment to provinces and/or regions as such.

Ideological Cleavage: Delegate Opinion at the 1976 Convention

Popular explanations for the outcome of the convention which chose Robert Stanfield's successor in February 1976, with few exceptions, emphasized the effects of ideological cleavages within the party. Joe Clark, who won a narrow victory over Claude Wagner on the fourth ballot, was commonly said to have had the support of the party's "left," "red tory," "progressive," or "moderate" wing, while Wagner was said to have had the support of its "right" or "conservative" wing.

There had been considerable public discussion of party doctrine in the months following Stanfield's announcement of his intention to resign. A vocal minority in caucus, seeking to explain the party's lack of success under Stanfield, challenged the direction in which he had led the party, arguing that the party needed to "return to true conservative" principles. In the spring of 1975, a caucus group calling itself the Chateau Cabinet met to draft a manifesto which could be used as a basis for creating a "conservative" bloc to influence the selection of the new leader.[1] Under pressure from Stanfield the Chateau Cabinet disbanded, but its attempt to organize drew attention to elite-level concern with the question of doctrine.

This question figured prominently in press accounts of the campaign for the leadership. The party was widely portrayed as being polarized between a "progressive," "red tory," or "moderate" left wing and a "conservative" right wing. Out of eleven candidates whose names appeared on the first ballot, seven—Clark, John Fraser, James Gillies, Heward Grafftey, Flora MacDonald, Brian Mulroney, and Pat Nowlan—were usually said to be on the left, and four—Paul Hellyer, Jack Horner,

Sinclair Stevens, and Wagner—were usually said to be on the right. In their campaign literature only three of the candidates—MacDonald, Horner, and Stevens—openly sought ideological identification, but during the campaign all were forced to deal with questions about where they stood ideologically.

In earlier chapters we found little evidence to substantiate the thesis that conflict within the party is the result of ideological cleavage—at least in the sense that ideological cleavage refers to systematic differences about principles of social, economic, or political organization. However, conflict within the party has frequently been described in these terms. Thus, it may be that the patterns we have observed are not typical and that under other circumstances, differences of this kind do have a role in the politics of the party. To explore this question further a survey was conducted among delegates to the 1976 convention. The survey does not permit an analysis of behaviour at the convention because it was conducted before the balloting, but it does provide data which can be used to analyse the extent and nature of ideological differences among the delegates.

Data from the survey show many delegates—at least when they are asked to do so—locate themselves in the party with ideological labels. Nineteen percent placed themselves on the left, 37 percent placed themselves in the centre, and 42 percent placed themselves on the right.[2]

This form of self-labelling does not in itself demonstrate a polarized party. Such an inference would depend on the distance the delegates perceived between the left and the right. Thus, delegates were asked questions about the extent of the differences between the party's left and right wings. While only 7 percent said that they believed the differences between the left and right are so great that they cannot be reconciled, a substantial minority of the delegates (47 percent) did see big differences between the left and right. In addition, there is evidence that ideological self-identification was related to behaviour at the convention. In data from a small sample gathered in a mail survey after the convention, Robert Krause and Lawrence LeDuc found a significant association between ideological self-identification on a left-right scale and voting choice on both the first and last ballots.[3] It would appear then that ideological differences expressed in these terms do have a bearing on the politics of the party.

ISSUES AND IDEOLOGY

Of course, the use of ideological symbols to describe differences does not demonstrate ideological cleavage. True ideological cleavage lies in the substance of opinion. Thus, to assess the significance of this evidence we

Table 30 **Percentage of 1976 delegates by ideological self-identification agreeing to or approving certain issue positions**

	Left	Centre	Right	All
Quebec's position in Confederation should receive special recognition	45	37	20*	30
French-speaking Canadians outside Quebec should be able to use French when they deal with their own governments	81	70	60*	67
Approve of the present policy for making the federal public service bilingual	45	37	19*	30
Approve of the principle of official bilingualism	85	86	72*	80
The monarchy is an essential part of the Canadian constitution	53	57	72*	64
The workers' right to strike should not be restricted	25	18	18	19
There should be laws to bring big unions under closer control	83	90	90	88
There should be laws to bring big corporations under closer control	77	61	46*	57
There are some cases in which government ownership in the economy is more desirable than private ownership	85	69	59*	68
There is too much government ownership in the Canadian economy today	46	71	83*	70
Government ought to interfere less with business	51	76	91*	77
We must promote economic efficiency even if that means more small businesses will be replaced by large corporations	21	32	24	26
Agricultural policy should ensure the preservation of the family farm—even at the cost of some economic inefficiency	68	64	74	69
Approve of the present policy of wage and price controls	17	17	17	17
Approve of the principle of wage and price controls	85	75	74*	75
The principle of a guaranteed annual income is wrong	30	48	60*	50

Table 30 *continued*	Left	Centre	Right	All
Social security programs (like old age pensions and family allowances) should be based on family income needs, and people who don't need this kind of assistance should not receive it	89	87	87	88
Canada should take steps to bring its foreign policy closely into line with that of the United States	18	33	39*	32
Canada should seek closer relations with Communist countries	43	27	17*	26
Canada's independence is threatened by the large percentage of foreign ownership in key sectors of our economy	78	53	48*	54
We must ensure an independent Canada even if that were to mean a lower standard of living for Canadians	68	52	56	57
Canada should have freer trade with the United States	51	61	74*	65
Generally favour lowering tariffs	35	46	54*	48
The federal government should give a bigger share of its tax revenues to the provincial governments	73	69	73	71
Provincial governments should have more power	66	63	62	63
Legislation which interferes with basic rights, like the special legislation in 1970 to deal with the FLQ, should be adopted only in wartime	64	53	57	57
Some restrictions on civil rights would be acceptable if it would help police reduce crime	47	64	65*	60
Approve of capital punishment	31	59	82*	64
Approve of abortion	62	55	63	61
N =	(150)	(311)	(341)	(802)

*Chi square significant at .001

need to ask to what extent and how the opinions of people who place themselves on the left and right actually differ.

Table 30 shows the percentage of delegates calling themselves left, right, and centre who agreed with each issue in a list of statements based on issues raised during the convention campaign. There were statistically significant relationships between ideological self-identification and opinion on eighteen out of the twenty-nine statements. But, on all but four statements, a majority of delegates on both the left and right took the same position—that is, for all but these four statements the balance of opinion in the party was the same regardless of where the delegates placed themselves on the ideological scale. The four statements on which the prevailing opinion among delegates of the left and right differed were those related to the principle of a guaranteed income, the desirability of imposing controls on big corporations, capital punishment, and the principle of free trade.

A further analysis was done to look for ideological cleavages in the distribution of opinion from issue to issue. It was assumed that if delegates' attitudes were structured ideologically, they would take consistent positions across a number of issues. But the linkages from issue to issue were relatively weak. The strongest association between any one pair of statements was at a level of $\pm.38$ and there were no clusters of three or more statements in which the association was stronger than $\pm.30$. The most interesting result, in terms of our concern with ideology, is the small number of associations between statements which could be construed to have some implication related to government intervention in the economy.[4] Out of twenty-eight possible pairs of correlations between statements of this kind, there were only six that were associated at a statistically significant level and the strongest association was only .28. The number of delegates who took wholly consistent interventionist or non-interventionist positions across all eight of these statements is less than 3 percent of the sample. The number who took wholly consistent positions, but did not express an opinion on some statements, is less than 2 percent. Even if one takes into account these delegates who gave one or more responses consistent with a predominant interventionist or non-interventionist position, the number who could be said to have adopted issue positions reflecting an ideological stance was barely one-third of the total sample. Thus most delegates appeared to respond to these issue statements not in terms of a rigid interventionist or non-interventionist view of the role of government, but in terms of a pragmatic orientation that leads to policy choices on a case by case basis.

To get a clearer picture of the structure of delegate opinion and its relationship to ideological self-identification, groups of issue statements were selected to reflect attitudes on a number of different dimensions. The selection consisted of statements which had been designed to express the essential idea or principle on each dimension. Thus, for the dimension of economic liberalism, only two statements were used—one dealing with the principle of government ownership in the economy and the other with the principle of wage and price controls. Altogether, six dimensions

Table 31 **Percentages of 1976 convention delegates giving consistent or predominant interventionist and non-interventionist responses on issue statements related to the role of government in the economy**[a]

Gave an interventionist response to every question	1.0
Gave consistent interventionist responses but did not express an opinion on some questions	0.4
Gave predominant interventionist[b] responses	8.5
Gave predominant non-interventionist[b] responses	20.5
Gave consistent non-interventionist responses but did not express an opinion on some questions	1.1
Gave a non-interventionist response to every question	1.2
Took no clear interventionist or non-interventionist position	67.3
	(N = 829)

(a) For a list of the questions used see note 4 to this chapter.

(b) A person was said to have taken a predominant interventionist or non-interventionist position on the following basis: if he answered four questions the ratio was 3:1; if he answered five questions the ratio was 4:1; if he answered six or more questions the ratio was 4:2 or greater.

Table 32 **Associations between ideological self-identification and six selected issue dimensions**

	Chi Square	V
Attitudes toward French Canada	0.0000	0.18
Economical liberalism	0.0000	0.22
Attitudes toward big business	0.0002	0.12
Attitudes toward decentralization in the federal system	0.0075	0.12
Political liberalism	0.0011	0.11
Economic nationalism	0.1065	0.09

were identified: economic liberalism, attitudes toward big business, economic nationalism, attitudes toward French Canada, political liberalism, and attitudes toward the distribution of authority within the federal system. Opinion on five of these dimensions was found to have some association with ideological self-identification. The exceptions were attitudes toward the distribution of authority within the federal system and economic nationalism. The strongest association was with economic liberalism (V = .22) and the weakest with political liberalism (V = .11).

A test was also conducted to look for linkages in opinion from dimension to dimension. As might be expected from the test for individual issues, few such linkages were found and those that did exist were very weak. Out of fifteen possible pairs of correlations, only three were associated at a significant level. (These were economic liberalism and attitudes toward French Canada, economic liberalism and economic nationalism, and economic nationalism and attitudes toward big business.) Therefore, although each dimension has some association with ideological self-identification, the associations are pretty well independent of one another. In sum, it would appear that to the extent that ideological self-identification has issue content, the kinds of issues which determine the choice of a delegate's ideological position vary from delegate to delegate.

THE MEANING OF IDEOLOGICAL SYMBOLS

This analysis has shown that for a large proportion of the party membership, ideological symbols have limited and varying issue content. Yet they are used and they have some relationship to behaviour. Three explanations may be suggested.

First, most people seek an orientation to the political world by devising short-hand terms for translating into meaningful form the multiplicity of messages they receive. Thus, in the literature on voting behaviour it has been observed that many members of the mass electorate become party identifiers—that is, they develop attachments to parties which endure through time, providing an element of constancy in their orientation to electoral competition. In internal party politics, where there are no formal structures like parties with clear identifying symbols, ideological labels are the only generalized symbols that have permanence and can perform this function. Therefore, we may hypothesize that party members develop an ideological identification in the same way that members of the electorate develop a party identification—as a means to sort out the messages that are transmitted in internal party conflicts. Their ideological identification orients them to each episode of conflict, helping them to recognize friends and rivals and to choose which side to support.

Second, ideological identification may be adopted as a means of giving legitimacy to behaviour rooted in causes that are not easily explained or lack moral approval. Any form of factional activity in a party is gener-

Table 33 **Tests of association between positions on selected issue dimensions**

	Attitudes toward French Canadians	Economic liberalism	Decentralization of federal system	Attitudes toward big business	Political liberalism	Economic nationalism
Attitudes toward French Canadians	—	.12[a] .001[b]	.07 .034	.06 .586	.05 .278	.04 .480
Economic liberalism		—	.07 .12	.08 .088	.09 .052	.13 .001
Decentralization of federal system			—	.14 .001	.03 .739	.04 .618
Attitudes toward big business				—	.07 .357	.14 .001
Political liberalism					—	.08 .050
Economic nationalism						—

(a) Test of strength of association using Cramer's V.
(b) Test of significance using Chi square.

ally disapproved. It is placed on the most defensible ground when it can be said to serve a matter of principle. By explaining one's dissent in terms of ideological disagreement, one can give it moral justification. This should not be seen to be entirely a manipulative tactic. A person may well need to adopt this form of expression to explain to himself motives which he does not fully understand or is subconsciously unsure of.

Third, ideological symbols have been used in the party to express attitudes which relate to political style. This point was made in chapter 6 in reference to O'Sullivan's comment that part of the difference between conservatives and progressives in the party was that the former used an approach to politics which was "more in touch with people," while the latter were technocrats. Joe Hueglin, a member of Parliament defeated in 1974, made a similar distinction in a letter to delegates during the 1976 leadership campaign:

> The left-wingers are, for the present, giving lip-service to the conservative virtues of encouraging the individual initiative, reducing government intervention in the economy, and demanding a strict accounting from those individuals who seek to abuse society for their own selfish, and often harmful, purposes. That these Red Tories are well organized and that they have the support of power brokers in every region, forming an interlocking directorship, is apparent. It is for them that the advance men from the machine are working. . . . Once in power they will drop their conservative facade, revert to their basic philosophy and their reliance on special advisers. A politics of people rather than of power must prevail . . .
>
> IN 1957 AND 1958 PEOPLE BASED POLITICS SUCCEEDED . . .
>
> As you stand in line to cast your ballot on the 22nd, please consider this:
>
> IF ONE OF THE POWER GROUP CANDIDATES EMERGES THE WINNER, WHAT ROLL [sic] WILL YOU OR I OR THE REST OF THE CONSTITUENCY DELEGATES PLAY IN DECIDING THE FUTURE OF OUR PARTY FROM THAT POINT ONWARD?[5]

It was argued in earlier chapters that the kind of anti-elite feelings expressed in Hueglin's letter were an important factor in conflicts during the tenure of both Diefenbaker and Stanfield. Their feelings were said to reflect the alienation of party members whose social characteristics placed them outside the centres of power and influence in the country. Thus, if similar feelings were finding expression as right-wing identification throughout the party, we would expect an association between right-wing identification and social distance from the national establishment among delegates interviewed in 1976. Although right-wing identification is fairly strong among all delegates, regardless of their location on the social distance scale, there is, in fact, a marked tendency for it to increase as the number of establishment social characteristics declines. The percentage of delegates who place themselves on the right is smallest (31 percent) among those who are closest to the national elite and largest (57 percent) among those who are most remote from the national elite.

POPULISM AS A SOURCE OF STRESS IN THE PARTY

A recurring theme in this study has been the role in the politics of the party of the alienation of social outsiders. It is clear that at least during the period with which we are concerned this factor has constituted a persistent source of stress on party unity. Diefenbaker's success in mobilizing this alienation has been ascribed to his populist political style. In fact, it appears that Diefenbaker captured and gave expression to a latent populist sentiment which is an enduring basis of cleavage in the party.

"The populist syndrome," as the British sociologist Peter Worsley has pointed out, "is much wider than its particular manifestation in the form or context of any particular policy, or of any particular class of polity . . . (P)opulism is better regarded as an emphasis, a dimension of political culture in general, not simply as a particular kind of overall ideological system or type of organization."[6] Adapting the definition of another sociologist, Edward Shils, Worsley sees the central idea in populism as an emphasis on "the supremacy of the will of the people over every other standard, over the standards of traditional institutions and over the will of other strata" and on "the desirability of a 'direct' relationship between people and leadership, unmediated by institutions."[7] This definition accords very well with what we have seen of Diefenbaker's approach to politics. It is consistent as well with O'Sullivan's description of the difference between conservatives and progressives in the party.

In making the point that populist ideas can be found on either the left or the right, Worsley provides a basis for explaining the apparent anomaly that, early in his career, Diefenbaker's supporters thought of him as a progressive, while during the Stanfield period he became identified with the party's right wing. The apparent shift in the ideological identification of Diefenbaker's supporters from left to right is perfectly consistent with the nature of populism and can be seen to be a response to changes in Canadian society. In 1957 Diefenbaker's government could be called progressive because it was an activist government that used the power of the state to undertake measures serving the interests of his social constituency—measures which included increases in social security benefits that directly aided the lower middle class, the symbolic opening of elite roles to minority ethnic groups, programs to rehabilitate rural areas, and transfers of tax revenues and capital to assist the weaker provinces. In the decade between 1957 and 1967, there was a continued extension of welfare state measures which had the effect of providing assistance to the middle as well as to the lower class. The concluding pieces of legislation were enacted under the Liberal administration of Lester Pearson: a national retirement pension plan and a national medicare plan. While this legislation benefited the middle class, one of its by-products was a very substantial increase in the size of public bureaucracies and in the proportion of national income controlled by government. In addition, the Trudeau government continued to expand the scope of government activity. Public assistance to poverty groups to help them organize more effectively, a broad liberalization of unemployment insurance benefits, the creation of make-work programs such as Local Initiatives and Opportunities for Youth, and the commitment to official bilingualism constituted an extension of the state role which became increasingly threatening to middle income groups, farmers, rural and small-town dwellers, and

Table 34 **Percentages of 1967, 1971, and 1976 delegates expressing agreement with selected issue positions**

	Percentage who agreed in[a]		
	1967	1971	1976
Provincial governments should have more power	32	45	63
Government ought to interfere less with business	61	69	77
The principle of a guaranteed annual income is wrong	—	39	50
Old age pensions and family allowances should only be paid to people who need them[b]	66	—	88
Legislation which interferes with basic rights, like the special legislation to deal with FLQ in 1970, should only be adopted in wartime	—	47	57
N =	(1091)	(551)	(829)

(a) — indicates that the question was not asked in that year.

(b) The wording, as an inspection of earlier tables will show, was slightly different in 1967 and 1976.

people in the hinterland provinces. Government intervention became less popular. It ceased to be identified with outputs that conferred benefits and became instead synonymous with increases in taxation, encroaching bureaucracy, the depersonalization of politics, technocratic decision-making, and the growing remoteness of political elites. In response to these changes, populism in the party took a new direction, adopting a more conservative view of the role of government in the economy and society.

This shift in the ideological identification of populists within the party was not manifest in conflict over social and economic policy because the change it involved coincided with the views of most other members of the party, including those whose social characteristics connected them to the national establishment. There are indications of this change in the distribution of opinion among delegates to the 1967 convention, 1971 annual meeting, and 1976 convention. Table 34 shows a general movement in the party toward a more conservative view of government's role. For example, over the three surveys, increasingly larger numbers of delegates agreed with the statement that "government ought to interfere less with business"; between 1971 and 1976 the number opposing the concept of a guaranteed annual income increased from 39 percent to 50 percent; and between 1967 and 1976 opposition to the principle of universality in social security programs increased from 66 percent to 88 percent. Some of the opposition to the growth of the federal government may also be reflected in the increasing percentages of delegates who expressed support for the proposal to shift power to the provincial governments. This figure grew from 32 percent in 1967 to 63 percent in 1976. The general shift in the party is expressed as well in the fact most members of caucus interviewed in 1973 and 1974—regardless of their backgrounds and self-described ideological positions—when asked what distinguished the Conservative party from the Liberal party drew attention to what several of them described as "Liberal statism." Even those members who proposed a guaranteed income program argued the merit of their proposal on the ground that it would reduce costs and eliminate bureaucracy by absorbing and consolidating existing programs.

It was argued in chapter 6 that the behaviour of social outsiders who rebelled against Stanfield's leadership lacked any positive orientation. It took the form of opposition to those in the party who appeared to be connected to the national establishment and to policy which appeared to favour or advance the claims of French Canadians. Two pieces of evidence suggest this is characteristic of many social outsiders at all levels of the party. First, among delegates who said they thought of themselves as belonging to "a Diefenbaker group" within the party, the feeling of hostility toward the party elite—as symbolized by Camp—appears to have been stronger than any positive feeling toward Diefenbaker. Only

36 percent of these delegates said they would be influenced to support one of the leadership candidates if that candidate had Diefenbaker's endorsement while 47 percent said they would be likely to oppose a candidate if that candidate had Camp's endorsement. Second, the social outsiders were the delegates most likely to be hostile toward French Canadians. As table 35 shows, the percentages of delegates with anti-Quebec or anti-French opinions increased in direct proportion to their social distance from the national establishment. In fact, with the exception of a statement related to the growth of big corporations at the expense of small business, the only issue statements significantly associated with the social distance scale were those related to the French-English cleavage.

Not all members of the party elite who adopt the populist style share this negative outlook. There are some who have tried to mobilize social

Table 35 **Percentages of 1976 delegates agreeing with selected issue positions[a] by their location on a scale of establishment social characteristics**

	Number of establishment social characteristics				
	4	3	2	1	0
Quebec's position in Confederation should receive special recognition	46	32	33	23	16
French-speaking Canadians outside Quebec should be able to use French in dealing with their own governments	79	63	75	63	48
Approve of the present policy for making the federal public service bilingual	51	30	35	24	11
Approve of the principle of official bilingualism	89	87	80	71	63
The monarchy is an essential part of the Canadian constitution	48	61	60	72	74
We must promote economic efficiency even if that means more small businesses will be replaced by big corporations	42	26	23	26	16
N =	(106)	(226)	(263)	(164)	(70)

(a) The issues chosen were those for which chi square was significant at .001.

outsiders with a more positive approach. In fact, in the competition for the leadership at the 1976 convention, it was this strain of populism that was most clearly identifiable—being represented in the candidacy of Flora MacDonald. MacDonald's speeches emphasized the importance of creating a mechanism for making the political process more participatory and her campaign was designed to exemplify this goal. Jack Horner came closest to representing the "negativist" outlook. Despite a more muted approach during the campaign, his record as an opponent of official languages policy was well known and he had been the leading spokesman of the anti-Camp (anti-establishment) elements in caucus. It would be wrong to equate this "negativist" outlook with the "conservative" turn of populism in the party because even populists with MacDonald's views share the consensual concern about the growth of government. The fact that MacDonald called herself a red tory and Horner placed himself on the party's right has to be viewed in the light of the fact that analysis of their published statements during the campaign reveals no discernible difference in their general opinions of the role of the state in the economy. In fact, they publicly disagreed on only one issue of social or economic policy: the proposal for the guaranteed income.

CONSENSUS AND CLEAVAGE

A major concern of this study is to determine the extent to which conflict in the party may be ascribed to enduring cleavages so deeply felt that they are inherently resistant to accommodation. Of particular interest in the context of this chapter is the extent to which the party is divided ideologically. Given that the prevailing ideology in the party endorses the welfare state and a mixed economy, we can measure the extent of ideological cleavage by looking at the number of delegates who adopted the economic liberal position of opposition to government intervention. Across the set of issues that could be related to this dimension, only 3 percent of the delegates took a wholly consistent non-interventionist position. Including those who gave some interventionist responses but took a predominantly non-interventionist position, the total of non-interventionists was 23 percent of the sample. Although there was a larger percentage of economic liberal responses on some individual questions, this figure would appear to constitute a reasonable estimate of the number of delegates who were potential ideological dissenters.

It is more difficult to estimate the extent of cleavage on the dimension reflected by the appeal of populism because we have no data which directly relate to the dispositions that populism mobilizes. We have assumed that such dispositions would be strongest among people whose characteristics placed them at the remote end of the social distance scale, but a person might feel himself an outsider even if he possessed only one of the characteristics that placed him outside the elite. Given Diefenbaker's role as the symbol of social outsiders, we might assume that identification with the Diefenbaker faction was one indicator which would compensate for this weakness in the social distance scale. This, too, is a rather crude measure, but it is the only other one available. Moreover, it certainly has validity as a measure of the number of delegates who thought of themselves as outsiders in the context of the politics of the party. The number of delegates—across all divisions on the social distance scale—who described themselves as members of "the Diefenbaker group in the party" was 15 percent of the total sample.

It has been argued that attitudes of hostility toward French Canadians are closely related to feelings of status insecurity. However, these attitudes may arise from other causes, in particular from the affective dispositions created through socialization in a political environment in which linguistic conflict has been a persistent feature. Therefore, attitudes on this dimension should be treated as a third, at least partly, independent form of enduring cleavage. As an indicator of the intensity of cleavage on this dimension, we can look at the number of delegates who took a negative stance on every issue statement involving some expression of sympathy for French Canadians. These delegates also constitute a fairly small proportion of the sample—about 15 percent of the whole group and 20 percent of the anglophone delegates.

All of these data point to the conclusion that, in the long term, it is a relatively small minority which is likely to feel so intensely on any cleavage as to resist accommodation with the majority. This suggests that party discipline is accepted by a large preponderance of the party's membership. This conclusion is supported by responses to a question which asked delegates what they would do if the party chose a leader whose policies or personality they strongly disliked. Eighty-one percent said they would continue working for the party.

If party unity is made vulnerable by a relatively small minority, it is nonetheless a problem—as Stanfield's successor, Joe Clark, has discovered. Clark has found the party as fractious and undisciplined as at any time in the past. Within a few months of his succession—even while the party held a commanding advantage in public opinion polls—his authority had been challenged and there were recurring challenges during the period leading up to the annual meeting in November 1977. Before the annual meeting there was speculation in the press that he might be overthrown. This speculation proved to be unfounded, but it seemed to demonstrate the extent to which the party's past has created expectations that may transform what in another party would probably be considered trivial or passing incidents into major disruptions of party unity.

CONCLUSION

We may summarize the conclusions of this discussion as follows:

1. A majority of the delegates were prepared to identify themselves as belonging to either a left or right wing in the party—43 percent on the right and 19 percent on the left. And nearly half of the delegates said there are big differences between the party's left and right wings.

2. There are statistically significant associations between self-identification with these ideological terms and positions on a large number of issues, although on most issues the division of opinion in the party cuts across these self-described ideological distinctions.

3. Only a small proportion of the delegates take wholly consistent interventionist or non-interventionist positions on issues related to government's role in the economy and the linkages between opinions across the eight issues which had an interventionist connotation were generally weak.

4. By using issue statements that refer unambiguously to the principle of government intervention, a scale was constructed to test economic liberalism and this scale was found to be significantly, although not very strongly, associated with left/right identification. Left/right identification was found to be significantly associated with four other issue dimensions: attitudes toward big business, economic nationalism, French-English relations, and political liberalism. But the associations between all of these dimensions and left/right identification were found to be relatively independent of one another. Thus, the use of these terms cannot be identified with any comprehensive set of issue positions. Delegates evidently place themselves on the left or right for different reasons.

5. We hypothesize that ideological self-identification has the same function in internal party politics in the Conservative party that party identification has for members of the electorate. It is a perceptual screen which helps party members identify allies and opponents in internal party conflicts.

6. Ideological language is used by some party members to describe a position which reflects attitudes that we associate with populism—defined as a dimension of political culture emphasizing the participation of the people in government through a direct relationship between people and political leadership.

7. Attitudes on the social distance scale cut across most issue positions, with the principal exception of those related to attitudes toward French Canadians and Quebec. The more remote a delegate from the national Establishment, the more likely he is to express an anti-Quebec or anti-French opinion.

8. However, members of the party elite who are most closely identified with populism in the party do not all express or seek to exploit nega-

tivist sentiment. There is a reformist-populist stream in the party which seeks to deal with the social forces generating anti-elite sentiment by creating devices to increase popular participation in and control over government.

10

The Tory Syndrome

A striking characteristic of the pattern of conflict in the Progressive Conservative party is that it carries on virtually without interruption. Changes in the leadership which might be expected to bring some abatement in conflict have often had little notable effect. Few leaders have been able to secure even the short-term compliance of the party as a whole. There always seem to be some party members who are unable to make the accommodations necessary to create at least the appearance of unity. Why is this so and what does it imply for the future of the party?

LONG-TERM CLEAVAGES

Most theories of conflict in parties emphasize the effects of enduring cleavages about issues of public policy. In the case of the Conservative party, the most popular theory relying on this form of explanation is that the party is riven by ideological cleavage. Our analysis has shown that issues with obvious or possible ideological content did not contribute significantly either to the breakdown of support for Diefenbaker's leadership, to behaviour at the 1967 convention, or to the conflicts over Stanfield's leadership. Ideological cleavage may have had some impact on behaviour at the 1976 convention, but it is difficult to assess how much—both because the terms party members use to describe their ideological positions have varying meaning and because very few party members give wholly consistent responses to questions that might be inferred to have ideological content. On balance, the evidence we have considered suggests that ideology has not been as serious a source of instability in the party as some analyses have assumed.[1]

The one set of cleavages that has consistently had a disruptive effect on the party has been that involving the social and cultural differences between French and English Canadians. Whenever an issue touching on these cleavages has arisen party unity has been breached.

The Conservative party has had particular difficulty in trying to manage these cleavages because it has been the political refuge for a minority of anglophone extremists who have challenged any hint of "concession" to Quebec and asserted a "British" conception of Canadian national identity that is anathema to French Canadians. The influence of this minority grew stronger in the party with the collapse of its Quebec wing. At the same time, because of the weakness of Quebec representation in the Conservative caucus, more moderate anglophones at the elite level have been deprived of the contacts with French Canadians which might have helped them acquire a better appreciation of French-Canadian concerns.

Another source of continuing strain within the party, particularly in recent conflicts, has been the alienation of party members who belong to social groups outside the Canadian establishment. It may be debatable to what extent there is a self-conscious establishment within the party, but there is certainly a self-conscious group of outsiders. While the effect of this cleavage has been apparent in disagreements over cultural issues, it has otherwise had no consistent manifestation in debates about party policy. This, as we saw in chapter 9, reflects the nature of populism. Populism is not an ideology; it may be of the left or of the right. Populism expresses an orientation to the exercise of leadership.

It is difficult to say how far back into party history this cleavage extends, but it certainly has been a factor since Diefenbaker's first campaign for the leadership in 1942. In that campaign Diefenbaker clearly cast himself in the role of populist tribune, a role he played to the hilt thereafter. He was particularly successful because he defined his attack on elites in such generalized form that any discontented group could attach itself to him.

Diefenbaker's importance as a rallying symbol for alienated groups may be explained at least in part by the fact that he has been the only populist to achieve the leadership of one of the major parties. It is not an accident of history that it was the Conservative party in which he was successful. The Conservative party itself, when Diefenbaker won the leadership in 1956, had become a symbol for outsiders—a party of opposition which had held office for only five of the previous thirty-five years. Diefenbaker's victory in the party identified it much more clearly as the vehicle for people with anti-elite feelings.

Regional cleavages have had an effect on the politics of the party independently of their effect through the cleavage mobilized by Diefenbaker's populism. There have been substantive disagreements based on differing regional economic interests and persistent regional economic inequalities, but regional cleavage is equally the result of a widespread regional particularism in the Canadian political culture. This sentiment has a foundation in cultural distinctions among all of the provinces (not just between Quebec and the predominantly anglophone provinces) and in feelings of attachment to provincial identities which have been shaped by the more intimate relationships between provincial governments and their populations.

The tensions along these regional cleavages have been re-enforced by the institutional tensions between the caucus and the extra-parliamentary party. Representation in the caucus has rarely reflected a proportional balance of regional interests, while the institutions of the extra-parliamentary party have been deliberately designed to ensure that balance. The conflicts between the party's parliamentary and extra-parliamentary elites, therefore, have social as well as institutional causes.

Social cleavages do not always express themselves as disagreements about policy. They may have effect simply through the antipathies they create between people who belong to different groups. In fact our analysis has shown that disagreements about policy were not the most important factor in leadership politics in the Diefenbaker-Stanfield period. Party members themselves take this view when they are asked about conflict, not in terms of explaining their own motives, but in analytical terms. Thus, out of thirty-three members of Parliament interviewed in 1973 and 1974 who were asked to rank the importance of various factors as a source of instability in the caucus, only eight ranked disagreements about policy first.[2] And, as table 36 shows, delegates to the 1976 convention took a similar view when they were asked what they thought was the main cause of the conflicts between the "Diefenbaker" and "Camp" factions. Only 19 percent ascribed these conflicts exclusively to disagreements about policy and only 14 percent ascribed them to policy in conjunction with other causes.

THE ROLE OF PERSONALITY

We have just noted that even in the absence of disagreements about policy, long-term cleavages may have effect in the form of affective dispositions between people who belong to different groups. Of course, affective motives also take the form of dispositions toward personalities, and motives of this kind were another major factor in conflicts over the leadership of Diefenbaker and Stanfield.

This point is also supported by the analytical comments of party mem-

Table 36 **Percentages of 1976 convention delegates ascribing conflicts between the Diefenbaker and Camp factions to policy motives, competing ambition, and conflicts of personality[a]**

	Percentage of delegates
Conflicts of personality	28
Competing ambition	22
Disagreements about policy	19
All three	14
Don't know	17
	(N = 829)

(a) The question asked: "Do you think the disagreements between the Camp and Diefenbaker factions have been mainly the result of a conflict of personalities, mainly the result of competing ambitions, or mainly the result of disagreement about policy?"

bers themselves. Twenty out of the thirty-three members of Parliament said conflicts of personality were the most important source of instability in the caucus and 42 percent of the delegates said personality conflicts, alone or along with other factors, were the main cause of the factional cleavage between the "Diefenbaker" and "Camp" groups.

Emotional responses to personalities have had a substantial part in contributing to and perpetuating conflict throughout the entire history of the Conservative party. One reason has been the nature of the leader's role in the party. This has had an effect in at least five ways:

1. Electoral competition in federal politics has tended to stress the personalities of leaders—or teams of leaders—which has created a general disposition to relate to politics in terms of personalities.

2. The central role of leadership in federal politics—and in the party—makes the leader the potential scapegoat for every party failure.

3. The party's early success under Macdonald has established a myth of heroic leadership against which all of his successors have been judged. "The Conservatives," John R. Williams wrote in 1956, "have been searching for another Sir John A. Macdonald, and when a new leader turned out to be an ordinary mortal he was subjected to constant criticism until he was forced to resign."[3]

4. Because of the leader's role in giving symbolic representation to the party and because of the broad scope of his authority, the leader's personality dominates the party. The idiosyncratic style, attitudes, and temperament of each leader are felt in every aspect of the party's internal life.

5. The leader's exclusive right to make party policy has meant that any disagreement about policy is likely to become a direct personal challenge. The only way in which party policy can be changed is to persuade the leader to change it. Thus, any expression of dissent from existing policy tests the leader's authority.

Another factor which contributes to the emphasis on affective motives in party conflicts is the importance of social relationships in the formation of political relationships among members of the party. We have seen that friendship networks are the chief means for the development of convention organization. In addition, anecdotal accounts and some partial data on the social networks of members of Parliament suggest that there is a close congruence between social relationships and political alliances within the caucus.

The emphasis on affective motives in party conflict also reflects the importance of personality as a mobilizing agent in leadership campaigns. The "mass politics" nature of the convention process, which is dictated by the structure of the party, leads to a style of convention campaigning that emphasizes personality images.

We have observed that one way in which factionalism develops in a party is through the effect of the emotional residues of conflict: the group feelings created by one conflict become the basis for the formation of alliances in the next. It seems reasonable to argue therefore that the tendency for Conservatives to act on the basis of affective dispositions increases the likelihood of factionalism because conflict is more likely to leave emotional residues when it originated in this kind of motivation. And this is a self-regenerating process. Each time there is an episode of conflict that activates factional ties it will add to the strength of these ties. In this way, the pattern of affective interaction within the Conservative party can be seen to feed upon itself—adding a dimension to the party's internal politics which makes any enduring accommodation in conflict difficult to achieve.

THE ROLE OF PATRONAGE MOTIVES

Many of the conditions which have contributed to the high level of affective interaction in Conservative leadership politics are present in the Liberal party. The divisive effect of this element in the Conservative party has been more serious because of the party's electoral weakness. The nature of conflict in the Conservative party has been profoundly influenced by the fact that it is normally the party of opposition.

One obvious result is that it has been difficult for leaders to secure sustained support from members of the party who have very strong patronage motives. While the rewards of a place in Parliament may be sufficient to satisfy the patronage-motivation of some party members, there are others whose ambition can only be satisfied by government office or access to benefits that come from controlling government. It is particularly difficult for the leader in opposition to deal with patronage-motivated party members outside Parliament because, without the resources of government, he cannot even bestow minimal honorific benefits.

Furthermore, a party which suffers repeated defeats is likely to have fewer members whose primary motivation is for the rewards of office. The significance of this lies in the fact that, as was noted in chapter 1, the person who is patronage-motivated is more likely to be governed by rational calculations of outcomes and to suppress his emotional responses to other people in order to achieve the outcome he seeks. This person will generally be more favourably disposed to accommodation and compromise and more willing to conform to party discipline in the interests of achieving power.

There are two reasons for supposing that there will be fewer people of this kind in a party which is normally in opposition.

First, when people enter politics they will be attracted to the party which offers them the best opportunity for fulfilment of the gratifications they seek. Those whose primary motivation is for power, status, or achievement will be attracted to parties which seem to have the best chance of winning.

Second, regardless of the initial motive for activism, the experience of being close to power or not being close to power is likely to have a socializing effect. People who act habitually under conditions in which patronage motives cannot be satisfied will likely acquire a disposition to act on the basis of other motives. Other gratifications will become more important in their behaviour.

The fact that the Conservative party is a federal party which—in most provinces—competes more effectively at the provincial level is also significant in this regard. It is likely that patronage-motivated Conservatives have focused their interest on provincial politics where the rewards of office have been more readily available. Even when they are involved in national roles—as delegates to meetings of the association or to leadership conventions—they may be less disposed to act on the basis of their patronage motives because their ambitions have been or appear likely to be satisfied in the provincial party.

Tables 37 and 38 provide some data which suggest few members of the party are primarily patronage-motivated. The tables report the distribution of answers to questions which asked delegates to the 1971 meeting of the association why they were party activists and why they had joined the Progressive Conservative party rather than some other party. In

Table 37 **Percentages of 1971 respondents ranking selected reasons very important, very important or important, or not important for "being active in party work"**

	Very important	Very important or important	Not important
"There are certain policies I strongly believe in and I want to see something done about them"	76[a]	95[a]	3[a]
"Participation in party politics is the best way to bring about social change"	60	88	9
"I like the excitement of politics"	34	77	20
"I enjoy the friendships I have within the party"	21	69	29
"I want to hold public office"	14	40	56
"Party work gives me a feeling of recognition from people who are important to me"	9	39	58
"Party work helps me in my career"	7	25	70
"I like being in public view"	6	28	68

(a) Percentages in each case are percentages of the total sample, that is, of the 553 respondents who completed the questionnaire. The sum of the percentages in the columns "very important or important" and "not important" does not come to 100 because some delegates did not answer particular items. In no case, however, does this non-response rate exceed 5 percent.

explaining their party activism, the number who ranked any of the four patronage reasons as "very important" was only 18 percent and the number who ranked any of these reasons as "important" was only 28 percent. The number who gave a patronage reason for choosing the Conservative party in preference to other parties was even smaller. Only 7 percent made any reference to patronage, and only 3 percent referred to it first.

Regrettably, there are no similar data which would permit a comparison of the motives of people attracted to the Progressive Conservative party and people attracted to the Liberal party. But the argument that there is a difference in the significance of patronage motives in the be-

Table 38 **Percentages of 1971 respondents who gave "patronage," "affective," or "policy" reasons for joining the Progressive Conservative party rather than some other party**[a]

Reasons	Percentage who mentioned reason	
	First[b]	At all
Patronage	3	7
Affective (including personality)[c]	28	35
Affective (not including personality)	25	30
Policy	61	74

(a) The question was open-ended, that is, it asked the delegates to write their spontaneous responses rather than to deal with a pre-determined list. Each reason mentioned was separately coded. All of them were then recoded to conform to the basic categories.

(b) Since most respondents gave more than one reason, each reason was coded in the order in which it was mentioned: that is, "mentioned first," "mentioned second," and so on. The column headed "First" records the percentage of respondents who mentioned a reason of that particular type as his or her first reason. The column headed "At all" records the percentage of respondents who gave any reason of the particular type to which each category refers.

(c) The category "affective" included responses of the type "because my family was Conservative," references to recruitment by friends, and attraction to the party through particular personalities. Because there may be some question about the "affective" content of attraction to the party through a particular personality, affective responses have also been reported without this kind of reason.

haviour of Conservatives and Liberals is buttressed by one piece of evidence. In a survey of members of the House of Commons in 1964 and 1965, David Hoffman and Norman Ward found that Liberal members were more likely than Conservatives to say that they hoped some day to attain a position in the cabinet.[4] Looked at the other way around, more of the Conservative members expressed satisfaction with the role of MP as such. This suggests one final comment about the significance of patronage motives in the behaviour of members of the Conservative caucus.

We may speculate that there are some Conservative members of Parliament who are not merely content with their role in opposition but actually prefer to be in opposition. There are two reasons for this. First, some people seek active roles in politics because of their feelings of status insecurity and, as we observed in chapter 6, there are different ways of dealing with status insecurity. One way is to try to change one's status by rising to a higher, more secure position. Another way is to seek a negative object on which to displace one's frustration. Thus, the Conservative party may contain some people whose motivation is to find an emotional outlet for their status insecurity by criticizing those who have power. The critic's role is the role they seek. Second, some people find their gratification in active political roles in the public attention they receive; their needs are met by the psychic satisfaction of popular esteem. For people of this sort, the opposition role is likely to be more satisfying than a backbench role in government because the opposition member has far more opportunity to attract attention in the House and from the press. We may assume that people who prefer the opposition role will be willing to comply in the norms of party discipline only to the extent that they feel it is necessary to ensure their opportunities for re-election.

MINORITY PARTY SYNDROME

On the basis of this analysis it may be argued that there is a reciprocal relationship between the Progressive Conservative party's electoral defeats and its vulnerability to internal conflict. This relationship is an aspect of what might be described as the minority party syndrome—characteristics acquired by minority parties which tend to re-enforce their weakness. This aspect of the syndrome may be explained as follows. Because of the party's exclusion from office, its members tend to interact in internal party politics on the basis of motives that make conflict difficult to resolve. Because conflicts recur frequently and the party is subject to manifest or latent factionalism, it is unable to achieve optimum organizational effectiveness and it projects an image of internal instability which undermines public confidence in its ability to govern. Thus, electoral defeats contribute to conflict in the party and conflict in the party contributes to its electoral defeats.

A second aspect of the minority party syndrome relates to the level of ability of the people attracted to activist roles in the party. In general, when two parties pursue the same basic goals the party which has the greater chance of winning is likely to have greater success in recruiting people of first-rate ability. There has been frequent criticism of the quality of the Conservative party's candidates—both from journalists and from members of the party. The party has usually been able to present a credible front bench, but it has clearly lacked deep resources of parliamentary talent. As John C. Courtney observes, "the Liberals have succeeded in dominating most of the predictable areas from which the Conservatives might attempt to co-opt their parliamentary notables: the civil service, universities, businesses and corporations."[5]

In addition, the Conservative party has had difficulty in getting imaginative and innovative people to assist it in policy development. There appear to be two dimensions to this problem. The first is that such people will be more likely to become involved in a party which offers them a better chance of getting their ideas translated into public policy. The second is that many Conservatives have developed an attitude of mistrust toward intellectuals—an attitude illustrated by the controversy which has attended every "Thinkers" conference in the party's history. There is a widespread suspicion that intellectuals will never make a commitment to the Conservative party—that sooner or later they will be beguiled by the Liberal party. This suspicion tends to be self-fulfilling. The party does not make intellectuals welcome, with the result that they turn away.

This re-enforces the effect of a third aspect of the minority party syndrome—the existence in a minority party of an "opposition mentality." A party which is habitually in opposition becomes absorbed entirely in the strategy and tactics of criticism. It tends to approach all debate with an attacking, destructive style. It, therefore, appears to lack ideas of its own and projects a negative popular image. Edwin R. Black has provided some insight into the "opposition mentality" of the Conservative party in his description of the establishment of the party's parliamentary research office. Black's comments on his efforts—as the first director of the research office—to interest the party in in-depth research on major issues is particularly telling both in illustrating the effect of this opposition mentality and in demonstrating the lack of cohesion in the caucus: "Party leader, committee chairmen, and backbench MP's all piously agreed on its desirability. Never, however, would the opposition caucus agree on a set of basic priorities. Tory members remained a gaggle of political private enterprisers who selfishly preferred to pursue their separate ways to the electoral gallows rather than hang together and work as a united opposition."[6]

A fourth aspect of the minority party syndrome relates to the competence of the party's leaders. One factor is that a minority party normally must choose from potential leaders of more limited experience than those available to a dominant party. In the past four decades the Progressive Conservative party has had few leadership candidates with federal ministerial experience.[7] Not one of the last five leaders had sat in a federal cabinet before his election. The only convention since 1937 at which there has been more than one candidate with cabinet experience was in 1967. The one source of experienced leadership for the party has been the provinces. But, although they have had the experience of governing, premiers are at a disadvantage when they enter federal politics. Their perspective is more parochial, the issues with which they must deal are different, they must work under a different set of constraints, and they exercise their leadership in an unfamiliar political milieu.

Another factor relating to the competence of leaders in parties caught in the minority party syndrome is the divisiveness of the party. In a party which is badly fragmented, the candidates who win are those who are least offensive to the largest number. As one member of Parliament put it, convention delegates must decide "not who they are for, but who they are not against." This is hardly the criterion by which the most able person is likely to be chosen.[8]

The interpretation of the Conservative party's weakness which is being presented here may be seen to have wider application to the study of political parties, helping to explain the development of single-party dominant systems. The concept of the minority party syndrome deals directly with the weakness of minority parties in such systems. Its concomitant is that the dominant party will be more cohesive, attract members and leaders with more effective personal resources, and be more positive in its outlook. Thus, indirectly, this concept also helps to account for the resilience of the dominant party.[9]

THE FUTURE OF THE PARTY

Explanations for patterns of party competition commonly focus on the social context in which the party system operates. They relate the electoral strength or weakness of parties to their ability to appeal to certain social groups. The approach of this study draws attention to the variable of the party's capabilities and effectiveness as an organization. To emphasize this variable is not to suggest that social group explanations have no relevance. The Conservative party's alienation of Quebec was obviously crucial in that it put the party at a permanent disadvantage which precipitated its reduction to minority status. But we have seen that the party's defeats have reflected a lack of support in other provinces as well as in Quebec. Moreover, analysis of data from survey research shows that its weakness cuts across most other social cleavages. Thus there is good reason to infer that explanations for the party's minority status must take account of some other factor.

The thesis I am proposing in this study is that conflict in the party—in particular, conflict involving the party leadership—has been a key factor in its electoral decline. There is no analysis of voting behaviour which permits a direct test of this thesis, but the inferential evidence is strong. The party's defeats in such critical elections as 1896, 1921, 1935, 1940, 1963, 1965, and 1974 were all preceded by conflicts over the leadership or by widely publicized disagreements with policy positions adopted by the leader; the party's internal divisiveness has been a frequent subject for critical comment from journalists and has been used as a weapon by the Liberal party in election campaigns; and there is evidence from survey studies that voters value party unity and rank the Conservative party behind both the Liberal party and the NDP on the extent to which it possesses this characteristic.[10]

Despite its weakness, the Conservative party continues to be the only party with sufficient popular support to challenge the Liberal hegemony in federal politics. The party can be expected to win elections from time to time—when there is serious social, economic, or political strain or when the Liberal party falls victim to what John Meisel has argued is its tendency (as a result of its habituation to office) to become too arrogant in its exercise of power.[11] However, the nature of the social cleavages that weaken the party would take some time to change. So too would the attitudes and dispositions associated with the minority party syndrome because they are deeply rooted in the party's internal culture. Therefore, any Conservative government can expect to go through an extended period in which it is vulnerable to disruption from within. The party's ability to avoid this danger and survive in office long enough to change its competitive position would appear to require exceptionally adroit leadership and some considerable luck.

APPENDIX A

Persons Interviewed

A. General[a]

Aldred, Joel
Amaron, Robert
Arpin, Maurice
Atkins, Norman
Balcer, Léon
Baldwin, G. W.
Bedard, Robert
Bell, R. A.
Bell, Elmer
Bell, Thomas
Camp, Dalton
Chilcott, D.
Churchill, Gordon
Clark, J.
Clarke, Joseph H.
Coates, Robert C.
Dinsdale, Walter
Dillon, R. M.
Faibish, Roy
Fairclough, Ellen
Fairweather, Gordon
Flynn, Senator Jacques
Flynn, Bernard
Fulton, E. D.
Goodman, E. A.
Grogan, Bill
Grossart, Senator A.
Guthrie, H. Donald
Hales, Alfred
Hamilton, Alvin
Hatfield, Richard P.
Hees, George
Horner, Jack
Johnson, D.
Johnston, James
Kowall, E. J.
Lambert, Marcel
Laschinger, John
Lyon, Sterling
MacAulay, R. A.
MacDonald, David
MacDonald, Finlay
MacDonald, Flora
MacLean, J. A.
MacQuarrie, Heath
Martin, Joe
Matthews, Don
McCutcheon, E.
McCleave, Robert
Meighen, Michael
Molyneux, Geoffrey
Monteith, J. Waldo
Mulroney, Brian
Murray, Lowell
Nielsen, Erik
O'Brien, Liam
Patillo, Arthur
Poole, R.
Porter, Julian H.
Rhéaume, Gene
Ricard, Théogène
Roblin, Duff
Rhomer, Richard
Schipper, Lionel
Spivak, Sidney
Stanfield, Robert L.

Starr, Michael
Symonds, T. H. B.
Thrasher, Richard
Trepanier, Paul
Walker, Senator David
Whiteacre, William
Wickson, Malcolm

B. Members of Parliament[b]

Alkenbrack, A. D.
Andre, H.
Arrol, I.
Atkey, R.
Baker, W. D.
Balfour, J.
Bawden, P. C.
Beattie, D.
Beatty, P.
Blenkarn, D.
Carter, W. C.
Clarke, W.
Cossitt, T.
Crouse, L. R.
Danforth, H. W.
Darling, S.
Dick, P.
Ellis, J. R .
Epp, J.
Forrestall, J. M.
Frank, W. C.
Fraser, J. A.
Gillies, J.
Haliburton, C. E.
Hamilton, F.
Hargrave, B.
Higson, K. J.
Hollands, D. F.
Holmes, J. R.
Horner, N.
Hueglin, J.
Hurlburt, K. E.
Jarvis, B.
Jelinek, O.
Knowles, W. D.
Kuntz, H.
LaSalle, R.
Lawrence, A.
Lundrigan, J.
MacKay, E.
Marshall, J.
Masniuk, P. P.
Mazankowski, D.
McCain, F. A.
McGrath, J. A.
McKinley, R. E.
McKinnon, A. B.
Mitges, C. G.
Morgan, T.
Munro, D. W.
Murta, J.
Neil, D. C.
Oberle, F.
O'Connor, T.
O'Sullivan, S.
Reilly, P.
Ritchie, G.
Roche, D.
Schumacher, S. S.
Skoreyko, W.
Stevens, S.
Stewart, C.
Towers, G.
Wagner, C.
Whittaker, G. H.
Wise, J.
Woolliams, E.
Yewchuk, P.

C. Other Informants[c]

Black, E. R.
Greene, Richard
Horswill, Les
MacMillan, Tom
Scott, Graham
Vernon, Patrick

D. Correspondence

Fairclough, Ellen
Flemming, Hugh John
Harkness, Douglas

(a) There was some overlapping in the lists of persons interviewed. To avoid confusion each name is reported on only one list. This first list includes people who were interviewed because they had a direct role in some particular event or series of events or because they held a leading position in the party.

(b) This list includes those who were interviewed primarily about their perceptions, opinions and actions as members of Parliament.

(c) This list includes persons who provided information in informal conversations rather than in a structured interview setting.

APPENDIX B

Supplementary Data

Table 39 **Percentages of the delegates approached by each of the candidates and/or his workers**

	Candidate and worker	Candidate only	Worker only	Total approached
Diefenbaker	1	1	5	7
Fleming	4	6	7	17
Fulton	8	13	12	33
Hamilton	3	5	8	16
Hees	6	10	12	28
McCutcheon	3	5	9	17
Roblin	7	8	17	31
Stanfield	6	6	18	30

Table 40 **Percentages of the delegates approached by one or more of the candidates and/or one or more workers**

Approached by both	54
Candidate(s) only	8
Worker(s) only	25
Approached by none	12
Did not answer	1
N	1091

Table 41 **Ballot one and ballot five votes of the delegates by demographic groups**

	Ballot 1									Ballot 5		
	D[a]	Fl	F	Ha	He	M	R	S	N	R[b]	S	N[c]
Income												
Over $20,000	10	5	16	5	11	9	21	22	282	39	61	237
$15,000–$20,000	14	4	19	5	11	7	11	24	176	38	62	163
$10,000–$15,000	11	3	15	7	12	8	14	29	247	35	65	219
$5,000–$10,000	12	7	15	7	12	6	14	25	242	45	55	204
Under $5,000	21	6	8	2	14	11	19	17	84	43	57	74
Education												
Post univ. degree	9	6	18	6	4	7	16	30	111	36	64	86
University degree	7	4	17	4	13	11	19	23	342	41	59	303
Post high school, no degree	15	3	13	7	13	7	12	29	209	35	65	183
Grades 12–13	18	6	15	6	14	6	15	17	182	46	54	160
Grades 9–11	13	6	13	6	9	6	16	29	158	44	56	142
Grade 8 or less	23	6	17	6	11	4	9	23	53	22	78	41
Occupation of the main wage earner												
Professional	9	4	18	5	11	8	18	24	414	39	61	361
Owners, managers, executives	11	4	16	7	12	7	15	28	262	35	65	224
Sales	13	4	15	4	14	11	15	21	114	36	64	98
Clerical	12	9	15	—	15	6	21	15	33	48	52	31
Skilled labour	8	10	15	6	15	15	8	21	48	38	63	40
Farmers	27	—	8	19	13	2	8	19	64	54	46	57
Widows, pensioned, retired	25	12	8	—	8	2	12	29	49	49	51	43
Sex												
Men	13	5	15	6	12	8	17	25	832	40	60	732
Women	15	7	18	4	13	5	12	25	165	38	62	151
Religion												
Roman Catholic	8	7	19	2	16	5	22	20	268	46	55	233
Anglican	16	4	17	7	6	9	13	25	268	40	60	234
United	14	5	12	7	12	9	14	26	285	30	61	247

Table 41 *continued*

	Ballot 1									Ballot 5		
	D[a]	Fl	F	Ha	He	M	R	S	N	R[b]	S	N[c]
Other	11	4	9	8	9	9	13	34	164	29	71	142
None	14	4	21	7	19	6	14	11	70	43	57	61
Country of origin												
England	15	5	17	6	8	9	11	25	334	34	66	278
Scotland	15	3	14	5	7	5	13	36	190	32	68	170
Ireland	14	3	12	7	12	11	11	27	177	39	61	159
France	7	7	16	3	20	6	27	14	162	52	48	146
Other European	9	4	20	6	18	3	18	18	120	49	51	104
Other	10	7	9	7	10	9	31	14	59	51	49	47
Community size												
Over 250,000	8	3	22	5	16	8	21	17	305	44	57	269
100,000–250,000	12	3	17	7	12	10	15	22	117	47	53	96
10,000–100,000	17	8	12	4	9	6	12	28	225	39	62	200
1,000–10,000	11	7	14	5	9	10	13	29	214	31	69	183
Rural non-farm	15	8	7	11	8	3	18	26	91	44	56	79
Farm	18	2	9	13	9	7	6	33	55	34	66	47
Age												
Under 20	13	3	27	3	17	3	3	30	30	43	57	28
21–30	8	4	20	8	12	13	15	21	185	42	59	159
31–40	8	1	20	5	12	6	18	26	216	35	66	194
41–50	11	4	13	7	11	7	17	26	271	43	58	221
51–60	19	8	9	4	11	8	18	22	187	41	59	174
61–70	14	10	16	5	10	5	14	26	116	35	65	96
Over 70	36	5	5	5	13	8	5	21	39	44	56	32
Sample	12	5	15	6	12	8	16	24	1032	61	39	927

(a) The candidates are arranged alphabetically as follows: Diefenbaker, Fleming, Fulton, Hamilton, Hees, McCutcheon, Roblin, and Stanfield.

(b) R and S stand for Roblin and Stanfield respectively.

(c) Using chi square and the .001 level of significance, the variables significantly related to ballot one vote were religion, country of origin, and community size. Only country of origin was significantly related to ballot five vote.

Table 42 **Percentages of delegates who gave each reason for changing their votes on ballots 2 to 5[a]**

	Ballots			
	2	3	4	5
One of his workers approached me and those of the other candidates did not	1[b,c]	2	2	2
I thought he would be the best vote-getter for the party	7	9	9	11
I agreed with his views on policy matters	8	10	9	12
I thought my own position in the party would be stronger if he were the leader	1	1	1	1
His personal characteristics were more appealing to me	7	8	8	11
I knew him better than the other candidates	3	3	3	2
A person prominent in the party whose judgement I respect was supporting him	2	3	4	5
I was asked to vote for him by a person prominent in the party who has helped me in the past or may be able to help me	1	1	1	2
He has helped the party in my community in the past	2	1	1	1
He has helped me personally in the past	—	1	1	—
I liked his political style	6	7	6	9
I thought he was going to win the leadership and I wanted to be on the winning side	2	2	2	2
He understands my part of the country better	3	3	5	4
The candidate I was supporting supported him	1	3	5	6
His views were closest to those of my first choice	5	7	8	10

Table 42 *continued*

	Ballots			
	2	3	4	5
Other unclassifiable[d]	1	1	2	2
Did not answer/does not apply	87	87	86	83
N	(1091)	(1091)	(1091)	(1091)

(a) The question asked was: "If you changed your vote on subsequent ballots indicate, *in each case*, what reasons were most important in your choice." The list of reasons followed.

(b) For instance, 1 percent of the delegates said that they had changed their votes on the second ballot because of a worker's approach.

(c) Since delegates were asked to give more than one reason, the total of the answers exceeds 100 percent.

(d) "Other" reasons were classified according to the policy-affective-patronage schema. Those which did not fit the schema were left in a category of their own. None of these reasons was given by 1 percent of the sample.

Table 43 **Pairs of issues and issue questions used to compare perceived positions of the candidates with the delegates' own positions**

Issues[a]	Issue questions[b]
Free enterprise	Government ought to interfere less with business
French Canada	French Canadians should have no more privileges than other ethnic groups
Canadian independence of the United States	There should be special laws to regulate American capital invested in Canada
A "deux nations" policy	Quebec's position in Confederation should receive special recognition
Social welfare	Governments spend too much money on social welfare
More aid to underdeveloped countries	Canada ought to devote much more effort and money to aiding the underdeveloped countries
Loyalty to the monarchy	The monarchy is an essential part of the Canadian constitution

Table 43 *continued*

The farmer	Farmers should have more say in determining the policy of the Conservative party
Less spending on defence	Canada should spend less on defence
The poorer provinces	More federal government money should be used to develop the economies of the poorer provinces
Trade unions	The workers' right to strike should not be restricted
A strong central government	Canada needs a strong central government
Restricting medicare to those who need it	Free medicare should be available to everyone

(a) Question 27 asked, "Which of the candidates, in your opinion, were most favourable or most unfavourable to each of the following? Use these symbols: Most favourable, Fl; Next most favourable, F2; Most unfavourable, U1; Next most unfavourable, U2." The list of issues followed. One item, "A strong stand against Communism," was omitted because the issue questions about Communism did not elicit the same opinion.

(b) The issue questions (question 31) were prefaced with, "Please indicate whether you agree, disagree or have no opinion, on the following statements."

Table 44 **Percentages of the total sample whose issue positions are consistent with their perceptions of those of the candidates**

	Diefen-baker	Fleming	Fulton	Hamilton	Hees	Mc-Cutcheon	Roblin	Stanfield
Free enterprise	10[a]	9	6	7	10	29	7	16
French Canada	17	5	12	5	5	6	26	17
Canadian independence	26	6	5	10	6	7	6	10
Deux nations	23	4	7	6	4	4	18	22
Social welfare	8	10	6	9	5	18	6	8
Aid to underdeveloped countries	6	4	8	10	5	5	8	13
Monarchy	34	8	5	4	4	4	4	10
Farmer	8	10	4	11	6	14	3	4
Less defence spending	8	5	6	8	5	6	6	11
Poorer provinces	18	3	4	7	3	2	15	44
Trade unions	7	12	3	4	5	17	3	4
Strong central government	28	7	12	5	4	8	9	25
Restrict medicare	6	9	7	4	5	21	11	21

(a) For instance, 10 percent of the delegates named Diefenbaker as most or next most favourable to free enterprise and themselves favoured free enterprise or named Diefenbaker as most or next most unfavourable and themselves opposed free enterprise.

Table 45 **Distribution of the delegates by those candidates perceived as closest to their own issue positions at the second (press issues), third (discriminating issues), and fourth (all issues) stages of the policy test[a,b]**

	Press issues	Discriminating issues	All issues
Diefenbaker	13[c]	16	18
Fleming	2	2	2
Fulton	4	3	3
Hamilton	1	3	3
Hees	2	2	2
McCutcheon	8	10	7
Roblin	6	6	6
Stanfield	11	13	17
Ties	21	17	14
Non-responses	32	30	28
N	(1091)	(1091)	(1091)

(a) Similar figures for the "deux nations" test are not available since only two favourable responses could be given by a respondent. See table 48 for the figures used at this stage of the "deux nations" test.

(b) The design of the policy test is explained in chapter 8, pp. 156–57.

(c) For instance, 13 percent of the delegates perceived Diefenbaker as closest to their own issue positions on the press issues.

Table 46 **Number of delegates who perceived the candidates as having the most similar positions to their own on the "deux nations" issue**

	Diefenbaker	Fleming	Fulton	Hamilton	Hees	McCutcheon	Roblin	Stanfield
Diefenbaker	103[a]	17[b]	9	61	8	23	4	17
Fleming	17[b]	4	1	—	3	3	6	3
Fulton	9	1	6	1	5	1	15	35
Hamilton	61	—	1	3	—	—	—	3
Hees	8	3	5	—	5	3	8	8
McCutcheon	23	3	1	—	3	3	2	6
Roblin	4	6	15	—	8	2	27	129
Stanfield	17	3	35	3	8	6	129	29
N	(242[c])	(37)	(73)	(68)	(40)	(41)	(191)	(230)

(a) The numbers along the diagonal represent delegates who named only one candidate; for example, 103 people mentioned only Diefenbaker.

(b) Seventeen delegates mentioned both Diefenbaker and Fleming. This number has been entered twice in the matrix.

(c) For instance, 242 delegates held positions consistent with what they perceived John Diefenbaker's to be.

Table 47 **Percentages of delegates who voted for one of the candidates whom they perceived as closest or second closest to their position on the "deux nations" issue**

	Percent	Of total N[a]
Diefenbaker	19	242
Fleming	30	37
Fulton	38	73
Hamilton	19	68
Hees	38	40
McCutcheon	12	41
Roblin	25	191
Stanfield	27	230

(a) For instance, of the 242 delegates who named Diefenbaker as closest or second closest to their own position, 19 percent voted for him.

Table 48 **First ballot votes of delegates who voted for their highest ranked candidate at each stage of the policy test and in the four stages combined[a,b]**

	Deux nations	Press issues	Discrim-inating issues	All issues	Com-bined tests	Total sample
Diefenbaker	21	13	16	17	18	12
Fleming	5	4	—	3	4	5
Fulton	12	14	2	14	12	15
Hamilton	6	3	9	8	6	6
Hees	7	7	13	6	8	12
McCutcheon	2	12	22	8	8	8
Roblin	21	20	4	8	18	16
Stanfield	27	26	33	36	28	24
N	(227)	(106)	(45)	(36)	(414)	(1042)

(a) The table does not include delegates who voted for Starr or McLean, non-voters, and delegates who did not report their first ballot vote.

(b) The four stages of the policy test are explained in chapter 8, pp. 156–57.

Table 49 **First ballot votes of delegates who gave affective reasons or patronage reasons or whose vote was consistent with their ratings of the candidates on the dimensions vote-winning ability and understanding of their region**[a]

	Affective[b]	Patronage[c]	Vote-winning ability	Understands region	Total sample
Diefenbaker	12	18	9	10	12
Fleming	4	3	2	2	5
Fulton	17	15	11	15	15
Hamilton	5	7	2	8	6
Hees	13	15	11	10	12
McCutcheon	4	4	1	4	8
Roblin	18	15	26	22	16
Stanfield	28	22	38	31	24
N	(527)	(381)	(473)	(416)	(1042)

(a) The table does not include delegates who voted for Starr or McLean since they were not included in the tests. Non-voters and delegates who did not indicate how they voted on the first ballot have also been excluded.

(b) This category consists of those delegates who gave two or more affective reasons for their vote.

(c) This category includes all delegates who gave one or more patronage reasons for their vote.

Table 50 **Percentage of each candidate's first ballot voters who gave two or more affective reasons or one or more patronage reasons for first ballot votes**

	Percentage who gave		
	Affective reasons	Patronage reasons	N
Diefenbaker	46	51	132
Fleming	44	25	52
Fulton	57	36	159
Hamilton	40	45	60
Hees	54	48	123
McCutcheon	27	20	83
Roblin	58	34	165
Stanfield	56	32	258

Table 51 **Percentage of the delegates in each province who gave two or more affective reasons or one or more patronage reasons for their first ballot vote**

	Percentage who gave		
	Affective reasons	Patronage reasons	N
Newfoundland	62	23	13
Nova Scotia	73	65	80
New Brunswick	49	36	53
Prince Edward Island	44	31	16
Quebec	52	37	170
Ontario	46	24	378
Manitoba	61	58	66
Saskatchewan	46	68	59
Alberta	49	21	76
British Columbia	52	44	88

APPENDIX C

Tests of Representativeness for the 1967 Questionnaire

Table 52 **Percentage distributions of the votes on each ballot for (1) the actual vote of the convention and (2) the sample**

	Ballot 1		Ballot 2		Ballot 3		Ballot 4		Ballot 5	
	(1)	(2)	(1)	(2)	(1)	(2)	(1)	(2)	(1)	(2)
Stanfield	23	24	28	28	32	36	40	45	54	61
Roblin	15	16	19	20	25	26	36	33	46	39
Fulton	15	15	15	16	16	18	17	16	—	—
Hees	13	12	13	11	13	8	—	—	—	—
Diefenbaker	12	12	8	9	5	5	—	—	—	—
McCutcheon	6	8	3	4	—	—	—	—	—	—
Hamilton	6	6	6	6	5	6	7	6	—	—
Fleming	5	5	5	5	3	1	—	—	—	—
Starr	2	2	2	—	—	—	—	—	—	—
Others	1	1	—	—	—	—	—	—	—	—
N	(2253)	(1069)	(2212)	(1003)	(2192)	(1002)	(2160)	(976)	(2119)	(927)

Table 53 **Percentage distribution of the convention delegates and the sample by type of credentials**

	Convention	Sample
Constituency delegates	56	54
MPs, senators, privy councillors[a]	6	6
Members of provincial legislatures	8	8
National executive, senior women's, YPC, PCSF executives	4	5
Montmorency participants	4	3
Delegates-at-large	23	24
N	(2372)	(1035)

(a) This category also includes nominated candidates.

APPENDIX D

A Note on Questionnaires and Data Sets

Copies of the questionnaires (in either French of English) used in the surveys of convention delegates can be obtained at a nominal cost covering overhead and mailing charges from the Data Unit, Department of Political Studies, Queen's University, Kingston, Ontario K7L 3N6. The Data Unit will also provide copies of the codebook and data sets on a similar basis.

NOTES

CHAPTER 1

1. John Diefenbaker, text of speech delivered to the Progressive Conservative annual meeting, November 1966.
2. Robert Stanfield, text of speech delivered to the Progressive Conservative leadership convention, February 1976.
3. For summaries of the main interests and findings in this literature see, inter alia, Alan C. Elms, *Personality in Politics* (San Francisco: Harcourt Brace, 1976), Gordon J. DiRenzo, *Personality and Politics* (Garden City, N.Y.: Doubleday Anchor, 1974) and Jeanne N. Knutson, ed., *Handbook of Political Psychology* (San Francisco: Jossey-Bass, 1973).
4. For another typology, created for the purpose of trying to identify the kinds of incentives which parties must offer if they are to retain the interest and involvement of their members, see Peter B. Clark and James Q. Wilson, "Incentive Systems, A Theory of Organization," *Administrative Science Quarterly* 6 (September 1961): 129–65.
5. This important point was developed by Peter M. Blau, in *Exchange and Power in Social Life* (New York: John Wiley, 1964), p. 35: "A crucial analytical distinction is that between associations that are intrinsically rewarding and those that furnish extrinsic benefits, which are, in principle, detachable from the association itself. In the first case, another's company as such is the source of the attraction, while in the second, specific benefits he supplies are the inducement for associating with him. Conceptualized in abstract terms, discriminations and corresponding generalizations along two different lines can be derived from gratifying social experiences. First, the discrimination is between this attractive individual and others who are not, the generalization is from this pleasurable experience with him to the expectation that other experiences with him will be gratifying too, and an intrinsic attachment to him develops. Second, the discrimination is between the person and the object or activity that is enjoyable, the generalization is that similar objects from, or activities with, other persons will be gratifying too, and an extrinsic interest in these benefits from any source results."
6. There are several studies of competition among groups which report this effect. Cf. J. Thibault, "An Experimental Study of the Cohesiveness of

Under-privileged Groups," *Human Relations* 3, no. 2 (June 1950): 251–78, cited in George C. Homans, *Social Behavior, Its Elementary Forms* (New York: Harcourt Brace, 1961), p. 144; William Foote Whyte, "Corner Boys: A Study of Clique Behavior," *American Journal of Sociology* 46, no. 5 (March 1941): 647–67.

7. J. L. Payne and O. H. Woshinsky make an analogous distinction between "program" oriented political activists and "mission" oriented political activists. See J. L. Payne and O. H. Woshinsky, "Incentives for Political Participation," *World Politics* 24 (1972): 518–46. The "program" oriented person is concerned with "devising and managing public policy" (p. 528) and has "a positive orientation toward compromise" (p. 531) while the "mission" oriented person focuses "upon the doctrine or ideology of his cause" (p. 533), and is therefore less amenable to compromise.
8. James Q. Wilson, *The Amateur Democrat* (Chicago: University of Chicago Press, 1962), pp. 3–4.
9. Peter B. Clark and James Q. Wilson, "Incentive Systems, A Theory of Organizations," *Administrative Science Quarterly* 6 (September 1961): 129–66.
10. A list of the people interviewed will be found in Appendix A.
11. One of the candidates for the party leadership in 1967, Senator M. W. McCutcheon, died while the research was in progress and another, Donald Fleming, refused to be interviewed. The conditions specified for an interview with John Diefenbaker were such that it was decided the interview would not be useful. In considering Mr. Diefenbaker's role in the conflict, I have relied on extensive interviews with a number of his close associates; his own public statements in newspapers and, where it was possible to get access to them, radio and television interviews; secondary sources, including an extensive account of the 1966–67 period by James Johnston, the party's national director, *The Party's Over* (Don Mills, Ontario: Longmans Canada, 1971); and Mr. Diefenbaker's memoirs, *One Canada, Memoirs of The Right Honourable John G. Diefenbaker, The Crusading Years, 1895–1956, The Years of Achievement, 1956–1962*, and *The Tumultuous Years, 1962–1967* (Toronto: Macmillan, 1975, 1976, 1977).
12. Four tests, comparisons of the distribution of the sample and the total delegate body by the characteristics of sex, province of residence, credentials type, and voting behaviour were undertaken to try to determine the representativeness of the 1967 survey. The sample was representative within acceptable standards of error on all but one test, voting behaviour on the last ballot, and this was not as serious as might have been expected, given that in all such studies there is usually a "bandwagon effect," that is, a tendency to overrepresent the support for the winning candidate. One part of the problem was created by the fact that many delegates did not say for which candidate they had voted on the last ballot. The size of the sample was approximately 50 percent of the total delegate body. There were 1,091 completed returns and questionnaires were mailed to 2,180 delegates. The 1971 survey produced a sample of exactly 50 percent of the total delegate body of 1,100 persons. The 1976 survey was designed to produce a sample of 850 delegates (one-third of the number who attended) and yielded a sample of 837. There was no significant error in any of the tests of representativeness for either of these samples.

CHAPTER 2

1. Hugh McD. Clokie, *Canadian Government and Politics* (Toronto: Longmans, Green & Company, 1944), p. 91.
2. See, for example, J. M. Beck and D. J. Dooley, "Party Images in Canada" and J. R. Mallory, "The Structure of Canadian Politics," in Hugh G. Thorburn, ed., *Party Politics in Canada* (Scarborough, Ontario: Prentice-Hall, 1969).
3. For example, Norman Atkins, a principal figure in the Conservative campaigns of 1972 and 1974, commented in an interview that the leader's image "is everything" in designing campaign strategy.
4. John Meisel, *Working Papers on Canadian Politics*, enl. ed. (Montreal: McGill-Queen's University Press, 1973), table VIII.
5. William Christian and Colin Campbell in *Political Parties and Ideologies in Canada* (Toronto: McGraw-Hill Ryerson, 1974) have argued that there are distinctive Conservative and Liberal ideologies. They describe the Conservative ideology as a mixture of nostalgia, hostility to rapid change, toryism, and liberalism and the Liberal ideology as a doctrine of pure liberalism (see pp. 76–78). The more widespread view is that expressed by a prominent Conservative member of Parliament, Heath MacQuarrie, who, in a brief history of the party, wrote that "He who looks for deep philosophical differences between Canadian Liberals and Conservatives will be disappointed." See his *The Conservative Party* (Toronto: McClelland and Stewart, 1965), p. 1. Gad Horowitz, who first developed the thesis that the two parties had been influenced by a somewhat different blend of ideas from tory-collectivist and liberal-individualist thought, has said that while he believes "toryism has been stronger in the Conservative party than in the others . . . the Conservatives like the Liberals are a 'business oriented party' and the 'primary component of the ideology of such a party' is liberalism." See his "Notes on Conservatism, Liberalism and Socialism in Canada," *Canadian Journal of Political Science* 11, no. 2 (June 1978): 392.
6. For a comparison of party policies see Conrad Winn and John McMenemy, *Political Parties in Canada* (Toronto: McGraw-Hill Ryerson, 1976), chaps. 11, 12, 13, and 14.
7. Cf. Mildred Schwartz, *Public Opinion and Canadian Identity* (Scarborough, Ontario: Fitzhenry, 1967), pp. 83–123, 146–58, et passim.
8. Denis Smith, "President and Parliament: The Transformation of Parliamentary Government in Canada," in Thomas A. Hockin, ed., *Apex of Power, The Prime Minister and Political Leadership in Canada* (Scarborough, Ontario: Prentice-Hall, 1971), pp. 224–41. For a general discussion of the role of the prime minister in Canada see in the same volume Thomas A. Hockin, "The Prime Minister and Political Leadership: An Introduction to Some Restraints and Imperatives," pp. 2–21, and Fred Schindeler, "The Prime Minister and the Cabinet: History and Development," pp. 22–48.
9. W. L. Morton draws attention to the tory belief in strong leadership in his discussion of the characteristic elements of Canadian Conservatism. See his "Canadian Conservatism Now" in Paul Fox, ed., *Politics Canada* (Toronto: McGraw-Hill, 1962), p. 287.
10. A recent example was a paper prepared by the party leader for a caucus debate on the principles of Conservative policy in the autumn of 1974. "Notes for Remarks by Robert L. Stanfield," mimeo, November 1974.

11. Macdonald's role in the early history of the party is described in Donald Creighton's two-volume biography: *John A. Macdonald*, vol. 1, *The Young Politician*, and vol 2, *The Old Chieftain* (Toronto: Macmillan, 1952, 1955).
12. *Communique*, published by the Progressive Conservative Association of Canada (Ottawa: February 1972), p. 3.
13. Geoffrey Molyneux, director of the PC Parliamentary Research Office (interview).
14. For a description of the role of the 1922 committee in the British Conservative party, see Robert McKenzie, *British Political Parties*, 2nd ed., rev. (London: Heinemann, 1963), pp. 57–61 et passim.
15. *Constitution*, of the Progressive National Association, 1974, article 9(e).
16. Leonard Jones, the candidate Stanfield rejected, exploiting the issue of interference with party democracy and local autonomy, ran as an independent and won—aparently taking most of the Conservative vote. This may be a deterrent to any future effort by a national leader to interfere in a local nomination.
17. Regrettably, this aspect of regionalism in Canada has not received much attention in national opinion studies. In surveys in which the author has been involved in Newfoundland and New Brunswick, substantially larger proportions of the samples expressed closer ties to provincial rather than federal political objects. The limited evidence which is available from national studies suggests that this pattern is not uniform across the country. For example, when respondents in one study were asked which level of government they would first approach if they had a problem, the federal government was mentioned more often in Ontario, British Columbia, and Alberta and the provincial government was mentioned more often in the Atlantic provinces, Quebec, Manitoba, and Saskatchewan. Even in Ontario, however, this study found that 30 percent of the sample would first approach the provincial government, compared to 39 percent who would first approach the federal government. In other words, if this is an accurate measure of how close people feel to the two levels of government, it indicates that there is still a relatively large proportion of the Ontario population which has a closer sense of identity with the provincial level. The same is true of British Columbia and Alberta, the other two provinces in which a larger number of respondents said they would first approach the federal government. See Raymond N. Morris et al., *Attitudes Toward Federal Government Information* (Toronto: Institute for Behavioural Research, York University, 1969), p. 142.
18. *Constitution*, article 9(b).
19. The notion of what constitutes an "active" association is highly subjective. As used here it means that an association has an annual paid-up membership of at least 0.5 percent of the registered electors in a constituency (roughly one member for each polling division in the constituency) and conducts functions and meetings other than those required under the party constitution. Party officials have not been able to provide data which could be used to apply this test to all constituencies. General comments are therefore based on the estimates of persons familiar with the situation in each of the provinces.
20. John R. Williams, *The Conservative Party of Canada: 1920–1949* (Durham, North Carolina: Duke University Press, 1956), p. 117.
21. There is some evidence to demonstrate the effect this has had on the recruitment of campaign workers in a study of party organization in

three ridings in Hamilton, Ontario. See Henry Jacek et al., "The Congruence of Federal-Provincial Campaign Activity in Party Organizations: The Influence of Recruitment Patterns in Three Hamilton Ridings," *Canadian Journal of Political Science* 5, no. 2 (June 1972): 198–200 et passim.

22. This point is illustrated by a comparison of the status characteristics of delegates to the 1967 leadership convention and party identifiers interviewed in John Meisel's national election study in 1968. Sixty-nine percent of the delegates compared to 23 percent of the identifiers were (or came from families in which the main wage-earner was) in a professional, executive, or managerial occupation; 69 percent of the delegates, compared to 15 percent of the identifiers, came from families with a total annual income of $10,000 or more; and 63 percent of the delegates, compared to 10 percent of the identifiers, had some post-high school education.
23. *Constitution*, 1974, Article 11.

CHAPTER 3

1. In fact, party unity had not been long established. During Macdonald's first term, from 1867 to 1873, there were several members of Parliament who supported and participated in his government but did not regard themselves as Conservatives. Even among the nominal Conservatives there was a good deal less cohesion, as measured by consistent support for government measures, than is now the case. Among all members of Parliament the incidence of consistent party support in 1867 was 28 percent over 30 divisions while in 1963 it was 78 percent over 124 divisions. See Roman R. March, *The Myth of Parliament* (Scarborough, Ontario: Prentice-Hall, 1974), table 3.5, p. 58. It took Macdonald a decade to establish a stable parliamentary coalition wholly committed to the Conservative party, as such. For a brief description of the emergence of stable party coalitions see Escott M. Reid, "The Rise of National Parties in Canada," *Papers and Proceedings of the Canadian Political Science Association*, 1932, reprinted in Hugh G. Thorburn, ed., *Party Politics in Canada*, 3rd ed. (Scarborough, Ontario: Prentice-Hall, 1972), pp. 15–22. On the general history of the Macdonald period there is a very extensive body of scholarly literature. The best sources on the party are the biographical studies (including a large number of theses) of Macdonald and other leading figures. The most comprehensive and the best known biography of Macdonald is the sympathetic study done by Donald Creighton, *John A. Macdonald*, vol. 1, *The Young Politician*, and vol. 2, *The Old Chieftain* (Toronto: Macmillan, 1952, 1955).
2. For discussion of the situation in the Quebec wing of the party in this period see Barbara Fraser, "The Political Career of Sir Hector Louis Langevin," *Canadian Historical Review* 42, no. 2 (June 1961): 93–132, and H. Blair Neatby and John T. Saywell, "Chapleau and the Conservative Party in Quebec," *Canadian Historical Review* 37, no. 1 (March 1956): 1–22.
3. Sources consulted for this discussion of the period from 1885 to 1896, in addition to those cited in other notes include Lovell Clark, ed. *The Manitoba School Question: Majority Rule or Minority Rights* (Toronto: Copp Clark, 1968); J. F. O'Sullivan, "D'Alton McCarthy and the Con-

servative Party," M.A. thesis, University of Toronto, 1949, and J. R. Miller, *Equal Rights: The Jesuits' Estates Act Controversy* (Montreal: McGill-Queen's University Press, 1979).

4. Fraser, "The Political Career of Sir Hector Langevin," p. 125; Neatby and Saywell, "Chapleau and the Conservative Party in Quebec," pp. 13–14; and L. L. LaPierre, "Joseph Israel Tarte and the McGreevy-Langevin Scandal," *Report of the Canadian Historical Association* (Toronto, 1961), p. 54.
5. Quoted in Lovell C. Clark, "The Conservative Party in the 1890's," *Report of the Canadian Historical Association* (Toronto, 1961), p. 62.
6. Cf. Alan W. MacIntosh, "The Career of Sir Charles Tupper in Canada, 1864–1900," Ph.D. thesis, University of Toronto, 1959, p. 399.
7. J. P. Heisler, "Sir John Thompson, 1844–1894," Ph.D. thesis, University of Toronto, 1955, p. 294.
8. Clark, "The Conservative Party in the 1890's," p. 64.
9. Maurice Pope, ed., *Public Servant: The Memoirs of Sir Joseph Pope* (Toronto: Oxford University Press, 1960), p. 104.
10. John T. Saywell, "The Crown and the Politicians: The Canadian Succession Question 1891–1896," *Canadian Historical Review* 37, no. 4 (December 1956): 324–25.
11. For a discussion of the attitude of the Quebec church toward the Liberal party see H. Blair Neatby, *Laurier and a Liberal Quebec* (Toronto: McClelland and Stewart, 1973), chap. 1, and Mason Wade, *The French Canadians*, vol. 1 (Toronto: Macmillan, 1968), chap. 7 et passim.
12. "McCarthyites" contested ten ridings in Ontario and one in Manitoba.
13. See, for example, Paul Crunican, *Priests and Politicians: Manitoba Schools and the Election of 1896* (Toronto: University of Toronto Press, 1974), pp. 298–99 et passim.
14. Neatby and Saywell, "Chapleau and the Conservative Party in Quebec," pp. 11–16.
15. Outside Quebec the Conservatives won seventy-two seats and the Liberals sixty-nine. Others elected included McCarthy and three of his followers.
16. See, for example, Neatby and Saywell, "Chapleau and the Conservative Party in Quebec," p. 1, and Clark, "The Conservative Party in the 1890's" pp. 58–61.
17. See Clark, "The Conservative Party in the 1890's." The desire to frustrate Tupper's succession was also a factor in Bowell's behaviour in January 1896. There are comments in some of the correspondence of leading participants which suggest a strong emotional undercurrent in Bowell's reaction. See, for example, the letter to Bowell of T. Mayne Daly, one of the ministers who did not resign, and the memorandum to the governor general of the six ministers who resigned which are cited in W. Stewart Wallace, *The Memoirs of the Rt. Hon. Sir George Foster, P.C. G.C.M.G.* (Toronto: Macmillan, 1933), pp. 89–95.
18. Robert Craig Brown, *Robert Laird Borden, A Biography*, vol. 1, *1854–1914* (Toronto: Macmillan, 1975), pp. 55–59. In addition to Brown's biography and sources cited in other notes, the principal sources for the Borden period are John Andrew Eagle, "Sir Robert Borden and the Railway Problem in Canadian Politics, 1911–1920," Ph.D. thesis, University of Toronto, 1972; John Richard English, "Sir Robert Borden, the Conservative Party and Political Change, 1901–1920," Ph.D. thesis, Harvard University, 1973; Catherine P. Warner, "Sir James P. Whitney and Sir Robert L. Borden: Relations Between a Conservative Provincial

Premier and his Federal Party Leader, 1905–1914," M.Phil. thesis, University of Toronto, 1967; and Brian Smith, "Sir Richard McBride," M.A. thesis, Queen's University, 1959.

19. Brown, *Robert Laird Borden*, p. 166. Borden's own account of the challenge to his leadership ascribes it to "Failure . . . the unforgivable sin of a political leader." See Henry Borden, ed., *Robert Laird Borden: His Memoirs*, vol. 1, *1854–1915* (Toronto: McClelland and Stewart, 1969), p. 106.
20. For a discussion of the Ontario schools issue see Marilyn J. Barber, "The Ontario Bilingual Schools Issue, 1910–1916," M.A. thesis, Queen's University, 1964.
21. Henry Borden, ed., *Robert Laird Borden, His Memoirs*, vol. 2, *1916–1920* (Toronto: McClelland and Stewart, 1969), pp. 21–34.
22. Roger Graham, *Arthur Meighen*, vol. 1, *The Door of Opportunity* (Toronto: Clarke Irwin, 1960), pp. 295–97.
23. Ibid., p. 295.
24. Ibid.
25. Roger Graham, *Arthur Meighen*, vol. 2, *And Fortune Fled* (Toronto: Clarke Irwin, 1963), pp. 15–18.
26. Graham, *Arthur Meighen*, 1: 253–72 and *Arthur Meighen*, 2: 149–64. See also references in n. 30 below.
27. Graham, *Arthur Meighen*, 2: 24–32 and 117–20.
28. For a discussion of the parliamentary role of the Progressives see W. L. Morton, *The Progressive Party in Canada* (Toronto: University of Toronto Press, 1950), chaps. 5 and 6, pp. 130–209.
29. On Rogers' motives see Graham, *Arthur Meighen*, 1: 46, 214, and 255–56; for an account of Rogers' campaign against Meighen see Graham's, *Arthur Meighen*, 2: 176–80, 244–58.
30. Graham, *Arthur Meighen*, 2: 149–50, 161–64, 241–45; 253–56, 259–83, 337, 453.
31. J. Murray Beck, *Pendulum of Power, Canada's Federal Elections* (Scarborough, Ontario: Prentice-Hall, 1968), pp. 163–65.
32. Graham, *Arthur Meighen*, 2: 293–94.
33. Beck, *Pendulum of Power*, pp. 182–87, and Graham, *Arthur Meighen*, 2: 467–71, et passim.
34. *Canadian Annual Review*, 1927–28, pp. 45–46; for a more complete account of the campaign, and the convention proceedings see the Montreal *Gazette*, October 11, 12, 13, 1927. All newspaper accounts of party affairs in the period covered by this chapter must be treated with some caution because of the highly partisan nature of reporting. There is no other source, however, for information about leadership campaigns and convention proceedings.
35. Beck, *Pendulum of Power*, pp. 198–200.
36. Quoted in J. R. H. Wilbur, "H. H. Stevens and R. B. Bennett, 1930–34," *Canadian Historical Review* 43, no. 1 (March 1962): 8.
37. Ernest Watkins, *R. B. Bennett, A Biography* (Toronto: Kingswood, 1963), p. 200.
38. The speech had been reproduced as a pamphlet, although it is not altogether clear that this was done at Stevens' direction. However, he was certainly responsible for the fact that it was distributed to some members of the press. See Wilbur, "H. H. Stevens and R. B. Bennett, 1930–34," pp. 11–12, and Watkins, *R. B. Bennett*, pp. 205–6.
39. H. H. Stevens, *Canada, House of Commons Debates* (1935), vol. III,

pp. 2668–75, in J. R. H. Wilbur, ed., *The Bennett New Deal: Fraud or Portent?* (Toronto: Copp Clark, 1968), p. 133.

40. Quoted in Wilbur, "H. H. Stevens and R. B. Bennett, 1930–34," p. 14.
41. Cf. Norman Riddell, "The Bennett New Deal: An Essay," M.A. thesis, University of Saskatchewan, 1967, chap. 2, et passim.
42. Cahan was a spokesman for the Montreal business community in the cabinet. Wilbur suggests he wanted to get rid of Stevens in order to prevent or curtail an investigation by the price spreads inquiry of a textiles firm to which he was connected. See Wilbur, "H. H. Stevens and R. B. Bennett, 1930–34," pp. 15–16.
43. For evidence about and some analysis of these aspects of Bennett's personality see Watkins, *R. B. Bennett*, pp. 20, 30, 171–73, 177, 179 et passim, and R. J. Manion, *Life is an Adventure* (Toronto: Ryerson, 1936), pp. 292–93. Bennett's correspondence provides revealing insights into his character. For a published example see Wilfred I. Smith, "R. B. Bennett and Sir Robert Borden," *Canadian Historical Review* 45, no. 2 (June 1964).
44. The account by Watkins, *R. B. Bennett*, pp. 198–213, which includes evidence from interviews with Stevens and others and a lengthy memorandum from Leon Ladner who tried to serve as a mediator in the quarrel, observes the importance of Bennett's personality in the break between the two men.
45. In late 1933 both Stevens and R. J. Manion had tried to persuade Bennett to take some action to re-build party organization, which had been neglected since the 1930 election, but Bennett was unwilling to approve more than token efforts. See J. R. H. Wilbur, "H. H. Stevens and the Reconstruction Party," *Canadian Historical Review* 45, no. 1 (1964): 5–6.
46. Wilbur concludes that there were sixty-two constituencies in which the combined Conservative and Reconstruction vote was larger than that of the winning Liberal candidate. See "H. H. Stevens and the Reconstruction Party," p. 16.
47. Harold A. Naugler, "R. J. Manion and the Conservative Party, 1938–1940," M.A. thesis, Queen's University, 1966, p. 98.
48. Ibid., p. 105.
49. See Manion, *Life is an Adventure*, pp. 292–93.
50. Naugler, "R. J. Manion and the Conservative Party, 1938–1940," p. 106.
51. Ibid., p. 101.
52. Roger Graham, *Arthur Meighen*, vol. 3, *No Surrender* (Toronto: Clarke Irwin, 1965), p. 82.
53. Naugler, "R. J. Manion and the Conservative Party, 1938–1940," p. 116.
54. Graham, *Arthur Meighen*, 3:82.
55. Manion's concern on this point is reflected in a letter to Meighen which he drafted in 1939 but evidently did not send. The text is reproduced in ibid., pp. 85–86.
56. J. L. Granatstein, *The Politics of Survival: The Conservative Party of Canada, 1939–1945* (Toronto: University of Toronto Press, 1967), pp. 44–45.
57. Ibid., pp. 50–51.
58. Ibid., p. 88.
59. Graham, *Arthur Meighen*, 3:127, et passim, argues that Mackenzie King did not need the specific provocation of Meighen's speeches to instruct party workers to assist the CCF candidate. Certainly King took a hand

in the campaign when he announced two weeks before polling day that the government would conduct a plebiscite asking public approval for the use of conscription if conscription were to become necessary. The effect was to deprive Meighen of his main issue.

60. Granatstein, *The Politics of Survival*, p. 110, attaches more importance than Graham (*Meighen*, vol. 3) to the independent effect of the CCF campaign.
61. Despite his earlier disagreement with Manion on issues of social policy, Meighen was prepared to shift his views when confronted with their adverse political consequences. Thus, Granatstein observes that in York South under the attacks of the CCF "Meighen began to modify his stand on social welfare as the campaign drew to a close." Ibid., p. 108.
62. In the words of one of the other candidates, "The party power brokers in Montreal and Toronto, and these included Mr. Meighen, decided that they would give a public imitation of Pharaoh's daughter. 'Was not Moses found in the bulrushes; why should not we go out and shake those bulrushes to find ourselves a leader?' They did; they concluded that the politician above all who filled the needs of the hour was the Honourable John Bracken, Premier of Manitoba. There was one difficulty. Although it was rumoured that his mother, before women had the right to vote, appeared to think as a Conservative, Mr. Bracken had never evinced even slight interest in being a Conservative." John G. Diefenbaker, *One Canada, Memoirs of the Right Honourable John G. Diefenbaker, The Crusading Years 1895–1956* (Toronto: Macmillan, 1865), p. 25.
63. For a time Bracken considered a strategy aimed at securing an alliance with Quebec nationalists, but when the conscription issue broke he was driven toward a position which ultimately took the form of an attack on Quebec to win votes in other provinces. Cf. J. L. Granatstein, *The Politics of Survival*, pp. 185–86 and 193–94.
64. The desire to remove him was said to be so strong that a fund was being established to provide him with a guarantee of an income if he would retire. "Backstage at Ottawa," *Maclean's*, LXI, no. 15, August 1, 1948, and no. 17, September 1, 1948.
65. John R. Williams, *The Conservative Party of Canada: 1920–1949* (Durham, North Carolina: Duke University Press, 1956), p. 75.
66. Diefenbaker, *The Crusading Years, 1895–1956*, p. 267.
67. The *Globe and Mail*, Toronto, September 20, 1948.
68. The *Globe and Mail*, Toronto, October 2, 1948.
69. Diefenbaker, *The Crusading Years, 1895–1956*, p. 268.
70. Pierre Berton, writing about Drew in *Maclean's*, commented that in his speeches the word "'Britain' has a stature similar to the word 'God' in an evangelist's sermon." *Maclean's*, LXI, no. 19, October 1, 1948, p. 64.
71. In his memoirs Diefenbaker says that after the 1949 election "things went along very well" in his relationship with Drew. He adds, however, that "there was still apparent among some of the palace guard a feeling that I should in no way be 'preferred' to use the expression that was bandied around by two or three of them. I wasn't preferred." Diefenbaker, *The Crusading Years, 1895–1956*, p. 270.
72. Drew's differences with Leslie Frost, the premier of Ontario, deprived him of the active support of the Ontario provincial party which he had led to power in 1943. These differences were never mentioned by either of the principals in public. In contrast, Drew's dispute with the provincial leader of the British Columbia party took the form of an extended

public struggle for control of party resources in that province. For an analysis of this conflict see Edwin R. Black, "Federal Strains Within a Canadian Party," *The Dalhousie Review* 45, no. 3 (1965).

73. Cf. the comment by George Hees in Peter Stursberg, *Diefenbaker, Leadership Gained, 1956–62* (Toronto: University of Toronto Press, 1975), p. 4.
74. Drew had led an opposition filibuster against the government's attempt to rush through legislation providing financial support for the Trans-Canada Pipelines Company. At issue was the opposition's claim that the government had provided inadequate time to debate the measure. The conflict developed into a fundamental test of the rights of Parliament and is widely believed to have contributed to the defeat of the government in the following year.
75. Grattan O'Leary, *Recollections of People, Press and Politics* (Toronto: Macmillan, 1977), pp. 114–16.
76. It has been asserted that they went so far as to approach an expatriate Canadian, Beverly Baxter, who was a Conservative member of the British Parliament. See Patrick Nicholson, *Vision and Indecision* (Don Mills, Ontario: Longmans Canada, 1968), p. 65.
77. For the views of some of the principals see Stursberg, *Diefenbaker, Leadership Gained, 1956–62*, pp. 16–21.
78. Pierre Sévigny, *This Game of Politics* (Toronto: McClelland and Stewart, 1965), pp. 45–46.
79. This strategy has been interpreted as a manifestation of hostility toward French Canada. Gordon Churchill, who was the author of the strategy, argues that it was nothing more than an attempt to achieve a more rational allocation of resources. Churchill's thesis was that the party would have to win the rest of the country and form a government before it could hope to make substantial gains in Quebec. Thus, resources should be allocated to maximize the party's opportunity to win seats where there was a real chance of gain—in other provinces. Gordon Churchill interview.
80. John Meisel, *The Canadian General Election of 1957* (Toronto: University of Toronto Press, 1962), p. 274.

CHAPTER 4

1. Canadian Institute of Public Opinion, "Liberals edge ahead in party standings," *Release*, September 28, 1960.
2. The problem with Coyne originated in the position of the previous government accepted by the Conservative minister of finance, Donald Fleming, soon after he assumed office, that the Bank of Canada had complete autonomy in the determination of national monetary policy. In early 1960 when the government began to consider a policy of economic expansion to deal with unemployment, Coyne was one of the senior public servants who advocated a restrictive policy. Unlike the other opponents of expansion, Coyne was in a position because of the autonomy doctrine, to act on his own and resist any movement toward expansion by maintaining tight credit.
3. Cf. Roy Faibish, cited in Peter Stursberg, *Diefenbaker, Leadership Gained, 1956–62* (Toronto: University of Toronto Press, 1975), p. 211.
4. Cf. Douglas Harkness, Roy Faibish, Davie Fulton and Donald Fleming, ibid., pp. 177–78.

5. There had been discussion of pegging the dollar (which had been allowed to float since 1950) for eighteen months. The immediate crisis was created by a run on the dollar but the government had had ample warning of this danger since there had been an intensive drain on reserves, reducing them by nearly 25 percent, in the four previous months.
6. The minister of finance, Donald Fleming, claimed he had not been informed of the decision to increase the pension, and it ought not to have been taken without his approval. Coyne responded that Fleming should have known about it since his deputy minister was aware of it. Fleming has since said that the deputy minister came to him after the controversy developed and apologized to him for not reporting the decision. Cited in Stursberg, *Diefenbaker, Leadership Gained*, p. 240. While it was Fleming who recommended to cabinet that Coyne be removed, it is not clear that he was responsible for emphasizing the pension issue. Some members of the cabinet said in interviews that they thought Diefenbaker had been responsible. Certainly, Diefenbaker emphasized this aspect of the controversy when he spoke to caucus about it. Cf. R. A. Bell, cited in Stursberg, *Diefenbaker, Leadership Gained*, pp. 241–42.
7. It was Fleming who refused the opposition request that the matter be submitted to commitee. He subsequently claimed he had consulted with Diefenbaker and had had cabinet approval for his decision (cited in Stursberg, *Diefenbaker, Leadership Gained*, p. 245), although at least three ministers—Alvin Hamilton, Davie Fulton, and David Walker—say they had wanted to let Coyne be heard. (Interviews.) Fleming does not appear to have foreseen that Coyne would be able to get a hearing in the Senate where the Liberals held a large majority. Thus Coyne did get his opportunity to testify—in a situation controlled by the government's political enemies.
8. Diefenbaker was allegedly involved in an attempt to suppress a CBC program, *Preview Commentary*, on which there had been criticism of the government. There is no direct evidence to support this allegation. When it was investigated by a parliamentary committee, the CBC official who had been responsible for the decision to suspend the program testified that "never at any time has an offer or directive been given to me, or to my president, by [the minister responsible for the CBC] or by any member of parliament, or by anyone else who could be said to wield political influence." Cited in Peter C. Newman, *Renegade in Power: The Diefenbaker Years* (Toronto: McClelland and Stewart, 1963), p. 235.
9. Ibid., p. 244.
10. On aspects of the Conservative party's problems in Quebec, see Marc La Terreur, *Les tribulations des Conservateurs au Québec* (Quebec: Les Presses de l'Université Laval, 1973).
11. These included the appointment of the first French-Canadian governor general, Georges Vanier, the decision to have all government cheques printed in both official languages, and the provision of simultaneous translation facilities in the House of Commons.
12. Léon Balcer, interview.
13. Ibid., Paul Sauvé who succeeded to the leadership of the Union Nationale and the premiership of Quebec upon the death of Maurice Duplessis in 1959 appeared to be more sensitive than Duplessis to the changes occurring in the province. He introduced a series of social and political reforms intended to respond to these changes. However, less than four months after his succession, Sauvé died.

14. Senator Jacques Flynn, interview. Senator Flynn said Union Nationale officials had wanted patronage support from the federal Conservatives and were "furious" when they did not receive it.
15. Between 1958 and 1962 the proportion of voters in Canadian Institute of Public Opinion surveys who said Diefenbaker "would make the best leader for Canada at present" fell from 50 percent to 35 percent. Cited in Peter Regenstreif, *The Diefenbaker Interlude* (Don Mills, Ontario: Longmans, 1965), p. 71.
16. Cf. the comments by Howard Green and Angus MacLean in Stursberg, *Diefenbaker, Leadership Gained*, p. 179.
17. Alvin Hamilton, interview.
18. Cf. the comment by Merrill Menzies in Stursberg, *Diefenbaker, Leadership Gained*, p. 125. Of eight ministers whom Menzies identified as supporters of the "progressive" policy of economic expansion, there were only three whom he described as unqualified "progressives" and there were three to whom he said the term definitely did not apply. None of the other ministers interviewed for the study accepted the thesis that such policy blocs existed.
19. Diefenbaker was himself sufficiently concerned about the perception of the government in big business circles to look for a representative of big business to sit in the cabinet. In August 1962, he appointed Wallace McCutcheon, an executive and director of several large corporations, to the Senate and made him minister without portfolio.
20. Cf. Newman, *Renegade in Power*, pp. 94–95, and Pierre Sévigny, *This Game of Politics* (Toronto: McClelland and Stewart, 1965), pp. 177–78, et passim. In an interview, Davie Fulton, the minister of justice, who had been a rival candidate for the leadership in 1956, gave an example of the extent of Diefenbaker's mistrust. He said that twice in 1958 he was called into the prime minister's office and accused of being disloyal, although Diefenbaker did not cite any evidence or any specific ground for his accusation. Fulton later came to the conclusion that the accusation arose from a newspaper article which described him as, next to the prime minister, the most powerful man in the cabinet.
21. Cf. Sévigny, *This Game of Politics*, pp. 179–80, and Patrick Nicholson, *Vision and Indecision* (Don Mills, Ontario: Longmans Canada, 1968), p. 140. In an interview, Ellen Fairclough described him as a person who was "mercurial and given to temperamental outbursts." Another minister, see p. 81, described him as "unstable."
22. Cf. the comments by George Hees in Stursberg, *Diefenbaker, Leadership Gained*, p. 180.
23. One of Diefenbaker's closest and most loyal associates who asked not to be identified made the following comment in an interview: "John Diefenbaker was a highly principled man . . . but there was one way in which you could say he was unprincipled. He would talk to some ministers about other members of the cabinet behind their backs and this would get back to them."
24. For a full discussion of the background to this issue see Newman, *Renegade in Power*, pp. 333–54, and Nicholson, *Vision and Indecision*, pp. 145–78, 196–226.
25. Cf. Nicholson, ibid., pp. 243–46. Nicholson had helped arrange the meetings between Thompson and representatives of the government.
26. An indication of the strength of party feeling is the fact that despite an appeal from Diefenbaker not to tie his hands in the matter, one-third of

the delegates to the annual meeting of the National Association in January supported a resolution calling on the government to accept nuclear weapons if no progress had been made toward nuclear disarmament by the end of the year.

27. Newman, *Renegade in Power*, pp. 363–78 and Nicholson, *Vision and Indecision*, pp. 230–63, have both provided fairly full descriptions of the events between 3–6 February. While they both agree on the main points, there are differences between the two accounts on some of the details.
28. E. A. Goodman, interview.
29. Sévigny, *This Game of Politics*, p. 284.
30. Léon Balcer, interview.
31. Cf. Newman, *Renegade in Power*, p. 363. Hees and Sévigny had both indicated to other ministers before they resigned that they accepted this proposal.
32. J. W. Monteith, interview. Diefenbaker claimed that Fulton asked him at a private meeting on February 4 to designate him as his successor.
33. Howard Green, the minister of external affairs, was the only minister strongly opposed to the acquisition of nuclear weapons.
34. All of the ministers who were interviewed stressed this point.
35. Michael Starr, interview.
36. Diefenbaker ran ahead of Pearson in every published survey prior to the 1963 election, even though his support had declined substantially from 1958.
37. Gordon Fairweather, interview.
38. Léon Balcer, interview.
39. Typical of the replies were these:

(a) My sympathies have been with the Conservative party for many years, however, I would be less than frank in saying that I cannot subscribe to the philosophies being expounded by the present leader of the party. Mine is a very small voice of complaint and no doubt I am very much in the minority in suggesting that the time is long overdue when the party should look for a new leadership . . .
In the meantime because I feel so strongly about the present situation, I think it would be hypocritical to send a contribution to you, at this time. However, if and when this situation is rectified, I hope you will feel disposed to ask me again. In the meantime I should say that I have not abandoned the Conservative cause and my allegiance and financial support is directed to the Provincial Party."

(President, large Toronto real estate company)

(b) On the other hand I would be less than frank if I did not tell you that my support of the two-party system does not go so far as to support any party headed by Mr. Diefenbaker. I think his leadership in itself is a great deterrent to the success of the party he heads, and it would be inconsistent with my views and my principles were I to support anything with which he is identified.

(Partner, Toronto law firm)

(c) I support Conservative principles where I can find them, but the Conservative party at present is seemingly without any adherence to such principles—and the last Conservative Prime Minister was a travesty while in office. Why then, is he retained as Leader? Surely not on the thoroughly disproven basis that he is a vote-getter. I think you must act in this matter before soliciting funds for support. If I am wrong, please let me know.

(General Manager,
national life insurance company)

(d) On a corporate basis, we have taken the position that we believe in the two party system, and it is right and proper that the national funds of the party in power and the opposition should be given an annual contribution. We make no secret of it and seek no quid pro quo. However, after giving it a good deal of thought, I can't bring myself to quite such an objective position. I no longer have confidence in Mr. Diefenbaker's ability to govern and, therefore, I do not feel that I wish to give tacit approval by contributing to the party funds now. Should the situation change and you still want help from me, I will be glad to reconsider.

(President,
national communications and
publishing company)

These quotations are derived from a file provided the author by a confidential source.

40. Peter C. Newman, *Distemper of Our Times* (Toronto: McClelland and Stewart, 1968), p. 117.
41. This group had no formal constitutional status but acted on its own authority in dealing with questions of agenda and procedure.
42. Dalton Camp, interview.
43. Marcel Lambert, chairman of a caucus subcommittee directed to consider one of the controversial pieces of legislation, said in an interview he knew nothing of Diefenbaker's decision until he was told by the party's house leader on the afternoon the bill was to be introduced for second reading that he would lead off the debate. Lambert was surprised since he had opposed Diefenbaker's apparent intention to make an issue of the bill on the grounds that "there was nothing in it. It was a 'Mickey Mouse' bill." When he asked what the party's position was to be, he was told to do as he saw fit. Lambert says he believes Diefenbaker had lost interest in the bill because he could no longer see any political advantage to it. Marcel Lambert, interview. Another explanation is that Diefenbaker's plan to fight on this issue had brought protests from three of the four Conservative provincial premiers, including John Robarts of Ontario.
44. Léon Balcer and others, interviews.
45. E. A. Goodman, interview.
46. George Hees and Davie Fulton, interviews.
47. One reason was an inquiry ordered by the Liberals into the relationship between Pierre Sévigny, when he had been associate minister of defence, and Gerda Munsinger, an immigrant from Germany who was once alleged to have been an espionage agent. The inquiry touched upon both the extent to which the relationship had constituted a security risk and the role of Diefenbaker, as prime minister, and Fulton, as minister of justice, in handling the case. Although the inquiry was being conducted by Wishart Spence, a justice of the Supreme Court, it was widely seen by Conservatives as an act of partisan vengeance, having been provoked

in the heat of a difficult debate in the House. Its immediate effect, therefore, was to unite the party.

48. Dalton Camp, interview.
49. Ibid.
50. Perhaps the most important reason was money. Constituency delegates were expected to meet most of these costs from personal resources, while there was some party support, from their provincial association, for the ex-officio delegates.
51. The Progressive Conservative Student Federation had challenged Diefenbaker as early as 1964 when it voted to ask the National Association to conduct its vote of confidence in the leader by secret ballot. Both the PCSF and YPC representatives had supported the motion for a leadership convention at the National Executive meeting in February 1965, and a few weeks later a delegation of officers from the PCSF (led by its president, Joe Clark) had called on Diefenbaker to urge him to resign.
52. See chap. 2.
53. James Johnston, *The Party's Over* (Don Mills, Ontario: Longmans Canada, 1971).
54. Robert Coates, *The Night of the Knives* (Fredericton, New Brunswick: Brunswick Press, 1969), p. 60.
55. Data from the survey of delegates to the 1967 leadership convention support this view.
56. Léon Balcer, interview.
57. Robert Stanfield and Gordon Fairweather, interviews.
58. Marcel Lambert, interview.
59. Ibid.
60. Confidential interview.
61. Tom Bell, interview.
62. David MacDonald, interview.
63. Ibid.
64. A. D. Hales, interview.
65. Coates, *The Night of the Knives*, p. 53.
66. Ibid., pp. 55–57.

CHAPTER 5

1. Robert Coates, *The Night of the Knives* (Fredericton, New Brunswick: Brunswick Press, 1969), p. 73.
2. James Johnston, *The Party's Over* (Don Mills, Ontario: Longmans, 1971).
3. Various interviews.
4. Johnston, *The Party's Over*, p. 168.
5. Only one member of Parliament, Gordon Fairweather, from New Brunswick, escaped the purge. Fairweather was re-elected because Commons representatives on the national executive were elected by separate meetings of the members from each province. Of the other three New Brunswick members, one, Tom Bell, was opposed to Diefenbaker and another, Hugh John Flemming, "owed [Fairweather] a favour." Confidential interview.
6. James Johnston, interview.
7. Camp himself commented on this point in an interview.
8. Camp says he did not want or seek the job. Interview.

9. Johnston, *The Party's Over*, p. 179.
10. Ruth Bell, "Conservative Party National Conventions, 1927–1956, Organization and Procedure," M.A. thesis, Carleton University, 1956, 104–5, reports "a heated exchange between the National Director and the Editor of the Winnipeg *Free Press* during late August and early September, 1948 [in which] the latter attacked the method of choice as being undemocratic, permitting 'bossism' and 'packing' the convention . . . . The *Free Press* suggested rather pointedly that there probably would not be a change in the rules, 'for Mr. Drew [the candidate against whom Diefenbaker was running], for one, has made no complaint.' A few weeks later the *Globe and Mail* joined in the fray and wrote, 'There is no foundation for these insinuations. It is significant that Mr. Diefenbaker himself . . . has given no credence or support to the complaints voiced by some of his supporters on this score." The rationale offered for the appointment of delegates-at-large by R. A. Bell, the national director, was to ensure the representation of a "full cross-section" of the party's support in each province. Ibid., p. 105. Similar arguments were used to justify the appointment of delegates-at-large at the 1967 convention. "Convention Committee Minutes," mimeo.
11. "Convention Committee Minutes," mimeo.
12. Cited in Johnston, *The Party's Over*, p. 184.
13. Ibid., pp. 70–71, and Coates, *The Night of the Knives*, pp. 78–86.
14. Some studies have defined factions more narrowly as groups pursuing policy objectives, but even these definitions appear to share the emphasis placed here on organized activity. See, for example, Richard Rose, "Parties, Factions and Tendencies," in Richard Rose, ed., *Studies in British Politics* (London: Macmillan, 1967), p. 318. Joseph Schlesinger's article "Political Party Organization," in James G. March, ed., *Handbook of Organizations* (Chicago: Rand McNally, 1965) suggests the more general definition adopted here: "When [a group within a party] is in conflict with others of the same party . . . it may be called a faction" (p. 796).
15. As was noted in chap. 1 (note 6) there are several studies of competition among groups which report this effect.
16. Both in specific references and tone the Coates and Johnston books convey a good deal of this feeling. Cf. Coates, *The Night of the Knives*, and Johnston, *The Party's Over*.
17. James Johnston, interview.
18. Alvin Hamilton, interview.
19. Michael Starr, interview.
20. Gordon Churchill, interview.
21. Confidential interview.
22. Arthur Patillo, interview.
23. Dalton Camp, interview.
24. Confidential interviews.
25. Duff Roblin, interview.
26. Ibid.
27. Robert Stanfield, interview.
28. Federal constituency associations in Nova Scotia have virtually no independent existence, being assembled only to perform constitutionally required tasks. In federal campaigns, the constituency committee is usually an ad hoc structure consisting of persons drawn from the provincial district associations which comprise the constituency. Most of the funds for federal candidates came from the provincial party.

29. Robert Coates, interview.
30. Cited in Michael Vineberg, "The Progressive Conservative Leadership Convention of 1967," M.A. thesis, McGill University, 1968, p. 89.
31. Johnston, *The Party's Over*, p. 213.
32. See chap. 4.
33. Coates, *The Night of the Knives*, pp. 118, 122.
34. Senator David Walker, interview.
35. Johnston, *The Party's Over*, p. 230.
36. Senator David Walker, interview.
37. This description is based on analysis of newspaper coverage of the campaign. The description is comprehensive and, therefore, does not reflect the relative frequency of discussion.
38. See, for example, their responses to fourteen questions asked by the *Toronto Star*, September 7, 1967.
39. Although making no public commitment, Johnson had ordered the Union Nationale to give Roblin organizational help in his Quebec campaign and a large number of Quebec delegates were known to be Union Nationale supporters.
40. Staff of the *Toronto Telegram, Balloons and Ballots* (Toronto, 1967).
41. *Toronto Telegram*, September 9, 1967.
42. Gordon Churchill, interview.
43. R. A. MacAulay, interview.
44. The distinction between a token candidate and a serious candidate is not an easy one to establish. It may be argued that serious candidates are those who are regarded as such by other candidates and the press. By their responses these two groups, particularly the press, can validate their own analyses. If this distinction is accepted then it is doubtful whether Hamilton, McCutcheon, and Starr could be called "serious" candidates. Or to carry it a step further, as Michael Vineberg observes, if press judgements alone are considered, then only Stanfield and Roblin were serious candidates. (See Vineberg, "The Progressive Conservative Leadership Convention of 1967.") The distinction here between McLean and Mrs. Sawka and the rest of the candidates is made on two grounds. First, neither McLean nor Mrs. Sawka had held any position in the party or had been active in any role to which particular esteem was attached in the community. Second, neither of them had seriously campaigned. McLean had announced his candidacy in January and took advantage of the opportunities for publicity afforded him by the mass media and convention rules. Mrs. Sawka was a last-minute candidate whose nomination gave her an opportunity to speak on national television. Convention rules had tried to screen out frivolous candidates by requiring the signature of twenty-five delegates to place a name in nomination. McLean's nomination had received help from the Stanfield organization because he had made most of his allotment of hotel and convention space available to Stanfield. At the same time, both his nomination and that of Mrs. Sawka ensured that none of the serious candidates would be forced out on the first, or possibly even the second, ballot by the requirement that the candidate with the smallest vote on each ballot be dropped from subsequent ballots.
45. Michael Starr, interview.
46. E. McCutcheon, interview.
47. E. McCutcheon, Julian Porter, interviews.
48. Julian Porter, interview.

49. Sidney Spivak, interview.
50. Ibid.
51. E. A. Goodman, interview.
52. Ibid.
53. Lionel Schipper, interview.
54. R. A. MacAulay, interview. Hees would not discuss the reasons for his choice.
55. E. A. Goodman, interview.
56. R. A. Bell, J. W. Monteith, Richard Trasher, Ellen Fairclough, interviews.
57. R. A. Bell, interview.
58. Senator David Walker, interview.
59. Johnston, *The Party's Over*, p. 244.
60. Joel Aldred and Senator David Walker, interviews.
61. Lowell Murray, interview.
62. Ibid.
63. Brian Mulroney, interview.
64. Roy Faibish, interview.
65. Alvin Hamilton, interview.
66. Sidney Spivak, interview.
67. Alvin Hamilton, interview.
68. Ibid.
69. Roy Faibish, interview.
70. Data in chap. 7 show candidates had some difficulty in "delivering" their delegates.
71. Reasons categorized as patronage included (a) a sense of obligation to the candidate (or an intermediary) for some past favour, or (b) a desire for some personal advantage. Affective reasons included (a) an affective response to the personality attributes of the candidate (or an intermediary), perceived either negatively or positively, (b) leadership style, (c) friendship, (d) a sense of personal loyalty (as distinct from obligation on some past or anticipated reward allocation). Policy reasons included (a) ideological or doctrinal stance, (b) positions on specific issues. One person refused to give a reason for his second choice. The sum of reasons is greater than the number of persons interviewed because some respondents gave more than one reason.
72. Julian Porter, interview.
73. Norman Atkins, interview.
74. Sterling Lyon, interview.
75. Gordon Churchill, interview.

CHAPTER 6

1. Robert Stanfield, interview.
2. Ibid.
3. Ibid.
4. Roblin's refusal of a seat in Parliament added to the impression that he was nursing a grievance from his defeat. Roblin says his reluctance to run was based on his ambivalence toward a future political career. "I felt that in caucus I would be just another private member. I had been through all that. . . . I didn't want to go . . . under those circumstances.

They aren't about to accord you a position of automatic leadership." Duff Roblin, interview.

5. Dalton Camp, interview.
6. Ibid.
7. For example, on the first motion of non-confidence he moved after entering the House, he agreed to a pair with Prime Minister Pearson which had the effect of preventing him from voting on his own motion!
8. On February 19, while Prime Minister Pearson and several members of the cabinet were absent from Ottawa, a government tax bill was defeated on third reading. The Conservatives argued that this defeat, since it involved a financial measure, constituted a vote of non-confidence and, therefore, that Pearson should resign or call a new election without delay. Pearson returned to Ottawa and persuaded Stanfield to agree to a twenty-four-hour adjournment to permit the government to decide what to do. On the following evening, Pearson appeared on national television to announce that the government did not regard its defeat as a test of confidence and that it would introduce a motion asking the House to affirm this interpretation and vote confidence. Meanwhile, the secretary of state for external affairs, Paul Martin, had secured support for the government's position from the Quebec Social Credit caucus (which had voted with the rest of the opposition to defeat the tax bill). This ensured that there would be a majority for the government motion. Churchill wanted the Conservative party to delay proceedings in the House in an attempt to prevent the government motion from coming to a vote, but Stanfield rejected this course in the belief that it might lead to a run on the Canadian dollar by creating an impression of political instability in the country. (Stanfield had been warned of this danger by Pearson and by the governor of the Bank of Canada who had briefed him on the situation at Pearson's request.) As a result, Churchill resigned from the caucus to become an Independent Conservative.
9. Cf. Robert Coates, *The Night of the Knives* (Fredericton, New Brunswick: Brunswick Press, 1969), p. 141.
10. Lowell Murray, interview.
11. *Toronto Star*, March 11, 1969.
12. Dalton Camp, "Westerners' Erratic Success," *Toronto Telegram*, March 13, 1969.
13. Gerald Baldwin, interview.
14. Robert Stanfield, interview.
15. Liam O'Brian, interview.
16. Toronto *Globe and Mail*, September 6, 1971.
17. Wickson had resigned as national director in 1970 to return to British Columbia. He was invited in 1971 to work in the Ontario provincial election campaign.
18. The existence of the fund was to become a source of some embarrassment to the people who had been involved in setting it up. Stanfield said in an interview that it had been done with his knowledge.
19. Vernon Peter Harder, "A House of Minorities, Parties and Party Behaviour in the Canadian House of Commons," M.A. thesis, Queen's University, 1977.
20. Toronto *Globe and Mail*, January 5, 1973.
21. Toronto *Globe and Mail*, March 31, 1973.
22. Mitchell Sharp, cited in Harder, "A House of Minorities," p. 151.

23. *Toronto Star*, June 28, 1973.
24. *Montreal Star*, December 12, 1973.
25. Don Matthews, interview.
26. "Terms of Reference for Chairman of Campaign Planning," mimeo, no date.
27. Finlay MacDonald, interview.
28. Don Matthews, interview.
29. Interviews with several members of the caucus.
30. I have described the party's campaign in some detail in "The Progressive Conservative Party in the Election of 1974," in Howard R. Penniman, ed., *Canada At The Polls, The General Election of 1974* (Washington: American Enterprise Institute, 1975). See also in the same collection William P. Irvine, "An Overview of the 1974 Federal Election in Canada"; Stephen Clarkson, "Pierre Trudeau and the Liberal Party: The Jockey and the Horse"; and Frederick J. Fletcher, "The Mass Media in the 1974 Canadian Election."
31. Robert Stanfield, interview.
32. Jack Horner, interview.
33. Sean O'Sullivan, interview.
34. Ibid.

CHAPTER 7

1. See, for example, Nelson W. Polsby and Aaron Wildavsky, *Presidential Elections: Strategies of American Electoral Politics* (New York: Scribner, 1964), chap. 2; or, for a more extensive treatment, Paul T. David, Ralph M. Goldman, and Richard C. Bain, *The Politics of National Party Conventions* (Washington: Brookings Institute, 1960).
2. The most comprehensive study of the leadership convention in Canada is to be found in John C. Courtney, *The Selection of National Party Leaders in Canada* (Toronto: Macmillan, 1973).
3. Maurice Arpin, interview.
4. Joe Clark, interview.
5. Carl Baar and Ellen Baar, observe that Canadian leadership conventions "follow a 'mass-society' model in which each individual delegate operates within a commonly defined situation, with a common set of behavioural constraints and opportunities. National party conventions in the United States follow an intermediate leadership model . . ." See their "Party and Convention Organization and Leadership Selection in Canada and the United States," in Donald R. Matthews, ed., *Perspectives on Presidential Selection* (Washington: Brookings Institute, 1973), p. 74.
6. Some studies accept significance level of .05. The more stringent standard of .001 is used throughout this study. For a discussion of the issues involved in the use of these different levels of significance see Sanford Labovitz, "Criteria for Selecting Significance Level: A Note on the Sacredness of .05," *The American Sociologist* 3 (August 1968): 220–22; James K. Skipper, Jr., Anthony L. Guenther, and Gilbert Nass, "The Sacredness of .05: A Note Concerning the Uses of Statistical Levels of Significance in Social Science," *The American Sociologist* 2 (February 1967): 16–18; and Hubert M. Blalock, Jr., *Social Statistics* (New York: McGraw-Hill, 1960), pp. 122–28.
7. Cramer's V is a measure of the strength of association based on chi

square. For a discussion of this statistic see Blalock, *Social Statistics*, pp. 228–31, and G. David Garson, *Handbook of Political Science Methods* (Boston: Holbrook, 1971), pp. 157–58. For a discussion of the interpretation of measures of association see Herbert L. Costner, "Criteria for Measures of Association," *American Sociological Review* 30, no. 3 (June 1965): 341–53.

8. For community size the value of V was .14, for religion it was .12, and for ethnic origin it was .15.
9. The value of V for ethnic origin was .16; for religion it was .11.

CHAPTER 8

1. Delegates were given a list of statements and asked to name those which had been a factor in their behaviour. This list was based on an inventory created from a pre-test of the questionnaire. To ensure the fullest range of explanation, delegates were also asked to identify any other reasons—not included in the list—which had influenced their choices. Some 20 percent of the sample gave additional reasons and these were classified in one of the categories of the typology or assigned to a category defined as unclassifiable within this framework. The process of classification was crosschecked by independent coders.
2. It should be noted that the format and content of the questions used in this test were not identical. The issue statements on which the candidates were ranked were not replications of the statements in the other questions, but were framed to express the central concepts in these statements.
3. This ranking was determined by sampling coverage in daily newspapers in all ten provinces. In fact, there was little difference in the reports from province to province because most dailies outside the large metropolitan areas use the Canadian Press wire service for most of their coverage of national events.
4. This is an entirely arbitrary cut-off, which can be justified only on the ground of its inherent reasonableness.
5. The issues were derived from the ranking shown in Table 21.
6. Delegates were asked to rank the candidates on fourteen statements but one, "a strong stand against communism," had to be omitted from the test because there was no comparable issue statement about which the delegates had been asked to express their own opinions.
7. For a discussion of Yule's Q see James A. Davis, *Elementary Survey Analysis* (Englewood Cliffs, New Jersey: Prentice-Hall, 1971), pp. 48–49. In his table of conversions for describing Q values, Davis describes a Q ± .70 or higher as a very strong association and one of ± .50 to ± .69 as a substantial association (p. 49). See also John H. Mueller and Karl F. Schessler, *Statistical Reasoning in Sociology* (Boston: Houghton Mifflin, 1961), pp. 242–52, and L. A. Goodman and W. H. Kruskal, "Measures of Association for Cross Classifications," *Journal of the American Statistical Association* 49, no. 268 (December 1954): 732–64.

CHAPTER 9

1. Sean O'Sullivan, interview.
2. The question asked: "Generally do you think of yourself as being to the left or right of the party?"

3. Robert Krause and Lawrence LeDuc, "Voting Behaviour and Electoral Strategies in the 1976 Progressive Conservative Leadership Convention," paper delivered at the annual meeting of the Canadian Political Science Association, June 1967.
4. The statements were "There should be laws to bring big corporations under closer control"; "There are some cases in which government ownership in the economy is more desirable than private ownership"; "There is too much government ownership in the Canadian economy today"; "Government ought to interfere less with business"; "We must promote economic efficiency even if that means more small businesses will be replaced by large corporations"; "The present policy of wage and price controls"; "The principle of wage and price controls"; "The principle of a guaranteed income."
5. Letter to Progressive Conservative convention delegates, mimeo.
6. Peter Worsley, "The Concept of Populism," in Ghita Ionescu and Ernest Gellner, eds., *Populism, Its Meaning and National Characteristics* (London: Weidenfeld and Nicolson, 1969), p. 245.
7. Ibid., p. 244.

CHAPTER 10

1. The most thoroughgoing attempt to explain conflict in the party in terms of ideological cleavage is to be found in William Christian and Colin Campbell, *Political Parties and Ideologies in Canada* (Toronto: McGraw-Hill Ryerson, 1974).
2. The number of responses to this question is less than half the sample for two reasons. Some members were unwilling to discuss conflict in the caucus and some were not asked because there was not sufficient time.
3. John R. Williams, *The Conservative Party of Canada* (Durham, North Carolina: Duke University Press, 1956), p. 42.
4. David Hoffman and Norman Ward, *Bilingualism and Biculturalism in the Canadian House of Commons* (Ottawa: Queen's Printer, 1970), p. 128.
5. John C. Courtney, *The Selection of National Party Leaders in Canada* (Toronto: Macmillan, 1973), p. 159.
6. Edwin R. Black, "Opposition Research: Some Theories and Practice," *Canadian Public Administration* 15 (Spring 1972): 37.
7. For data on and discussion of this aspect of Conservative leadership recruitment see Courtney, *The Selection of National Party Leaders in Canada*, pp. 137–60.
8. The preference for provincial premiers is probably to be ascribed in part to the fact they are usually free of any association with the conflicts in the federal party. In this regard it is interesting to observe that 80 percent of the sample of delegates to the 1971 annual meeting when asked to name the person they would most prefer as leader if Stanfield were to resign mentioned one of the (then) three Conservative premiers—William Davis of Ontario, Peter Lougheed of Alberta, and Richard Hatfield of New Brunswick.
9. Lester G. Seligman develops this argument in a somewhat different way, proposing the hypothesis that "A permanent minority party with little hope or expectation of gaining a majority will choose a leadership proficient in opposing but lacking experience and/or capacity for governing.

Such minority parties tend toward purism and sectarianism; their candidates are more concerned with expressing ideological integrity than with winning the broadest spectrum of popular support. In contrast a party with expectations of governing will select candidates with the skills, abilities, and resources to win and to govern. The party will calculate more strategically about winning and will attract more of the politically ambitious, who will seek the party as an avenue to political advancement." Lester G. Seligman, "Political Parties and Recruitment of Political Leadership," in Lewis Edinger, ed., *Political Leadership in Industrialized Societies, Studies in Comparative Analysis* (New York: John G. Wiley, 1967), p. 303.

10. See John Meisel, "Party Images in Canada: A Report on Work in Progress," table III and chart I, pp. 70–71 in John Meisel, *Working Papers on Canadian Politics*, enl. ed. (Montreal: McGill-Queen's University Press, 1973).
11. John Meisel, "Howe, Hubris, and '72: An Essay on Political Elitism," ibid.

INDEX

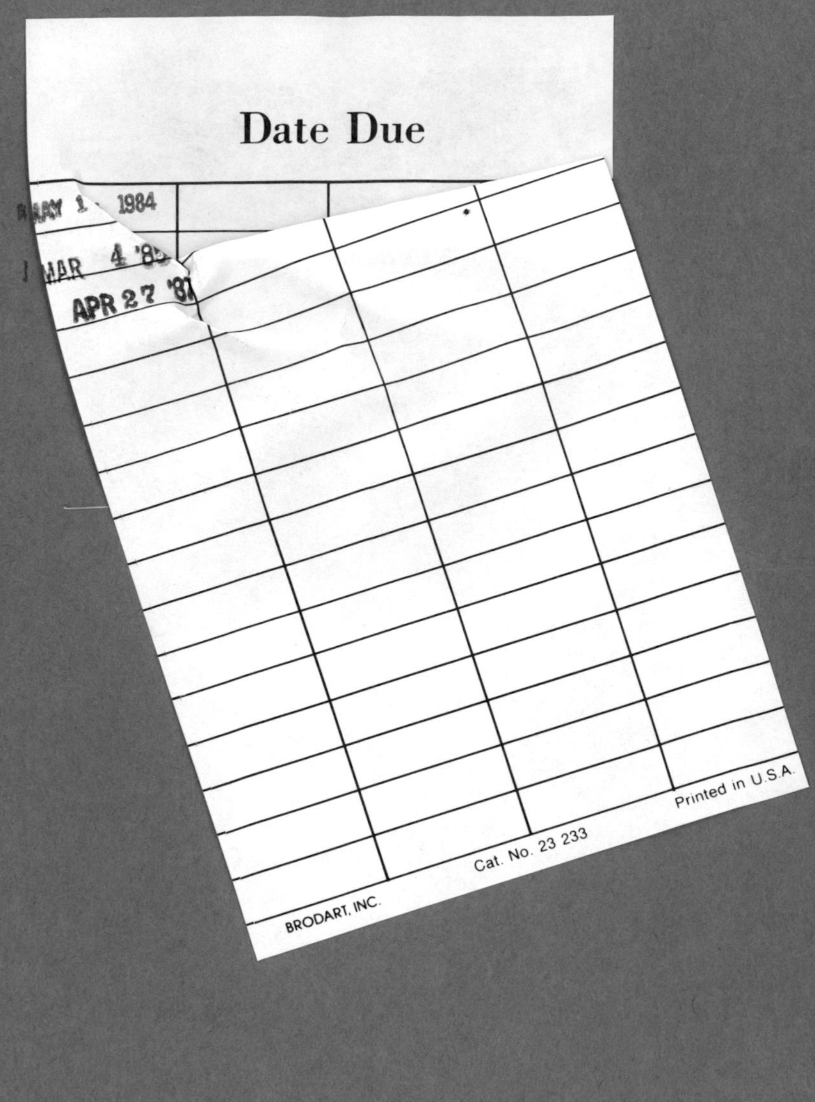
Date Due
MAY 1 - 1984
MAR 4 '85
APR 27 '87
BRODART, INC.
Cat. No. 23 233
Printed in U.S.A.